T0168006

A Zion Canyon Reader

A
ZION CANYON
R E A D E R

EDITED BY

Nathan N. Waite AND Reid L. Neilson

Foreword by Lyman Hafen

Published in partnership with the Zion Natural History Association

THE UNIVERSITY OF UTAH PRESS

Salt Lake City

Nathan N. Waite works for the Joseph Smith Papers Project in Salt Lake City, Utah. He holds an MA in American studies and environmental humanities from the University of Utah. Although he now resides in northern Utah, he still considers his native St. George his home.

Reid L. Neilson is managing director of the Church History Department of the Church of Jesus Christ of Latter-day Saints. He is the award-winning author or editor of over twenty books, including *Early Mormon Missionary Activities in Japan, 1901–1924* (University of Utah Press, 2010).

Copyright © 2014 by The University of Utah Press. All rights reserved.

The Defiance House Man colophon is a registered trademark of the University of Utah Press. It is based on a four-foot-tall Ancient Puebloan pictograph (late PIII) near Glen Canyon, Utah.

Library of Congress Cataloging-in-Publication Data
A Zion Canyon reader / edited by Nathan N. Waite and Reid L. Neilson ; foreword by Lyman Hafen.
     pages cm
Includes bibliographical references and index.

ISBN 978-1-60781-347-7 (pbk. : alk. paper)
ISBN 978-1-60781-348-4 (ebook)

1. Zion National Park (Utah)—Description and travel. 2. Zion National Park (Utah)—History. I. Waite, Nathan N., 1982- II. Neilson, Reid Larkin, 1972-
F832.Z8Z554 2014
979.2ʹ48—dc23

2014000046

Preceding pages: Thomas Moran, *Valley of Babbling Waters, Southern Utah* (chromolithograph of watercolor sketch), in F. V. Hayden, *The Yellowstone National Park, and the Mountain Regions of Portions of Idaho, Nevada, Colorado, and Utah* (Boston: L. Prang and Company, 1876). Courtesy of John and Melody Taft.

Printed and bound in the United States of America.

For Dustin and Roland, old companions in Zion adventures,
and for Michelle, more recent (and permanent) companion.
—NNW

⌇

For Steven Snow and Jeffrey Holland, fellow servants
in church history and two of Dixie's finest.
—RLN

If the Yosemite is Goldsmith's Dream Incarnate,
if the Yellowstone Milton's Paradise Lost,
and the Grand Canyon Dante's Inferno,
then Little Zion is the Revelation of St. John,
the Apocalypse of God,
the New Jerusalem let down from the skies;
the Mukuntuweap, the Home of God.

—FREDERICK VINING FISHER, 1916

Contents

Figures

Foreword

Most mornings I routinely leave my home near St. George, Utah, and drive into the rising sun. I travel eastward off the northern fringe of the Mojave Desert and the southern edge of the Great Basin and climb onto the vast and glorious Colorado Plateau. This daily ritual transports me from my home on a Chinle ridge above Santa Clara Creek to my office along the Virgin River, at the base of the towering walls of Kayenta and Navajo Sandstone in Zion National Park. Between the two points I pass through 200 million years of geologic deposition and erosion, all of which has resulted in a landscape so fascinating that more than three million people come from all over the world each year to see it.

Though the drive itself has become habitual, the awe and wonder it inspires have only heightened with time. Invariably, on the way to or from the office, something in the landscape will incite a memory, a line of poetry, a scientific fact, or a story that moves me—often to tears. Each trip is more than a commute, even more than a journey. The more I learn, and the more I immerse myself in this place, the more each drive becomes a sojourn full of wonder and enlightenment.

This excellent collection of Zion Canyon writing has enhanced that wonder and enlightenment, returning me to several pieces and excerpts that have long been close to my heart and introducing me to several more that I have never quite gotten to, or that have lingered in obscurity for ages. In all, it must be the most comprehensive, insightful, and inspiring compilation of Zion writing ever assembled.

I have never forgotten my first encounter with Zion National Park. I couldn't have been more than four or five years old the first time our family drove through the canyon. I must have been asleep in the backseat because I've always remembered it as coming out of a dream. I peered out the window at the passing shops and motels and service stations of Springdale. Then Dad reached his arm across the seat and placed his fingers gently under my chin. With a simple nudge, he tilted my head and raised not only my eyes, but my heart to a new level. My eyes flashed up and I caught sight of that wondrous scene, the higher level that had been passing unnoticed.

Those castles in the clouds.

A half century later, I am an eyewitness, almost daily, to someone's first encounter with Zion Canyon. I watch and listen as they stop in their tracks, look up, take a deep breath, and sigh something indecipherable as they exhale. It seems that for most people confronted by Zion's towers of stone for the first time, words fail them. They stand transfixed and utter something like "Wow," or "Awesome," or "Unbelievable" (often in a foreign language) and know that they have not come close to expressing what they feel. At a loss for the right words, they default to the camera, as if the only way to define what they are experiencing is to digitize it for later reference. As the old saying goes, a picture is worth a thousand words.

For hundreds of years people have been trying to communicate what this canyon means to them with symbols on rock and words on paper. The early explorers and scientists did a remarkable job of recording in prose the geology, flora, fauna, and human history of the area. But even they never set out into canyon country without illustrators, photographers, cartographers, and fine artists in tow, to back up their words with amazing images.

Frederick Dellenbaugh, who explored the area with John Wesley Powell in the early 1870s and returned to spend some serious time in Zion Canyon in the summer of 1903, was one of the few Zion chroniclers who could not only write but was also an accomplished illustrator, cartographer, and fine art oil painter. His work, as pointed out in these pages, played an important role in opening the eyes of the country to the importance of setting Zion Canyon aside as a national park. One might debate whether it was his words, published in the January 1904 edition of *Scribner's Magazine*, or his series of paintings that hung in the 1904 World's Fair in St. Louis that had the greatest impact.

I often find myself returning to Dellenbaugh's article in *Scribner's*, entitled "A New Valley of Wonders." It is written in the style of its time, perhaps "overwritten" by today's prose standards, but for me it comes as close as anything to communicating the beauty, the power, and the mystery of Zion Canyon. Whenever I read anew Dellenbaugh's impassioned response to his first view of the temples and towers of the Virgin, the words move me as deeply as any photograph or painting.

> Never before has such a naked mountain of rock entered into our minds! Without a shred of disguise its transcendent form rises preeminent. There is almost nothing to compare to it. Niagara has the beauty of energy; the Grand Canyon, of immensity; the Yellowstone, of singularity; the Yosemite, of altitude; the ocean, of power; this great temple, of eternity.

When I come to the word "eternity" at the end of that soliloquy, I am convinced that there are times when a word is worth a thousand pictures.

With the advent of digital photography, photos of Zion National Park have become as ubiquitous as air. On any summer day I would posit that more photographs are taken from the bridge crossing the Virgin River at Canyon Junction than the total number of articles and books published on Zion since it became a national park. Over the decades, hundreds of articles and scores of books have been published about Zion. The book you hold in your hands is one of the few that relies little on illustrations and photographs to tell the canyon's story. And with good reason, since this is one of the few books about Zion that doesn't *need* photos to support it. The words, stories, articles, and excerpts so thoughtfully and skillfully gathered here by Nathan Waite and Reid Neilson paint as magnificent a picture of Zion Canyon as any artist could render on canvas or photographer could capture on a digital storage card.

While photos and paintings are a wonderful conduit, nothing connects a person to a place more than story. In Zion, some find that connection in the epic saga of the canyon's geology. Others find it in the meandering Virgin River and its riparian oasis in the desert. For some, the story starts with the Ancestral Puebloan people who inhabited the canyon more than a thousand years ago, or the band of the Southern Paiute known as the Parus who lived along the river for centuries before Mormon settlers arrived. For others, it's the story of the Mormon pioneer experience in the canyon that connects them to this place. The development of the canyon as a national park is a fascinating story including the golden age of travel, camping, and the building of Zion Lodge and the Zion–Mt. Carmel Tunnel. For many folks, the stories that connect them most to Zion are their own stories of working summers at the lodge, or precious memories of a childhood visit, or canyoneering through the cliffs, or an encounter with a mule deer on the trail.

Stories such as the classic writings in this collection enliven the landscape and connect us with it more intimately than any other medium. It makes no difference whether they are fiction, nonfiction, poetry, essay, science, folklore, or history. The stories started millions of years ago when the landscape now known as Zion was covered by sand dunes thousands of feet deep. Over the ages, those dunes solidified into a continuous mass of solid sandstone. As the eons passed, streams began to erode and cut spaces through fissures in the stone. Canyons formed and widened as walls slumped off and washed away. What remained, as peaks and towers and mesas and spires, were those ledges with a harder, erosion-resistant cap of rock atop them. Those resistant caps allowed the majestic castle-like skyline to survive. With the passage of time, nature has continued to sculpt the artful horizon we recognize as Zion Canyon.

It strikes me now that each piece in this wonderful anthology of Zion writing is a kind of erosion-resistant cap that contributes to the formation of a beautiful landscape of understanding. Without the stories shared in these pages, that understanding would erode away, leaving a stark and featureless horizon offering little hope for the future. The more we learn about Zion Canyon—the more we immerse ourselves in the words that comprise its history, science, art, and lore—the more vividly that landscape will take shape in our hearts, and the more we will be inclined to help ensure that generations unborn will experience the same joy and renewal we do when we visit Zion.

Lyman Hafen
Executive Director
Zion Natural History Association

Acknowledgments

The history and literature of Zion Canyon, though scattered among various repositories, is remarkably well preserved, and we thank the curators of the many archives and special collections who were constantly ready to assist us. In particular we thank Justin D. Hall, museum curator at Zion National Park; Michelle Elnicky of the Utah State Historical Society; Jeffrey Cannon, Brittany Chapman, and their colleagues at the Church History Library, Salt Lake City; Paula Mitchell and Janet Seegmiller, special collections librarians at the Sherratt Library, Southern Utah University; Amber D'Ambrosio, special collections librarian at Dixie State College; and the staff members of special collections housed at the Harold B. Lee Library, Brigham Young University; and the J. Willard Marriott Library, University of Utah.

We appreciate Carole Ann West and Michelle Waite for their careful help in transcribing the texts and preparing them for publication. For generously answering questions and sharing their extensive knowledge of Zion's history, we thank Wayne K. Hinton and Walter J. Woodbury. For his characteristically well-written preface and for his enthusiasm and advice throughout the project, we are greatly indebted to Lyman Hafen of the Zion Natural History Association. Many thanks are also due to Peter DeLafosse, John Alley, Stephanie Warnick, and Jessica Booth of the University of Utah Press for shepherding the manuscript to final publication, as well as to our pitch-perfect copy editor, Laurel Anderton. Finally, thanks to the group of historian-adventurers that accompanied us down the Subway in September 2013. It made for a memorable conclusion to this project.

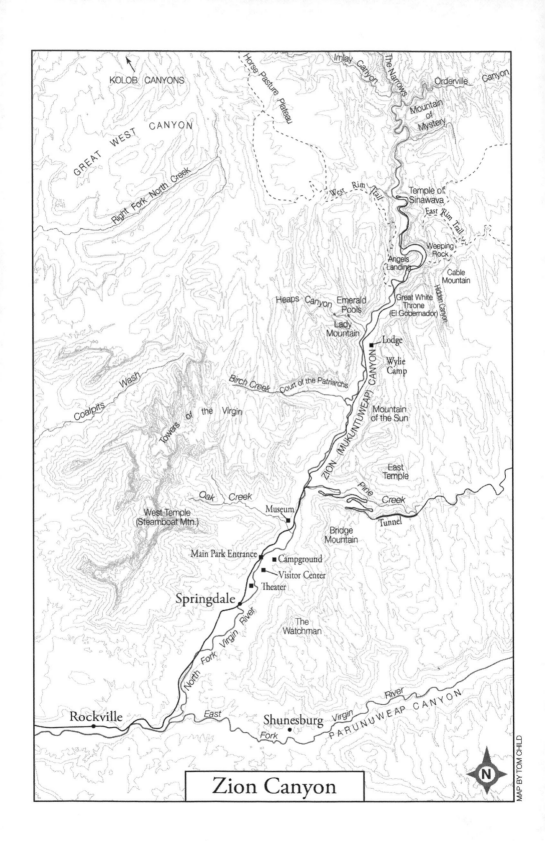

Zion Canyon

MAP BY TOM CHILD

Introduction

Imagining Zion

NATHAN N. WAITE

There are as many Zion Canyons as there have been ancient nomadic pass-ersby, pioneering settlers, railroad boosters, ranchers, herders, environ-mentalists, park rangers, hotel developers, adrenaline junkies, artists, and spiritual seekers who have laid eyes on this "Yosemite done in oils." A hand-ful of their stories are told in this reader, which endeavors to portray the many human perspectives of the canyon.

The stories of Zion I bring to this project derive from a lifetime of sed-imentary recollections. I have early childhood memories of Dutch oven cookouts in the shadow of the Great White Throne and of zigzagging up Walter's Wiggles to take in the stunning view at Scout Lookout (my mom wisely ended the hike there, thinking better of heading out to Angels Land-ing with rambunctious children). I remember driving through the Zion tunnel, Dad honking merrily away. It was my dad who instilled in me a love of this place, built on endless drives in the Colorado Plateau and ever-enthusiastic hikes in Zion, dragging along young children and, in later years, sometimes unappreciative teenagers. As I grew older, the layers of my imagined Zion Canyon became more complex: I spent a night on a narrow ledge, contemplating my own mortality as I waited for a helicopter rescue after a rappel into the wrong drainage. I learned of the competing interests of development and preservation, recreation and irrigation, and I came to understand (not least through the designation of Grand Staircase-Escalante National Monument in 1996) that federal protection of wild lands was not universally viewed as a good thing. One of the perils and promises of study-ing history and the humanities is that you can no longer see your world strictly from your own viewpoint: you see it for the contested space it is.

Two summers ago I read the spellbinding account (found in chapter 7 herein) of John Wesley Powell's descent of Parunuweap Canyon, carved by the East Fork of the Virgin River, and I decided I had to see it for myself. My adventurous wife agreed to come along. The portion of Parunuweap within park boundaries has long been closed to visitors because of its fragile Indian artifacts, and the only ready access to the upper canyon involves a grueling twelve-mile hike beginning and ending at Checkerboard Mesa, accompanied by a series of rappels, downclimbs, and swims through a tributary slot. Very occasionally, when I wasn't so tired I saw only the sand at my feet, a sense of what I can only call transcendence swept over me. We did not encounter another human being the entire day. We saw the color of the sandstone walls transform from charcoal to glowing ember to wildfire, and then as the day wore on and evening came, subside back to ashy grays. When finally we stood in the East Fork of the Virgin and looked up and up and up the walls of the narrow chasm, it was impossible not to relate to the breathless nature writing scattered throughout this book. The sense of vastness of space and time, coupled with the overwhelming aesthetic power of the rock layers, defied words but left indelible memories. I posed for a photograph next to the plaque dedicated to Powell's visit and marveled that anyone could manage such adventuring in the days before nylon ropes and neoprene socks—to say nothing of descending the canyon with only one arm, as Major Powell did. By the time we again reached Checkerboard Mesa, we had been baptized by water from murky potholes and fire from sore muscles, and the spiritual renewal I felt long outlasted the utter exhaustion.

NAMING THE CANYON

One way to approach the many historical and cultural Zion Canyons— Zion as impenetrable wall, as site of limited but sheltered farmland, as access point to timber and other natural resources, as aesthetic wonder and sign of God's hand in creation, as remote and inaccessible national monument, as overrun vacation getaway, as threatened wilderness, as locked-up resources, as home—is by tracing the names assigned it and the values such names carry. On one level, naming signals the obliteration of a place's past in order to begin anew. In 1925, the *New York Times* carried an article about Zion National Park, lamenting movements afoot to rename the features of the canyon and declaring, "Names which have become legends should be protected no less than the spots they adorn."[1] The writer makes explicit the notion that what is being preserved is not merely a place but a particular conception imposed on a place by its naming. It is not simply the preservation of a natural resource but a monument to the mindset of those exploring or inhabiting the land, as captured in the name.

At the same time that Euro-American naming represents an erasure of history and the projection of self onto the external world, it also signifies a willingness to enter into a relationship with a location, an insertion of self into landscape, and an investment in what's going on around here. To name a place is to consider it worth remembering and sharing; it is to begin a story of self and community in place.

According to Powell, the Indian inhabitants of the region called the canyon *Mukuntuweap*, which Powell said Paiutes told him meant "straight canyon."[2] As explained by historian Angus M. Woodbury in the 1940s, however, "there has been much dispute as to its derivation and application." Woodbury's Southern Paiute informants variously interpreted the canyon name as "red country," "red dirt," "big canyon," "arrow quiver," or "Mukun's canyon"—or they did not recognize the word at all. Woodbury's contemporary, the self-trained anthropologist William R. Palmer, speculated that it might be "derived from the Indian word yucca or oose, muk-unk, the whole word muk-unk-o-weap, thus meaning Oose Creek (or since the oose was sometimes used for soap simply Soap Creek)."[3] Further reinforcing their own interpretation of things, members of The Church of Jesus Christ of Latter-day Saints (Mormons) who pioneered the region told Woodbury the name meant "place of the gods" or "God's land." As probably became clear to Woodbury, the appellations we give places often divulge more information about the namers than the named.

The first white explorers to note the canyon's features in writing were Mormon scouts from Salt Lake City, reconnoitering the area for possible settlement. They did not name the towers and cliffs they saw from afar, but their description aptly conveys their view of the hostile southern Utah landscape as they approached what is now St. George:

> The great Wasatch range along which we had travelled during our whole journey here terminates in several abrupt Promontorys. The Country Southward opening to the view as it were a wide expanse of

chaotic matter [,] huge hills, Sandy deserts, cheerless, grassless, water-less plains, perpendicular rocks, loose barren clay, dissolving beds of Sandstone & various other elements, lying in inconceivable confusion, in short a country in ruins,...turned inside out, upside down by terrible convulsions in some former age.[4]

Springdale, at the entrance to Zion Canyon, offered only a narrow strip of arable land and was the last place along the upper Virgin River that the Mormons settled, in 1862. Still farther up the canyon, separated by more than a mile of rocky terrain, was an even smaller strip of land (in the vicinity of the present-day Zion Park Lodge), a richly fertile ancient lakebed. The first settler in the canyon, Isaac Behunin, also gave the canyon the name by which it was first known to locals—Zion.

At the designation of U.S. national monument status in 1909, the name *Mukuntuweap* was bestowed, pointedly following Powell's designation in preference to its local name. The name introduced immediate confusion. Reporters complained of the unintelligible moniker and tried to clear up the meaning in readers' minds. The *New York Times* reported that *Tuweap* meant farmable land and that *Mukun* derived from an old Indian named Muggins who resided there.[5] In 1917, a local paper reported that despite claims that the name meant "Land of Many Waters" or "Land of the Birds," "no Indian could be found who recognized the word Mukuntuweap as of Indian origin, or who could understand it."[6]

When Horace M. Albright, acting director of the National Park Service, visited in 1917, he fell in love with everything about the canyon, except its name. "I always preferred local names, especially native Indian ones, for natural wonders," he later wrote, "but 'Mukuntuweap' was too difficult to pronounce and really tough to spell." He learned from the local people that the common name of the canyon, *Zion*, meant "heaven" or a "heavenly place" and concluded, "That sounded about right to me."[7] The name was changed later that year and was codified in 1919 at national park designation.

The name *Zion* offers the same proliferation of meanings as does *Mukuntuweap*, and almost from the moment Behunin bestowed the name, visitors have interpreted its meaning differently. The connotation that has stuck, and that was most recently reiterated at the centennial celebration of the park, is that of sanctuary and refuge. Angus Woodbury interpreted this meaning in terms of Behunin's experience with the persecution of the early Mormon movement: "Here in Zion he felt that at last he had reached a place of safety where he could rest assured of no more harassments and persecutions. No wonder he proposed the name Zion, which implies a resting place. He went even further, maintaining that should the Saints again be harassed by their enemies, this would become their place of refuge."[8] A 1918 *Salt Lake Telegram* article interpreted the name as signifying a potential refuge from more imminent threats: "This difficult canyon was chosen as a refuge in the event of Indian attack."[9] How a box canyon could serve as an escape from an Indian attack is unclear.

Other sources say that the inspiration for the name was not safety and refuge but the beauty of the canyon. "My father named the place Zion Canyon," stated Elijah Behunin in 1930, "and said as he gazed up at the great Canyon walls, these are the Temples of God. One can worship here as well as in any man-made Temple."[10] The story is told that during a visit by Brigham Young in 1870, the underwhelmed Mormon prophet, irritable either from the bumpy ride into Zion Canyon or from finding among residents an open violation of the faith's proscription against tobacco, dismissed the canyon, saying, "This is not Zion," and perhaps adding, "Zion is the pure in heart." And the legend says that the settlers dutifully (or impudently) began referring to the canyon as "not Zion."

Outsiders interpreted the name in its traditional biblical sense. Nineteenth-century surveyor Clarence Dutton relied on the description in 2 Corinthians for his interpretation: "No wonder the fierce Mormon zealot, who named it, was reminded of the Great Zion, on which his fervid thoughts were bent: of houses not built with hands, eternal in the heavens."[11] Not all were satisfied with the name. A correspondent to the *New York Times* wrote in August 1873 of a trip into the canyon, which inspired him in every way other than in its name. "The valley vastly excels the famous Yosemite," he wrote. "It is called by the Mormons 'Little Zion Valley;' but as this name has been only a short time applied, it is to be hoped some other, more consonant with the character of the place, may be adopted."[12]

From Behunin's perspective, a complete understanding of the name takes into account ancient Zion—in the conventional Judeo-Christian tradition, it is the mountain citadel in the desert and site of the temple of God, beside a life-giving stream. Mormon founder Joseph Smith, however, added several layers of meaning. He made Zion a uniquely American site, located in Jackson County, Missouri. He made it the site of the primeval Garden of Eden, perpetually green in contrast to Jerusalem's desolate environs. And he added the apocalyptic New Jerusalem, bringing the sacred city of God, built without mortal hands, crashing to the earth in a melding of the sacred and the profane, heaven and earth. After the Mormons came to the Rocky Mountains, the idea of Zion evolved to embrace a conception of Zion as being found in the tops of the mountains as prophesied by Isaiah.

STORIES OF ZION

Interpretations of the names *Mukuntuweap* and *Zion* expose the values that different people brought to their encounters with the canyon, as well as the values and meanings they assigned *to* the canyon. Even more than the names we attach to a location, the stories we tell about it outline the contours of the place in our cognitive maps. The accounts in this volume trace those contours. An anthology necessarily involves the artificial sifting, dividing, and organizing of information. The collection that follows is our attempt to present an array of voices encompassing many different perspectives on Zion Canyon. The book is divided into five thematic sections, roughly corresponding to chronological periods in the history of the canyon.

The editorial method employed in this book is on the conservative side: to retain the character and flavor of the original texts, particularly the historical documents, we retain variant spellings and other idiosyncrasies. When such errors could lead to confusion, we clarify as best we can in square brackets or end notes. We have corrected obvious typographical errors and made other minor changes, such as smoothing out uneven punctuation, to improve consistency.

The opening section, "The Land and Its Earliest Inhabitants," has the immodest task of summarizing not only the 8,000 years of human history on the Colorado Plateau before European explorers came on the scene but also the preceding 240 million years of geologic and natural history.

"Water and the Geology of Zion National Park" provides a thumbnail view of the hydrologic forces that cut through the white-topped Navajo Sandstone layer and the sloping Kayenta Formation below it to form the cliffs and grottoes, hoodoos and oases in the park. These geologic formations are the habitat for an extraordinary diversity of life, including species found nowhere else (the tiny Zion snail, for instance) and the critically endangered (Mexican spotted owl, desert tortoise, Virgin River chub). The canyon is also home to reintroduced wildlife, including the bighorn sheep, woundfin minnow, and California condor. In "Flora and Fauna," Zion Canyon native J. L. Crawford gives a description of the plant and animal life found in the canyon. Born in 1914 in a cabin a stone's throw from where the visitor center now stands, Crawford contributed a bookshelf of work on Zion's history and was a popular speaker until his death in 2011.

Archaeological artifacts found in the canyon speak of a persistent human presence dating from the Archaic period, as early as 6000 BCE. The earliest cliff dwellings were home to bands of the Ancient Pueblo and date back to 500–1300 CE. Beginning about the same time, Numic speakers, particularly Southern Paiutes, or Nuwuvi, inhabited and cultivated the region that included the upper Virgin River valley. This volume contains three texts relating to the native presence in Zion Canyon. The first is a selection from Greer Chesher's *Zion Canyon: A Storied Land*. Chesher, a nature writer and former park ranger, brings to her writing an awareness of the many layers of environmental and human history operating in Zion, and she weaves together her own imagination of Zion Canyon with the story of the Ancient Pueblo and later Southern Paiute peoples. "Origin of the Pai-Utes" gives the creation story of the Southern Paiutes, as recorded by John Wesley Powell in the 1870s. In "From the Beginning," anthropologist Martha C. Knack explains the geography of the Southern Paiutes and describes their lifestyle at the time they first encountered white settlers. Those earliest settlers were Mormon migrants, who under the leadership of Brigham Young had fled the United States and in 1847 established headquarters on the shores of the Great Salt Lake. Young then sent vanguard companies to establish settlements throughout the Mountain West and, as author and historian Wallace Stegner vividly describes in "The Land Nobody Wanted...," they soon encountered the inhospitable beauty of the Colorado Plateau.

Part 2, "Euro-American Explorers," comprises firsthand reports by explorers and surveyors of Zion Canyon, documenting the first steps toward its discovery by tourists and vacationers. Before the Mormons arrived on the scene, other explorers had left their footprints in the vicinity of Zion Canyon. The Dominguez-Escalante expedition had passed close by in 1776, and the paths of explorers and trappers, notably Jedediah Smith and John C. Fremont, had crisscrossed the shadow of the cliffs of Zion. By about 1830, the Old Spanish Trail, running from Santa Fe to Los Angeles, passed within sight distance of the Kolob Canyons and the immense West Temple of Zion Canyon.

The geologist and Civil War veteran John Wesley Powell captured the nation's imagination in 1869 when he successfully navigated the Colorado River through Grand Canyon. The trip marked the start of the government-funded Powell Survey of the Colorado Plateau, and in 1872 he descended the East Fork of the Virgin River through what he named Parunuweap Canyon to its confluence with the North Fork. The canyon carved by the North Fork Powell called Mukuntuweap. His description of the exploration, published in *Scribner's Monthly* in 1875 and in the *Report on the Exploration of the Colorado River of the West and Its Tributaries* later the same year (expanded and republished in 1895), proved a key step in turning Zion Canyon into a world-famous natural wonder as reports trickled back to the eastern United States of this "newfound" marvel. The trickle grew to a steady stream as Powell's associates presented their findings to the nation. Grove Karl Gilbert, a member of the Wheeler Survey, descended the Narrows in 1872 and described Zion Canyon as "the most wonderful defile it has been my fortune to behold."[13] In 1873 Powell invited famed landscape painter Thomas Moran to tour the canyon country. One result of Moran's tour was his enormous painting of Grand Canyon, now hanging in the U.S. Capitol. Moran was particularly taken with the cliffs and river of Mukuntuweap, and he painted them in fine Hudson River school style. In the same party was Powell Survey photographer J. K. Hillers, who took some of the first photographs of the canyon, and Moran's traveling companion, journalist James Colburn, who published reports of the trip in the *New York Times*. Of Zion Canyon, Colburn wrote that "in beauty of forms, in color, in variety, in everything but size, [it] vastly excels the famous Yosemite."[14]

Geologist Clarence E. Dutton was brought on board the Powell Survey in 1875 and spent fifteen years surveying the high plateau country of southern Utah. His monumental *Tertiary History of the Grand Cañon District* included a description of Zion Canyon that strays from the field of scientific description to shout praises to God's creations. Accompanying the writer's breathless prose were a massive folio-size atlas and meticulously detailed drawings of the striated rock formations there, prepared by William Henry Holmes. Another of Powell's colleagues was Frederick S. Dellenbaugh, who had joined the second Powell expedition down Grand Canyon as artist and topographer and who spent several decades exploring and documenting the Colorado Plateau region. He promoted the park twice over in 1904— through paintings exhibited at the World's Fair in St. Louis and through a feature article for *Scribner's Monthly* focused on Zion, the "New Valley of Wonders." Such promotion did not go unnoticed.

In 1908, St. George resident Leo A. Snow surveyed the land that included the west rim of Zion Canyon for the Office of the U.S. Surveyor General. His field notes included his observation that from the precipice, "a view can be had of this canyon surpassed only by a similar view of the Grand Canyon of the Colorado.... In my opinion this canyon should be set apart by the government as a national park."[15] Acting on authority recently granted him by the Antiquities Act, President William Howard Taft set aside 15,840 acres of the canyon as Mukuntuweap National Monument the next year.

Part 3, "From Remote Outpost to Vacation Destination," follows the story of the canyon from national monument designation in 1909 up through 1956, when the Kolob Terrace was added to the northeast portion of the canyon, effectively giving the park its present-day boundaries. The writings in part 3 are best understood in the context of improved access to the park and the exponential growth in visitation in these years—up from 3,700 to 55,000 from 1920 to 1930 alone. In some cases, the pieces presented here contributed to that growth.

The nation did not at first come in droves to visit the newly designated monument. The building of railroads had already revolutionized transportation, and mass production of the automobile was not far in the future, but in 1909 the canyon was still extremely remote, involving a rail journey to Lund, Utah, in the desert west of Cedar City, followed by an automobile trip down the Black Ridge and back up the Hurricane Cliffs to the mouth of the canyon on what could only charitably be described as a road. From Springdale, a decades-old wagon trail led into the canyon itself. Of the few who braved the journey to the national monument, Wall Street lawyer and amateur geologist George D. Fraser left one of the most memorable accounts in his journal, excerpted here. Fraser, an intrepid forerunner to the modern national parks tourist, journeyed from New Jersey to make a series of expeditions to view the scenic wonders of southern Utah and northern Arizona in the 1910s.

Another who braved the rough roads to the canyon was Frederick Vining Fisher, a Methodist minister turned lecturer who traveled the country promoting the natural wonders of the United States, with a special focus on Utah. In summer 1916 he traveled to Mukuntuweap National Monument to capture slides to use with his lectures, and his trip left a lasting mark on the canyon. As described in the newspaper article "The Canyon Sublime," Fisher and his Mormon companions took turns naming the cliffs and promontories they spied from the valley floor. Some of their designations never took—for example, there is no longer a "Court of the Poets" with peaks named Homer, Milton, and Shakespeare—but many were ultimately codified on maps and in the public consciousness. When visitors today use names like the Court of the Patriarchs and the Great White Throne, they are unknowingly invoking Fisher's imagination of the canyon.

A principal supporter of improved access and increased visitation to the park was the Union Pacific–owned Los Angeles & Salt Lake Railroad. In the 1910s Union Pacific sponsored many trips to the canyon for government officials and journalists. By 1917, the state had improved the road to the monument and federal funding had built a modern road into the canyon itself. The first of many promotional pieces the railroad produced was the 1917 brochure *Zion Canyon: Utah's New Wonderland*, touting the convenient rail journey to Lund, the "interesting scenic motoring" to the monument, and the awe-inspiring spectacles of the canyon. The railroad partnered with the newly minted National Park Transportation and Camping Company to bus tourists from the rail station to the park and accommodate them in the "Wylie Camp," located south of the present-day lodge. The next year, a well-known mountaineering enthusiast named LeRoy Jeffers visited Zion.

The report he dispatched to *Scientific American* documents the remarkable breadth of his explorations there; Jeffers not only made the requisite trip to the mouth of the Narrows but spent time on the seldom-visited Kolob Plateau, west of the main canyon.

At the recommendation of Horace M. Albright, acting director of the National Park Service, Mukuntuweap National Monument was in 1918 renamed Zion National Monument and expanded to 76,800 acres, five times its original size. The next year, Utah senator Reed M. Smoot successfully shepherded a bill through the legislature, and President Woodrow Wilson signed a law on November 19, 1919, making Zion a national park, the first in Utah and the sixteenth in the nation. In "Zion National Park with Some Reminiscences Fifty Years Later," southern Utah historian Andrew Karl Larson recalls his participation in the dedicatory services held the next year and the visit from U.S. president Warren G. Harding in 1923.

Also included in part 3 is a brochure titled *All Aboard for Zion*, published by Union Pacific in 1926, shortly after the company bought out the other shareholders in the Salt Lake Route to gain complete ownership of the line. The advertisement is notable not only for its stunningly purple prose but also for the advancement of travel and accommodations it documents. The railroad now extended into Cedar City, where a modern hotel, El Escalante, awaited the weary traveler and good roads carried the adventurer to the front door of the recently built Zion Lodge (see part 4). By this time, of course, the railroads were beginning to lose their hold on the travel market as the country came to rely more and more on the private automobile.

The next two pieces serve as reminders that even with ready access and growing popularity, the canyon was still, for many, an untamed wilderness, full of danger and adventure. In 1927, a self-professed rock-climbing expert from California named William H. Evans attempted to scale the vertical walls of the Great White Throne. Angus M. Woodbury, who went on to write the definitive history of Zion National Park, was serving as the park's first naturalist at the time and wrote of the efforts he and others made to rescue Evans when he failed to return. And in the early 1930s, the celebrated nomad Everett Ruess turned his back on the frenzied pace of modern life to experience the canyons of southern Utah in a more primitive and solitary manner. With his poetry and woodcuts, his anachronistic burro, and his disappearance in 1934 at the age of twenty, Ruess left an enduring mark on the American Southwest. Presented here are letters he wrote while visiting Zion Canyon in 1931 as well as a poem he began while there.

The final piece in this section jumps ahead twenty years to describe the Zion Canyon of the 1950s, when modern highways and ubiquitous roadside motels put the national parks within easy reach of the casual vacationer. The trip down the Zion Narrows that wilderness advocate and writer Lewis F. Clark described for *National Geographic* has the spirit of adventure reminiscent of an earlier age in Zion, but it was now an adventure whose risks were mitigated by asphalt roads all the way to the Temple of Sinewava and a backcountry desk with rangers ready with advice and a rescue party. Even in this period, however, Zion was relatively unknown, with far fewer visitors than national parks like Yellowstone and Yosemite. Clark's full-color article introduced the park to millions.

Part 4, "Human Constructions," focuses on four artificial developments introduced in the canyon over the last century. A local named David Flanigan spent years advocating for a cable system to transport lumber from the forests above the canyon rim to the valleys below; when the idea gained no traction he built the system himself. After he completed the cable works in 1901, millions of board feet of lumber flew down the thousand-foot "Cable Mountain" to reach the settlements below. By the time operations ceased in the mid-1920s, the timber supply on the plateau had been decimated. The remnants of the cable works can still be seen north of the Great White Throne from the West Rim Trail.

The last major contract for wood from the cable was to build Zion Park Lodge. As part of its development of scenic tours in southern Utah and northern Arizona, the Union Pacific Railroad invested in several lodges in the national parks; the first of these was in Zion. Through her history of the lodge presented here, architectural historian Christine Barnes also tells the story of the evolving transportation and tourism movements in the American West.

On July 4, 1930, automobiles began to rumble through the Zion–Mt. Carmel Tunnel. The project had taken three years to complete, and the finished tunnel stretched just over a mile through solid stone. Twenty-six years after George Fraser made the torturous journey over bad roads to

visit the geologic curiosities of southern Utah, motorists could now journey from anywhere in the United States and drive not only into the canyon
but up a set of switchbacks and through the sandstone walls themselves to
reach the highway that would take them north to Bryce Canyon or south
to Grand Canyon. Donald T. Garate, a historian of the American West,
documents this engineering feat in "The Zion Tunnel: From Slickrock to
Switchback." The author of the next piece, environmentalist Edward Abbey,
would have vehemently opposed the Zion tunnel had he been born thirty
years earlier. In the excerpt from his classic *Desert Solitaire*, Abbey argues in
his distinctive cantankerous style against opening up Zion and the other
national parks to "progress"; he would rather have seen them remain as
difficult as possible to reach in order to dissuade all but the most devoted
from visiting.

The final chapter in the "Human Constructions" section is an account
by a reporter for the *Los Angeles Times* detailing a more recent major battle
over development in Zion Canyon—building the mammoth movie theater at the park's front door in the 1990s. The ensuing clashes over conservation and economic opportunity—often cast reductively as a clash
between outsiders and locals—highlight the contentious space that Zion
and other protected spaces embody. Balancing conservation and use is an
ongoing concern, and innovations such as instituting a shuttle transportation system into the canyon in 2000 and banning the sale of plastic water
bottles in 2008 will no doubt continue.

Part 5, "Senses of Place," presents a handful of the countless stories told
about present-day Zion by the more than 2.8 million people who visit each
year. In "The Land That God Forgot," Mormon historian Juanita Brooks,
who is better known for her unflinching historical scrutiny of southern
Utah, extols her homeland's beauty in the language of a booster. In her
essay, Brooks writes as a seasoned and well-spoken tour guide for the unini-
tiated visitor. The next chapter, "Rough Hike through the Wrong Canyon,"
is vacationer Edwin Reed's account of his perception of the Zion Narrows.
Though Reed was not oblivious to the beauty of the place, his view of
the park was forever changed by a night spent shivering on a rocky outcropping, clutching his young children after a flash flood roared down the
canyon.

In 1972, French composer Olivier Messiaen toured Utah to seek inspiration for a piece he had been commissioned to write for the bicentennial celebration of the United States. Messiaen had long before established himself as one of the century's most important composers, starting with his *Quartet for the End of Time*, composed and first performed while Messiaen was a prisoner of war during World War II. In the canyons of southern Utah, the musician found something uniquely and essentially American. The interview excerpted here gives Messiaen's explanation of how the piece he wrote for the bicentennial, *From the Canyons to the Stars...*, including its final movement, "Zion Park and the Celestial City," gives a musical rendition of the grandeur of the canyons, the songs of the birds he heard there, and even the colors of the rocks.

The next chapter, "The Spirit of Kinesava," presents Lyman Hafen's description of his own revelatory experience in Zion, this one obtained at one of the canyon's most popular and vertigo-inducing lookouts, Angels Landing. Hafen, who is director of the Zion Natural History Association and a longtime chronicler of his native southern Utah, experiences a vision of the canyon's guardian-god, who casts the history of Zion in mythological terms but ultimately leaves the meaning of the canyon to individual interpretation. In "Kolob Backcountry: Paradise Found," outdoor enthusiast and writer Paul Rea describes the revelations attendant to a backpacking trip in the Kolob Canyons region, far from the crowds and shuttles of the main canyon.

The final chapter, "Zion Pioneers and Spirituality in the Land of Zion," is taken from *Pioneer Voices of Zion Canyon*, a distillation of oral interviews with second- and third-generation residents of the upper Virgin River valley, many now in their eighties and nineties. These are the people who as children saw the first automobile drive into Springdale and who watched their sleepy farming communities transformed into the gateway to a world-famous attraction. In the chapter excerpted here, they tell of the connection they and their forebears have with the land as well as the responsibility they feel toward it. Their observations about stewardship and religion begin to complicate the conventional wisdom that those who are best equipped to understand and appreciate and care for Zion are the outsider, the artist, the aesthete; they offer hope that religious beliefs, which have always played a commanding role in determining land use policy and practice in the American West, need not be inimical to environmental ethics.

RESPONSIBILITIES

Of course, the stories we tell about Zion Canyon are not a complete representation of the canyon. The purpose of this reader is to convey a few of the "many Zions," as Chesher puts it in her book. A collection of writings about this landscape cannot convey the canyon's essence, but the writings can convey, perfectly, the understanding that humans are inextricably integrated—and implicated—in the landscape. The stories we tell ourselves about Zion give us a vested interest in the future of this place, and the more stories we hear, and the more disparate their viewpoints, the greater our ability to empathize with and respect other viewpoints and to foster an ethic of care for our fellow humans and the natural world. The more we learn about the ecology of our relationships (with both the human and more-than-human world), the more we sense that there is much we do not understand, and the more we realize that we must act with humility. This is not to say we should not fight passionately to protect places like Zion Canyon. It is to say that we need to be open to scrutinizing from what and for what we will be protecting them.

The environmental historian William Cronon has eloquently argued that we must problematize our understanding of place if we are to act responsibly in relation to our increasingly threatened world. He writes, "The flight from history that is very nearly the core of wilderness represents the false hope of an escape from responsibility, the illusion that we can somehow wipe clean the slate of our past and return to the tabula rasa that supposedly existed before we began to leave our marks on the world." He continues:

> If this is so—if by definition wilderness leaves no place for human beings, save perhaps as contemplative sojourners enjoying their leisurely reverie in God's natural cathedral—then also by definition it can offer no solution to the environmental and other problems that confront us....Worse: to the extent that we live in an urban-industrial civilization but at the same time pretend to ourselves that our real

home is in the wilderness, to just that extent we give ourselves permission to evade responsibility for the lives we actually lead. We inhabit civilization while holding some part of ourselves—what we imagine to be the most precious part—aloof from its entanglements. We work our nine-to-five jobs in its institutions, we eat its food, we drive its cars (not least to reach the wilderness), we benefit from the intricate and all too invisible networks with which it shelters us, all the while pretending that these things are not an essential part of who we are. By imagining that our true home is in the wilderness, we forgive ourselves the homes we actually inhabit.[16]

The stories told in this book serve to turn the reader toward Zion Canyon, to call up in our minds our own experiences there, and to reinforce or challenge our perceptions of the place. At the same time, they should teach us about ourselves, about how we form our identity around places like Zion Canyon, and perhaps how we too easily forgive ourselves of our responsibility for the other places.

NOTES

1.   Wallace Smith, "'Just Too Cuters' Now Invade Zion Park," *New York Times*, August 16, 1925.

2.   John Wesley Powell, *Explorations of the Colorado River of the West* (Washington, DC: Government Printing Office, 1875), 111.

3.   Angus M. Woodbury, *A History of Southern Utah and Its National Parks*, 2nd ed. (Springdale, UT: Zion Natural History Association, 1997), 114.

4.   Parley P. Pratt, "Report to the Legislative Council of Deseret, 5 Feb. 1850," in *Over the Rim: The Parley P. Pratt Exploring Expedition to Southern Utah, 1849–50*, ed. William B. Smart and Donna T. Smart (Logan: Utah State University Press, 1999), 181.

5.   Smith, "Just Too Cuters."

6.   "Mukuntuweap Canyon. Indian, 'Mogantuweap,'" *Washington County News*, February 1, 1917.

7.   Horace M. Albright, *Creating the National Park Service: The Missing Years* (Norman: University of Oklahoma Press, 1999), 243.

8.   Woodbury, *History of Southern Utah*, 157.

9.   "Wilson Gives New Name to Monument in Utah," *Salt Lake Telegram*, May 30, 1918.

10. "Interview with E. C. Behunin," *Deseret News*, August 1930.

11. Clarence E. Dutton, *Tertiary History of the Grand Cañon District* (Washington, DC: Government Printing Office, 1882), 60.
12. James E. Colburn, "The Colorado Canyon," *New York Times*, September 4, 1873.
13. George M. Wheeler et al., *Report upon Geographical and Geological Explorations and Surveys West of the One Hundredth Meridian* (Washington, DC: Government Printing Office, 1875), 3:77.
14. Colburn, "Colorado Canyon." Colburn's is the earliest known account of Zion Canyon printed outside Utah.
15. Quoted in Woodbury, *History of Southern Utah*, 187.
16. William Cronon, "The Trouble with Wilderness; or, Getting Back to the Wrong Nature," in *Uncommon Ground: Rethinking the Human Place in Nature*, ed. William Cronon (New York: W. W. Norton, 1996), 80–81.

Part 1

The Land and Its Earliest Inhabitants

Parunuweap Canyon. Engraving published in John Wesley Powell's *Exploration of the Colorado River of the West*, 1875.

1 | Water and the Geology of Zion National Park

ROBERT L. EVES

In this excerpt from his book Water, Rock, and Time: The Geologic Story of Zion National Park, *Robert Eves gives a summary of the hydrologic and geologic forces that combined to form Zion Canyon and expose the 150 million years of Earth's history exhibited on its walls. Eves is a professor of chemistry and geology and dean of the College of Science and Engineering at Southern Utah University.*

Water is an important component in the past and current story of Zion National Park. Climate is the controlling factor in precipitation, the source of the park's water resources. Average precipitation equals 14.4 inches (36.6 cm) per year. The maximum reported annual precipitation in Zion National Park, recorded in 1978, was 25.9 inches (65.8 cm). Precipitation during the driest year on record, 1956, was reported at 3.2 inches (8.1 cm). This extreme variation is not, however, unusual for the semiarid climate of Zion National Park.

Precipitation falling to Earth is called meteoric water, and it enters the park's hydrologic system in one of two ways: from summer thundershowers, locally known as monsoons, or winter frontal storms. Summer thundershowers generally flow or run off along existing drainage networks, eventually exiting the park via the Virgin River. Winter frontal storms are usually confined to the highest elevations and have a better opportunity to infiltrate porous sediments and rock, becoming part of the park's groundwater system. Let's examine these two important components of Zion National Park hydrology.

RIVER (FLUVIAL) SYSTEMS

Though often overlooked because of their flow variations, desert streams are major agents of erosion. They erode, carry, and deposit sediment. Although they carry only about one-millionth of the Earth's water, they are the most important agents of surface change, particularly in Zion National Park. A stream erodes down through uplifted land toward base level, the lowest level to which it can erode its channel. Worldwide base level is sea level; however, streams often encounter temporary base levels, such as lakes, that halt their downward erosion for considerable periods of time.

Stream behavior is a very dynamic geological process. Streams respond immediately to changes in their environment. When a summer cloudburst dumps several inches of rain on a drainage basin, the stream quickly rises, flows rapidly, erodes more sediment, and deposits that sediment downstream. In an unchanging environment a stream's gradient, or slope, is at such an angle that a stream would flow just swiftly enough to transport all the sediment supplied to it by its drainage basin, resulting in little net erosion or deposition of sediment. However, when a stream's gradient is changed, by transgression or regression of the sea, for example, the stream responds appropriately. A lowering of base level causes the stream to cut downward; a rise causes it to deposit coarse sediments onto its bed.

The principal result of a stream's erosive power is the creation and deepening of valleys. The composition of a valley's rocks and sediments strongly influences the stream's effect. More resistant rocks (like well-cemented sandstone) erode slowly, while loose, less resistant materials are eroded more quickly.

A stream left to its own processes would cut vertically, forming near-vertical walls. However, most river valleys have a distinctive V-shape. Why is this so? The answer lies in the relationship between a stream's downcutting and related geologic processes. For example, although downcutting by the Colorado River is largely responsible for the 5,940 feet (1800 m) of vertical relief in the Grand Canyon, landslides and overland flow eroded the 13-mile (21 km) width.

Streams erode their channels by abrasion, hydraulic lifting, and dissolution. Abrasion is the scouring of a streambed by transported sediment in the stream. This is particularly true in swift-flowing, sediment-laden floodwaters. Hydraulic lifting, which is erosion under water pressure, occurs when turbulent stream flow dislodges sediment and loosens large chunks of rock. This process is most active during high-velocity floods. As an example, a 1923 flood along the Wasatch Mountain front of central Utah lifted 90-ton (82-metric ton) boulders and transported them more than 5 miles (8 km) downstream. When a stream flows across and dissolves soluble rocks, such as limestone, dissolution also contributes to stream erosion. The Niagara River, which flows between Lake Erie and Lake Ontario, carries 60 tons (55 metric tons) of dissolved rock over Niagara Falls every minute.

The processes of erosion by running water are very much in evidence in Zion National Park. After the Colorado Plateau rose from its near sea level position, its western edge broke into large blocks bounded by faults. Over time, movement on these faults caused thousands of feet of displacement and tilted the rocks of the Colorado Plateau gently toward the northeast. The Virgin River and its tributaries removed thousands of feet of strata from the block that contains Zion National Park. The erosion was more rapid near the western boundary of this block, which created the current network of west-draining canyons.

Zion National Park, with its spectacular steep-walled canyons and unlimited vistas, owes its very existence to the interaction between the upward movement of these blocks and the erosional work of the Virgin River. Zion Canyon was carved by the Virgin River.

The Virgin River originates on Cedar Mountain in southwestern Utah [and] flows through the northwestern corner of Arizona and into Nevada where it joins the Colorado River at Lake Mead. The Virgin River has a much steeper gradient than the Colorado, which has contributed significantly to its erosive power. It is comprised of two main branches: the North Fork (Mukuntuweap Canyon), which originates from springs located outside the park's north boundary, and the East Fork (Parunuweap Canyon), which also originates from springs located east of the North Fork. The Virgin River is approximately 160 miles (258 km) long and empties into Lake Mead. The total loss in elevation along its course is about 7,800 feet (2340 m), an average gradient of approximately 48 feet per mile (9 m per km). The gradient in Zion Canyon proper is about 71 feet per mile (13 m per km).

Despite its significant gradient, the Virgin River is a small, gently flowing stream. It is not difficult to wade across during most of the year and it flows through the park at an average of 100 cubic feet (30 m³) per second (cfs). It is hard to imagine that this stream could have eroded such an immense canyon as Zion. Although it appears to be clear much of the year the Virgin River transports an estimated one million tons, or more, of rock waste each year. The flow in Zion Canyon is quite variable and the 65-year record suggests a peak flow range from 20 to 9,150 cfs (0.6 to 256 m³ per sec). During the high flow periods the amount of material transported is staggering. Normal flow carries approximately 120 cubic yards (29 m³) of suspended sediment each 24-hour period, 43,800 cubic yards (10,585 m³) per year. It's estimated that a flood of ten times normal flow carries two thousand times more rock waste. That means one flood event can result in more sediment removal than an entire year at normal flow. When the wetter climates of the ice age and post–ice age periods are considered, the ability of the Virgin River to carve Zion Canyon in so short a time seems far more plausible.

GROUNDWATER SYSTEMS

Some precipitation soaks into the ground and slowly migrates down through soil and loose sediment into the underlying rocks. Water that infiltrates the Earth's surface and resides in unconsolidated, or solid rock, is called groundwater. As it percolates downward, this groundwater may find permeable rock layers called aquifers, or it may encounter tightly sealed rocks called aquitards.

Groundwater accumulates below the surface creating a horizon below which all pore space in loose sediment or rock is completely saturated with water. This surface, which fluctuates with climatic conditions, vegetation, and topography, is called the water table. In desert climates like Zion National Park, groundwater resources are the primary agent sustaining living systems. Groundwater is currently being mined all over the Southwest to supply the drinking water needs of a growing population.

The Navajo Sandstone in Zion National Park is an excellent aquifer that allows infiltrating water to move between sand grains through solid rock. The water typically filters downward until it encounters an aquitard—either a more completely cemented horizon in the Navajo, or the contact between the Navajo and the Kayenta Formations. With its downward progress halted, the groundwater moves horizontally. When its movement intercepts a sheer cliff face, or when erosion lowers the ground surface until the water table is intercepted, a spring results. Springs are very important features in Zion Canyon.

Recharged annually by snowfall in the park's high elevations, springs feed the Virgin River through the dry summer months. Springs are also critical to the existence of numerous micro-climates and environments in park canyons. Take a walk along the Weeping Rock or Gateway to the Narrows Trails and look at the fantastic array of living things associated with these groundwater sources.

In an environment as hostile as Zion Canyon, water is a critical factor, not only as a geologic agent, but to sustain living systems. In Zion National Park, as much as anywhere, one merely has to be observant to recognize that two major hydrologic subsystems—rivers and groundwater—are intimately linked and interdependent. They combined their forces throughout the history of the canyon's development.

2 | Flora and Fauna

J. L. Crawford

J. L. Crawford was born in the shadow of the cliffs of Zion in 1914, on a family farm located near the present-day park visitor center. Here he draws on nearly a century of experiences in the canyon to list and describe the plants and animals of Zion National Park and to reflect on changes to its ecosystems.

Zion is home to a wide variety of plant and animal life. A wide range of elevations, shaded canyons, and open, sunny slopes create environmental extremes from moist forests to rugged deserts. Plants and animals suited to these diverse conditions have evolved over time and live side by side in a delicate ecological balance.

MAMMALS

Nearly everyone who visits the park sees some of Zion's 68 species of mammals, 36 species of reptiles, 7 species of amphibians, and 271 species of birds.

The mule deer is found throughout the area and is the largest mammal one is likely to see in the park. A few elk reside in the higher Kolob Plateau to the north, but generally they prefer more open country than the park provides. The desert bighorn sheep is native to the area but disappeared prior to 1950. Though it has been reintroduced, it is seldom seen.

Predators include the mountain lion (also commonly called the cougar), bobcat, coyote, gray fox, badger, and the weasel. The one known shrew is classed as an insectivore, along with several species of bats. The wolf and otter have long since left Zion. The raccoon was once numerous, but disappeared during the 1920s. Should you be driving through the canyon at night, you might spot a relative of the raccoon—the ringtail cat. This handsome creature is nocturnal and may raid your camp looking for food.

Of the many rodents in the park, the most obvious is the gray rock squirrel, which is sometimes a nuisance to campers. The little antelope ground squirrel is less numerous but more likely to be seen year-round. You may never catch a glimpse of the pocket gopher, but its mounds are present at all elevations. Likewise, the presence of the wood rat, or pack rat, is evidenced by the many "trash piles" this nighttime raider builds around the entrances to its dens. The porcupine is also found in the park, but is more numerous on the plateau than in the canyon. The beaver was absent from the park for 50 years, but reappeared in about 1940 while migrating up the Virgin River from the Colorado River. It is called a "bank beaver" since it lives in burrows and generally does not build dams. The cottontail and jackrabbit are found in the park, but the jackrabbit seldom ventures into the canyon.

REPTILES AND AMPHIBIANS

Nonvenomous reptiles and amphibians make up an interesting part of Zion's fauna. The most visible among these are lizards, the largest being the vegetarian chuckwalla, which may reach a length of 20 inches. The most colorful lizards are the hardest to see because they are less common and well camouflaged. These include the collared lizard, banded gecko, and western skink. The whiptail may also be colorful and is numerous. It has a long, slender, striped body, and the tails of the young range in color from blue to green. The two species of horned lizard are the desert horned lizard, which is nearly always seen below 5,500 feet, and the short-horned lizard, which stays above 6,000 feet.

Like the horned lizards, some of Zion's snakes have a narrow habitat range. For example, the black-and-white–banded common kingsnake is seldom, if ever, found above 4,500 feet, and its more colorful relative, the Sonoran Mountain kingsnake, has never been seen below 6,500 feet. This species is quite rare and is often persecuted because of its resemblance to the venomous coral snake. Note that there are no coral snakes in Zion.

The western rattler is a venomous snake that may be found at all elevations up to 8,000 feet. Though it may appear threatening if startled or cornered, it will usually retreat rather than strike. Its venom is not as virulent as that of some other snake species, but it can be deadly, nevertheless.

BIRDS

About 271 bird species have been recorded in Zion. Of this number, approximately 60 are permanent residents and over 100 are known to breed in the area, including three species of hummingbirds, the golden eagle, and the rare peregrine falcon. The song birds include the robin, black-headed grosbeak, lazuli bunting, Townsend's solitaire, and both the solitary and warbling vireo. The canyon wren's song—a clear, sweet cascade of descending notes—can be heard any month of the year. The ungainly, soot-colored dipper has a surprisingly pretty song, and it usually sings to the accompaniment of a babbling brook or stream where it dives for food. The dipper may build its nest in a hanging garden where it is hidden underneath a projection of dripping tufa (porous rock) and vegetation. Other choice nesting sites are behind waterfalls and in damp caves.

Seven members of the crow family are found in Zion, three of which nest here. The raven and scrub jay are ever present and the Steller's jay frequents the canyon from its normal range in the higher elevations. With the exception of the rare gray jay, these are the noisiest birds in the park. The call of the gregarious pinyon jay always precedes its arrival. This species is sometimes called the "blue crow." It appears in great flocks throughout the pinyon-juniper belt. The raven is a notorious clown and bully, and delights in making life miserable for the soaring hawks and eagles, whom it dive-bombs repeatedly. The raven usually wins these encounters.

The roadrunner, a member of the cuckoo family, is also considered a clown by some. Its methods of locomotion and obtaining food may appear comical, but the roadrunner is deadly serious when it flails a rattlesnake to death and swallows it whole. The roadrunner is a desert dweller, but has been observed among the aspen trees in late summer at an elevation of 9,000 feet....

PLANT LIFE

A great variety of plants thrive in Zion. Shady side canyons, a wide range of elevations, and disparate sources of water provide diverse environments for biotic communities. Consequently, plants requiring very little water cover desert hills and live only a short distance from the lush greenery that grows along the banks of the Virgin River.

The most noticeable plant community below 5,000 feet is composed of pinyon and juniper, two evergreen species that grow together in an association known throughout the West as the "pygmy forest." It dominates the talus slopes and sandy benches below the vertical cliffs of Zion. Scattered among these evergreen species are serviceberry, single-leaf ash, round-leaf buffaloberry, manzanita, joint fir, cliffrose, and various types of cacti. Gambel oak, scrub live oak, and bigtooth maple also appear in patches.

Also found in the canyon is the riparian woodland, a narrow band of deciduous trees that grow along the river and its tributaries. The Fremont cottonwood is dominant, and is the largest of the riverbank varieties, followed by the box elder and velvet ash. Several types of willow are also common. Water birch occurs primarily in the very wet areas in side canyons. The ground cover in this community has undergone considerable change since the occupation of the canyon. Where sandbar willows and wild roses used to dominate, the exotic tamarisk, or salt cedar, has largely taken over and forms dense thickets in many places.

The terraces and plateaus from 5,500 to 7,500 feet are characterized by ponderosa pine (the largest of local conifers), Rocky Mountain juniper, and sagebrush. Gambel oak is also prominent at this elevation. Douglas fir and white fir are also fairly abundant, although they usually live, along with the quaking aspens, at higher elevations. The 14 varieties of cacti that have been identified in Zion are divided into three groups commonly called hedgehog, cholla (tree cactus), and prickly pear. Identification, especially between the prickly pears and chollas, is difficult and confusing because they hybridize so readily. The most colorful, if not the most abundant, of Zion's wildflowers belong to the cactus family. The claret cup, smallest of the hedgehogs, is the first to bloom. It sometimes blooms as early as March, followed by its larger relative, the purple torch. Some varieties of cacti may bloom as late as August, but you will find the most profuse display in May and June.

Two species of yuccas grow in Zion. One, the narrowleaf, or Spanish bayonet, produces a flower stalk of white blossoms reaching several feet above the spines, inspiring its popular name, Lord's Candlestick. The yuccas, which belong to the lily family, are erroneously called cacti by some and, along with the cacti, are considered "desert" plants. Zion is a desert canyon, and has an average annual rainfall of about 15 inches, so both cacti and yuccas are perfectly at home throughout the park, even up to 7,500 feet in areas with southern exposure.

If the desert plants seem out of place on the plateau tops, likewise, several mountain varieties are found at the bottom of the canyon in areas of limited sunlight and only adequate moisture. In Emerald Pools Canyon, for instance, entirely different plants grow on opposite sides of the canyon, though the canyon walls are only a few hundred feet apart. At the end of the Gateway to the Narrows Trail, a yucca grows on a cliff ledge just a few yards directly above a Douglas fir tree. Hanging gardens are found at several places where water seeps constantly from the vertical rock walls, depositing calcareous tufa, which gives footing and life to a variety of water-loving plants. The two most accessible hanging gardens are at Weeping Rock and along the Gateway to the Narrows Trail. In addition to grasses and banks of maidenhair ferns, such flowers as golden columbine, shooting star, purple violet, and cardinal monkey flower grow abundantly. The latter species blooms in spring and again in September. Scarlet lobelia, or cardinal-flower, while not a part of the hanging garden, may be found nearby in late summer.

From the east end of the Zion tunnel to the East Entrance to the park, the Zion–Mt. Carmel Highway winds about eight miles through cuts and around contours in the upper half of the massive Navajo Formation. On these sandstone slopes, ponderosa pine, littleleaf mountain mahogany, Douglas fir, and Rocky Mountain juniper appear to be growing out of solid rock. As this side canyon widens into a sandy valley bottom near the East Entrance, ponderosa pine and juniper are joined by Gambel oak, sagebrush, manzanita, and joint fir. Manzanita and joint fir are also found, though in fewer numbers, on the rocky slopes and sandy benches of the main canyon.

It seems odd that the first blossoms of spring may appear on the higher slopes instead of in the lower elevations. The tiny pink Japanese-lanternlike blossoms of the manzanita usually begin to appear in January, but have been known to bloom in December at an elevation of 6,000 feet. The low-growing sand buttercup blooms in March, or earlier, in the sandy areas near the east end of the tunnel. Small, brilliant, orange-scarlet clumps of slickrock paintbrush dot the slopes. Look for purplish blue spiderwort along the roadsides and other sandy areas. Red and purple penstemons bloom along the roadsides throughout the summer, but the last flower to bloom in this section of the park is the bright red hummingbird trumpet, which looks like penstemon but belongs to the evening primrose family.

Perhaps displaying the best color of all is the bigtooth maple, which turns brilliant shades of red before dropping its leaves in October. It grows along the streambed of Clear Creek, the drainage that the road follows through the slickrock area east of the tunnel.

A few species catch everyone's eyes, depending on the time of year. For a short period in early spring, the disturbed areas on the canyon floor become solid purple from the bloom of the foul-smelling member of the mustard family, *Chorispora tenella*, which seems to have been introduced within the last two decades and has no common name. Desert beauty, also known as "purple sage," is a blooming shrub that belongs to the pea family. The true purple sage blossoms earlier and is very conspicuous on the hills near the Zion Canyon Visitor Center[1] for only a few days. The tall yellow spikes of another mustard, the prince's plume, have a wide distribution on the rocky slopes and retain some of their blossoms throughout the summer. Perhaps the biggest attention-getter in the park is the sacred datura, a member of the nightshade family, which may have as many as a hundred large, white, funnel-shaped flowers. The blossoms open at night and usually close by midday. This plant is so abundant in the park that it has been given the nickname "Zion lily."

A small tree that is not widely distributed and could go unnoticed except when it is in bloom is the New Mexico locust. When it blooms, the aroma is intoxicating. Best seen along the road near Weeping Rock and near the west door of the Zion Canyon Visitor Center, the New Mexico locust's clusters of pink flowers bloom a second time if summer showers are abundant.

NOTE

1. Now the Zion Human History Museum.

3 | Zion's Story

GREER K. CHESHER

Greer Chesher is a former National Park Service ranger and a creative nonfiction essayist. In this piece she writes of her understanding of the "many Zions," focusing on the early human presence in Zion Canyon and providing an ecological perspective of the park.

I'm lying back on a fallen sandstone slab, eyes closed, sun on face. The autumn breeze billows around me, and cottonwoods along the Virgin River applaud the day's perfection with a yellow rustle. To my right another slab towers, implanted vertically by its plunge into Zion Canyon, its skin thick with the patina of time, dark moss, yellow lichen.

I hear the clack of rock on rock in the wash below and open an eye to see a young mule deer, her ears and tail flicking gnats, ambling on delicate feet between boulders. Unbound by time, current or ancient, slow or fast, for her there is only now. Gnat time. Cooling time. The yellow time of sunflowers and goldenrod. Her dun coat blends the color of grass and stone. I scan the entire bowl of sky to find only a small cluster of clouds like ripples on the river's bottom—otherwise the sky in the south, lazuli; to the north, mountain bluebird. Last time I walked here under a kingfisher sky.

In that dawn, claret cup and cliffs burned in the sun's first unoccluded rays of summer. I hiked to the rock as kingfisher skirted the river's bank, his wings lost in daybreak's blue-gray. Before me, a small crowd gathered to watch the rock mark time.

Just as the sun rimmed the canyon's eastern wall, a shadow exactly the shape, and close to the size, of a howling coyote leapt onto the standing rock. Ears up, front legs stiff, head thrown back, mouth wide, the coyote eats time. The crowd oohed and aahed, then grew silent as the shadow, over the next hour, descended the rock, mouth open, gulping five small petroglyphs: first a figure whose name or story is lost to our knowledge; then a bird's footprint; then a spiral; next the hand-pecked form of a canine; and last another bird print. Only at dawn on this one day, June 21, the summer solstice, does the coyote take shape. And only on this day does redrock reverberate with the clock's sole tick.

This solstice marker, set in motion perhaps a millennium ago by the Virgin Anasazi, is a case of fortuitous geology. Some eons ago, huge rock slabs fell hundreds of feet from the Springdale Member of the Moenave Formation; they landed in a creative jumble that, when the sun rises over its northernmost point on the redrock skyline, casts a shadow from one rock onto another which resembles a howling canid. Some few thousand years later, someone noticed the effect, took time to peck symbols into solid stone to mark the spot, and activated a perpetual time machine that will only wind down as time erodes bedrock or planetary orbits change. To what did this soundless alarm, going off, call people?

As the Virgin Anasazi transitioned from hunter-gatherers to semi-sedentary farmers, a calendar would have placed the people within the year's rotating story. A horizon-based calendar still consulted on the Hopi Reservation in Arizona links sunrise alignments before the solstice with farming chores—field clearing, early planting—indicating when to prepare regardless of weather. Calendars also compute precise dates of important events so proper ceremonies occur at correct times. It is impossible to date exactly when this clock was wound, or to know definitively if those who consulted it were farmers. We can surmise that they were people who inhabited or visited the canyon repeatedly.

It's an easy walk across the canyon and over the river from the stone clock to a treeless knoll where sacred datura bloom, moon white, and fade in the late day. I walk there as clouds gather and light fails. Globemallow, four-o'clock, and Mormon tea brush my legs as I climb the short hill. The view from the top is surprisingly robust: south all the way to

Eagle Crags and Smithsonian Butte; up canyon to the Sentinel Slide, and beyond to Lady Mountain; and canyon wall to wall—the Watchman towers overhead; West Temple across the canyon. Near the knoll's north end, in the lee of a large boulder, thin sandstone blocks, set on edge, trace two ancient rooms.

This Virgin Anasazi site—constructed and augmented between AD 700 and 900 and again from AD 1010 to 1300—consists of two storage rooms, three storage cists, and two hearths. This hilltop probably served as flood-safe storage for a stone and adobe dwelling below, closer to the river and now invisible. No foodstuffs remain within the room blocks, so it's not known if these people were farming the Virgin's floodplain, relying on a natural regimen, or creating a mixed economy of agriculture and wild resources.

Most archaeological features in Zion Canyon don't represent long-term living places. This may be a case of unfortunate geology. The forces that contributed to our tumultuous night in Great West Canyon[1] also made and make Zion Canyon a rather unsuitable living place. Zion's archaeological sites are primarily work sites for the seasonally sedentary Anasazi.

Prehistorically, lower Zion Canyon could feasibly support only a small family group, fewer than twenty people. This was a time when natural forage was probably still plentiful and individual families dispersed across the landscape, hunting, gathering seasonal edibles, and gardening small plots. They may have returned to their durable Zion Canyon homestead during specific seasons or multiyear periods; if conditions were especially conducive, they may have spent a lifetime in place.

There is not much we can state definitively anymore. The deeper we study any subject, the more we confront exceptions, nuances, and unexpected new information. Archaeologists now recognize there was no real culture we can name exclusively Anasazi, and they are fine-tuning their language. Even the word Anasazi is out, replaced by the generic term, Ancestral Puebloan. (I use Virgin Anasazi for readers who wish to learn more about Zion's cultures; looking up "Virgin Ancestral Puebloan" would be fruitless.)

We don't know what the Anasazi called themselves; it's doubtful they had one unifying name for the entire people. They, like us, may have had names for various groups (Rockvilleans, Springdaleans, New Yorkers, and so forth), just as the extant Puebloans do today (Hopi, Zuni, Jemez). Saying Anasazi is like saying American. We can characterize related traits and lifestyles—corn production, pottery, basketry techniques—as Anasazi, but localized technologies were a mix of adaptations dependent on immediate environment and each people's history. We could say that there were myriad ethnicities within an overarching lifeway. Archaeologists have long designated the Anasazi centered on southwestern Utah the Virgin Branch. We should probably address these knoll people as the Zion Canyon Branch of the Virgin Branch of the Anasazi. The "Zionsazi," as endemic as Zion snails, carefully adapted to Zion Canyon's very particular environment.

The knoll people adjusted to Zion by capitalizing on every part of the available environment, then seeking greener pastures, so to speak. I had always assumed that planting and reaping were easier than hunting and gathering, but it turns out I'm wrong. Collecting wild plants was not only easier than tending crops; natural fare also provided more calories. Cattail pollen and roots, pine nuts, bulrush seed, wild rye, acorns, four-wing saltbush, mutton grass (*Poa fendleriana*), sunflower, and Indian rice grass all provide better caloric gain than agricultural crops. Many scientists now reason that people resorted to farming only when native foods were scarce. Thus, finding corn in early archaeological sites may indicate environmental stress—that is, that an area's natural sustenance was impaired by climate change or overharvest.

During the time the knoll wasn't used, between AD 966 and 1010, conditions in Zion Canyon were unusually parched; some years the Virgin River may have run dry. From AD 1015 to 1100 moisture returned, until the notorious southwest-wide drought sizzled from AD 1125 to 1150. During the first drought, people may have clustered near reliable water and cultivated gardens. As the rains returned, they expanded garden plots to large-scale agriculture, and relied almost totally on the holy trinity of prehistoric agronomy: corn, beans, and squash. The population increased, and when the AD 1125 drought arrived, there were too many people to support with any mix of available economies. As the climate changed, the lifeway so scrupulously tailored to a particular environment no longer worked; and, as many of us have experienced, inventing a new lifeway under stress is difficult, if not impossible.

Thus, by about 1250 the last Anasazi migrated from their former homeland and concentrated along permanent rivers such as New Mexico's Rio
Grande. This was the people's standard operating procedure: Times are
tough? Leave. But this move catches our eye, so vast and total. The standard explanation: drought. But the people had withstood worse. Research-
ers now think moisture came, but at the wrong time. Changing climate
shifted rain from summer to winter; Anasazi provisions, both natural and
agricultural, withered, year after year, until native plants and stored grain
were exhausted, and survival lay elsewhere. The future, and the people, relo-
cated where weather dictated. Although we don't understand it yet, this is
also our future.

On the hilltop today, coyote scat sits atop a rock, red and seedy, the gut-
processed fruit of prickly pear; I think of cactus spines in coyote noses.
Exotic, inedible cheatgrass now fills rooms that once stored nutritious
rice grass seed. And across the canyon, easily in view, Solstice Rock still
beats with annual precision. Each year it marks ceremonies missed, songs
unsung. Technology continues without the technologists. To our good fortune, pueblo peoples still sing and dance to the silent chant and rhythm
of the seasons, insuring for all the world's people the sun's return to its
appointed rounds (thank you). The clock and the carefully ordered rocks
on this knoll also serve as placeholder, quietly marking home.

From my knoll-top perch I can't see the slightest indication of the people
who followed the Anasazi. For these people, permanent dwellings had little
meaning. These were the Southern Paiute, a people who called themselves
by many names, each descriptive of a particular group's environment or
lifeway. Thus there were, to name a few, the Pagu'its, the fish people, who
fished from Panguitch Lake; the Unkaka'niguts, red-cliff-base people, who
dwelled near Bryce Canyon; and the Ea'ayekunants, arrow-quiver people,
who ranged from the Virgin's headwaters to just below Zion Canyon.

The Numic-speaking Paiute migrated into southern Utah from the
Great Basin as early as AD 1000, perhaps overlapping and interacting with
our knoll-top Anasazi. The changing climate was pushing the sedentary
Anasazi farmers out, and may have impelled the Paiute into southern Utah
in search of their own greener pastures. Whenever two cultures overlap,
especially during hard times, resource competition ensues. Recent theory

suggests that southern Utah's Anasazi may have left as the Paiute increased, or that the two groups melded, each learning important survival techniques from the other.

In and around Zion, Paiute groups integrated into distinct regions centered on a river or spring. For the Ea'ayekunants, it was the Virgin River; for the Unkaka'niguts, it was the Sevier. The Pagu'its relied on Panguitch Lake. These territories, which modern anthropologists call *cultural ecosapes*, contained what was necessary for each band's self-sufficiency: dependable water for irrigated gardens of maize, squash, and beans (they may have learned farming from the Anasazi); upland forests for elderberry, chokecherry, and mule deer; midland elevations for piñon nuts, sego bulbs, serviceberries, and pronghorn; and lowland deserts for sunflower, grass seed, agave, and rabbit. Brush-shelter villages developed near central water sources, but the Paiute moved throughout their ecoscape seasonally, camping near outlying springs and harvesting wild plants and animals. This may sound similar to early Anasazi technology, and so it may have been. But the Anasazi evolved into homebodies, staying in place, becoming skilled agriculturists; and, as they consolidated into larger and larger stone-built towns, eventually overwhelming local environments and relocating. Anasazi town life, coupled with the intensive land use needed to support it, was ultimately unsustainable.

Both the Virgin Anasazi and the Southern Paiute centered their homelands on one of the Zions. The Anasazi stayed primarily on the lower reaches of the Virgin River's North and East Forks (Zion Canyon), while the Paiute focused on a larger Zion—the biotic Zion—in a sense, participating as members of the ecoscape. They ranged through its elevational gradients and resources in extended families capable of easy seasonal movement, quickly constructing brush shelters. The Paiute lifeway speaks to scale: few possessions, no wealth accumulation, small bands roving the land. I often wonder if this lifeway is a possible future we all share. If so, it might be wise to listen to the Paiute closely.

Just as the extant Puebloans hold rain and what we modern folk call "nature" sacred, so the Paiute hold in reverence their ancestral waters and traditional ecoscapes. They view the land in a way most people do not, believing that everything is alive—air, springs, plants, mountains, minerals, rivers, animals, rocks—and that each must be treated with respect. The Paiute believe their people were put in place, this place, to care not only for nature but also for the spirituality dwelling in the land. The Paiute term for homeland, Puaxante Tevip, translates as "Sacred Land." One way Puaxante Tevip is honored is by speaking directly to the land and its other-than-human inhabitants. Another is the passing on of story and song.

The Paiute lifeway may have continued into the deep future as it had in humanity's deep past, if not for the arrival of another wave of immigrants. The traditional Paiute economy was eventually overwhelmed. Puaxante Tevip was invaded by foreigners, and Paiute waters usurped. Incursion brought starvation, bloodshed, and devastating epidemics from European diseases. Alien creatures—cattle, horses, goats—were unleashed on Puaxante Tevip, decimating Paiute sustenance. Up to 90 percent of Paiutes died after contact.

The Paiutes say they were forced from this land when pioneers settled the only places water made habitable. Even though cut off from their cultural ecoscape, and depleted by disease and hunger, the Paiute survive today as the Paiute Tribes of Utah, Arizona, Nevada, and California. They remain a people deeply connected to Puaxante Tevip. The Southern Paiute still talk to the land. And the land still listens.

NOTE

1.   Earlier in her book, Greer describes being caught in a flash flood while descending the Right Fork of North Creek.

4 | Origin of the Pai-Utes

JOHN WESLEY POWELL

Centuries after the Ancient Pueblo constructed dwellings in the walls of Zion Canyon, the Southern Paiutes inhabited the Colorado Plateau and Mojave Desert. In this origin story, recorded by John Wesley Powell during his surveying work in southern Utah and northern Arizona, the Paiutes characterize their land as the "middle of the world" and as a rich source of resources.

Shin-au-av Pa-vits	The elder Shinauav
Shin-au-av Skaits	The younger Shinauav
Si-chom-pa Ka-gon	Old Woman of the Sea
[...]	
Kai-vwaw-i	Kaibab Plateau
Pa-ga We-wi-gunt	Grand Cañon of the Colorado
[...]	

Si-chom-pa Ka-gon came out of the sea with a sack filled with something and securely tied. Then she went to the home of the Shin-au-av brothers carrying her burthen with her, which was very heavy, and bent her nearly to the ground. When she found the brothers she delivered to them the sack and told them to carry it into the middle of the world and open it, and enjoined upon them that they should not look into it until their arrival at the designated point and there they would meet Ta-vwots, who would tell them what to do with it. Then the old woman went back to the sea disappearing in the waters.

Shin-au-av Pa-vits gave the sack to Shin-au-av Skaits and told him to do as Si-chom-pa Ka-gon had directed, and especially enjoined upon him that he must not open the sack lest some calamity should befall him. He found it very heavy and with great difficulty he carried it along by short stages and as he proceeded, his curiosity to know what it contained became greater and greater. "Maybe," said he, "it is sand; maybe it is dung! who knows but what the old woman is playing a trick!" Many times he tried to feel the outside of the sack to discover what it contained. At one time he thought [it] was full of snakes; at another, full of lizards. "So," said he, "it is full of fishes." At last his curiosity overcame him and he untied the sack, when out sprang hosts of people who passed out on the plain shouting and running toward the mountain. Shin-au-av Skaits overcome with fright, threw himself down on the sand. Then Ta-vwots suddenly appeared and grasping the neck of the sack tied it up, being very angry with Shin-au-av Skaits. "Why," said he, "have you done this? I wanted these people to live in that good land to the east and here, foolish boy, you have let them out in a desert."

There were yet a few people left in the sack and Ta-vwots took it to the Kai-vwaw-i to the brink of Pa-ga We-wi-gunt and there took out the remainder where the nant [*Agave utahensis*] was abundant on cliffs, and herds of game wandered in the forests.

These are the Pai-Utes, the true Utes, the others have scattered over the world and live in many places.

5 | From the Beginning

Martha C. Knack

The Southern Paiutes' way of life was remarkably attuned to the harsh conditions of the Colorado Plateau and Mojave Desert. They took advantage of the extreme variation in their region, migrating throughout their lands to gather food as it became available from season to season and cultivating crops where water was plentiful, including Zion Canyon. This essay is an ethnohistory of this people by Martha Knack, a professor of anthropology at the University of Nevada, Las Vegas, who has spent decades researching the history and culture of the Southern Paiutes.

Sheer walls of red sandstone plunge across Southern Paiute territory, through places now called Zion National Park, Bryce Canyon, Arches, and Canyonlands, slashing their way through southern Utah. Above them, pine-covered plateaus lift to isolated knots of mountains—the La Sals, the Pine Valley Mountains, and the southernmost Wasatch Front. Below, dry plains sweep across deserts only to tumble over the sharp edges of the Grand Canyon into the Colorado River.

For unknown years this land was home to Southern Paiutes. They lived in the southern halves of what are now called Utah and Nevada, a piece of Arizona above the Grand Canyon, and much of the eastern Mojave Desert of California. When Euro-Americans first met Paiutes, the Indians said they had always been there. They saw their lives replicating not only the way of their ancestors but also the form established by the supernatural powers who had set the world into motion at the beginning of time. Their land was lean and chary of its riches, but it did provide support to Paiutes through a series of techniques tested by long experience. Their life required hard work and vigilance; they were vulnerable to threats of drought, accident, disease, and the physical power of outsiders. But it was a way of life Paiutes understood, and they trusted it to carry them safely past any dangers.

Virtually everywhere within this territory, Southern Paiutes could walk in a day's time to some dramatic change in elevation; much of the secret of their success in this arid land lay in their systematic exploitation of that verticality. Stretching more than three hundred miles from south to north, Paiute territory included parts of the Colorado River Valley at only fifteen hundred feet as well as mountain peaks rising over eleven thousand feet. This was no smooth transition but was intercepted by escarpments, local massifs, and even isolated peaks looming out of the desert. Canyons sliced through plateaus to drop without warning to deceptive dry washes that might host torrents after brief cloudbursts.

The heights were cooler than the lower-lying flatlands, and they also snared passing storms to win more rainfall; the higher the elevation, the more dramatically different the climate. For instance, the valley floor at Las Vegas, only two thousand feet above sea level, baked at temperatures of over 100 degrees day after day for a third of the year, often blazing to 120 degrees in the shade, if any could be found, and cooling overnight to only 90 just before the sun returned. Within sight, the mountains of that valley's western wall stood to nearly twelve thousand feet and sported unthawed snowfields from November until May. The valley averaged five and a half inches of rain in a year, the mountain five times that much.

Each individual altitude zone, drainage slope, soil type, and even angle of sun exposure supported a distinctive variety of plant and animal life. On a single valley side, plant communities might well shift from creosote and cactus, through piñon and juniper, to white pine and spruce. Paiutes learned to harvest an eclectic assortment of nutritious seeds, berries, roots, nuts, leaves, and stalks, each in its own season, from each of these biotic layers.

They used not only resources but also their extensive botanical knowledge. They knew, for instance, that plants ripened at lower elevations earlier than at higher, so they stretched the harvest period of useful, food-producing species by following their ripening cycles uphill.

The resource that demanded their most careful husbanding was water. Everywhere Paiute country was arid, in spots true desert. Much of the rain came in winter, drizzling across broad areas over a number of days, but at a season when the dormant plants could not use it for growth; the only benefit lay in its rejuvenation of the uppermost shallow water tables. These winter rains were also undependable; southern Nevada, for instance, often got no rain at all through an entire winter, sometimes several winters in a row.

The short spring and fall were generally dry, but summer brought thunderstorms. Violent winds and lightning accompanied downpours of more than an inch an hour during a season when the ground was so dry that the water beaded up or ran off into the dry washes without soaking below the first soil level. If the storm path happened to parallel a drainage pattern, it could drop enough water to cause dangerous sheet washes that collected in normally dry ravines, turning into flash floods several feet high that shoved debris, boulders, and people before them.

Such summer thunderstorms were isolated; a mile or even a hundred yards aside there might be no rain at all. These cloudbursts left avenues of moisture, but plants were fixed to the ground, and statistically, chances were small that rain would fall on any particular hillside at an opportune point in a specific plant's growing cycle. As a result, desert plants, while often locally lush, produced in spots separated by seemingly barren stretches where their desert-adapted seeds hovered dormant until a luckier year. Even if a patch chanced to fall under a passing summer storm one year, it might well not be equally fortunate another, so the richest blooming of even the same species would shift location through time. For the animals that lived on those plants, whether lowly field mice, browsing deer, or humans, no single place guaranteed a reliable, ample food supply. Paiutes learned to move with flexibility to the most promising spots of any particular year.

Paiutes clearly could not rely on rainfall for drinking water. Perennial streams offered no solution. Southern Paiute country bordered the

Colorado River for over six hundred miles along its southern edge, and above it a few mountain massifs were high enough to generate run-off for permanent streams that flowed into it. These were easily counted: the Muddy River near the Nevada-Utah border; the Virgin in southwestern Utah slipping out of what is now Zion National Park; Kanab Creek easing down the eastern side of the Kaibab Plateau; the Paria in central Utah, hiding deceptive quicksand flats; and the San Juan, fed by the high mountains of southwestern Colorado that swung north into Ute country before it slipped into the Colorado River from the east. Between these five rivers lay hundreds of square miles of dry land full of seeds, roots, nuts, and game that Paiutes wanted to harvest; flowing streams were not the solution to Paiutes' daily domestic water needs.

The answer lay in springs. The same underlying layers of sandstone that produced the brilliant red cliffs of Paiute country created numerous impermeable planes that channeled water along until it broke out at a penetrating cliff wall or was pressed up an invisible fault crack. Sometimes the water actually bubbled out as a spring, such as the one that headed the Muddy River. At other times the water lacked pressure to force its way to the surface and hid under a layer of sand; such damp "seeps" were proclaimed by a patch of flourishing greenery, and Paiutes learned to dig down and wait until morning for enough liquid to leak into the hole to support a small family. Where there were no springs, fine sandstone, wind-eroded into shallow basins, might puddle passing rainfall until it evaporated. One such "tank," known as Jacobs Pools, was key to Paiute use of the seed-rich plateau between Kanab Creek and the northern rim of the Grand Canyon, for it held the only water for forty miles in any direction. Paiutes knew the location and condition of every tiny spring, seep, tank, and puddle for miles. Where water was hidden in tumbles of rocks or around the corner of a side canyon, they etched petroglyphs in stone to guide relatives to this life-giving resource....

Southern Paiute lands rarely offered a food surplus, let alone abundance. Productive spots were localized and widely dispersed because of unpredictable rainfall. Because no single place provided reliable sustenance, people had to be mobile. They traveled up and down mountain ranges to follow the sequential ripening of food plants, and they traveled out across the valleys to the places most productive that year. Even so, the food they produced was limited, and few people could ever live together; Southern Paiute camp groups of ten to fifteen people were normal, although richer areas, like the Muddy River Valley or along Santa Clara Creek in southwestern Utah, supported larger communities.

The people's movements were far from random; had Paiutes "wandered," as later Euro-Americans mistakenly described their mobility, they would have soon starved. Their movements were based on extensive knowledge of the growth preferences of specific plants and solid familiarity with the seasonal blooming and ripening of each species. Paiutes harvested one plant after the other as each matured. They ate what they needed and sundried whatever was left over for winter use. Once one species had ripened and loosed its seeds to the wind, Paiutes moved on to the next scheduled resource, which probably required that they relocate to a place where their past experience and careful observation predicted they would get the best return of food for their time and labor. If drought, plant disease, or insect pests interfered with that anticipated target, they had secondary and even tertiary alternatives in mind, plants that were perhaps harder to collect, less tasty, or less likely to store well....

Along the Muddy and Virgin Rivers and in a few other well-watered areas, Paiutes planted domesticated corn and squashes and transplanted such wild native plants as amaranth, sunflowers, and devil's claw. People on Santa Clara Creek had beans and gourds, too. Fields were small. Women used the same pointed digging sticks with which they uprooted desert plants to prepare the friable loams along permanent streams. On the Santa Clara and other tributaries to the Virgin, they scratched out short diversion channels to spread water for their favorite plants. Nineteenth-century Paiutes in the extreme south, called Chemehuevis, learned from Mohaves to use residual soil moisture left by Colorado River floods to germinate corn seed. Women's work, like their efforts to harvest wild plants, marked the resulting crops as their own. Other Paiutes knew where each family had worked in the spring and generally respected that garden as "theirs." Only a bona fide emergency justified taking crops from someone else's garden; anything less was rude theft and an offensive violation of customary ethics.

This labor, coupled with other obligations on their time, limited Paiutes' gardens to an acre or less. Such small plots could not produce enough to support a family year-round, and Paiutes could not afford to eschew harvesting wild plants in order to guard their gardens from insect or animal pests. They cleared as much land as they had time for in the spring, planted whatever seed they had left after a winter's eating, and left to find food for the summer. In the fall, they returned to harvest whatever had survived. They often treated horticultural crops as a lucky windfall, promptly sharing them around among their kin so that everyone could enjoy this rare treat. Whatever was not immediately consumed was dried for winter or kept for seed....

Because of its specific location, each Paiute group was a bit different in diet and seasonal movements. All groups relied, however, on an eclectic diversity of foods harvested with lightweight baskets and hand-held tools that were carried from one campsite to another throughout the year. Few of these foods produced a bumper crop that Paiutes could store, but those few were critical—rice grass, piñon nuts, rabbit meat. Fortunately, these were fairly reliable, if not in a specific location in a given year, then surely somewhere in a wider range.

Other foods varied immensely. If one failed to produce abundantly or even to appear at all, their very plurality assured that Paiutes had alternatives to which they could and did shift with great flexibility. They had preferences (foods that tasted best, were most easily harvested, or grew in clumps so that walking time was minimized), but they had secondary and even tertiary choices when necessary. Pollen and flower stalks of the ubiquitous sagebrush could be boiled; although bitter and with little nutritional value, still these would keep the family alive until they could walk to a better area. Juniper berries, even if dried and withered, could be softened and the thin layer of fruit nibbled off. If the periodic waves of locusts or cutworms destroyed the green plants, those insects themselves were systematically harvested for their high protein content. Frugal, hard-working, provident, and knowledgeable about the resources of their environment, Paiutes used what they had with great creativity and flexibility, adjusting when they had to.

Paiutes firmly believed that their land was nurturant and productive; they were secure in the knowledge that they could always make a living on their desert if they worked hard, with imagination and persistence. They did not look at their land as a harsh and barren place, as did some other people who came later....

In the years before the arrival of non-Indian people, Southern Paiutes traveled their desert on foot, gathered seasonal wild plant foods with lightweight basketry, and made small gardens when they could. They hunted wherever they were and saved whatever possible for winter. Each year was different, without a fixed sequence of resources to harvest or campsites to occupy. Camp groups aggregated when rabbit populations or piñon productivity allowed and then redivided into smaller groups. When resources failed, Paiutes visited their relatives elsewhere, perhaps staying a season or years. They socialized with their relatives, married nonkinfolk, and extended the privileges and obligations of kinship to these new affines. Without fixed rules of residence or rigid group membership, they found that intergroup reciprocity and social openness insured greater security than private ownership of property. They traveled lightly, avoiding personal possessions and distinctions of rank based on wealth. Individuals, male and female, were valued for the skills they had to share, whether to hunt, cure, mediate a dispute, or tell a good story on a winter evening. No person was subservient to the dictates of a chief or bound in a social hierarchy; obligations to others were defined by kinship relations, personal friendships, and social ethics. Flexibility and the absence of rigid, culturally defined rules for doing things "properly" as well as the corresponding presence of numerous alternative options enabled Paiutes to meet the varying unpredictable demands of the land in which they lived by means of wide-ranging individual creativity and response. Despite regional band variations, Paiutes formed one native "people." Their way of life was a culture that had supported them through past difficulties and that they trusted would continue to carry them through such new challenges as the future would bring.

6 | The Land Nobody Wanted...

WALLACE STEGNER

Wallace Stegner, dean of Western writers, describes in his excerpt from his 1924 book Mormon Country, *the Colorado Plateau, its extreme topographic and hydrologic features, and its improbable settlement by a people who believed themselves called by God to do so.*

Make a dot on a map of the western United States just off the southwestern corner of Yellowstone Park, at St. Anthony, Idaho. Make another at Grand Junction, Colorado, and another at Safford, Arizona, on the Gila River, and draw a long segment of an oval connecting the three. The segment will mark approximately the north, east, and south extensions of the Mormon Country. The western boundary is harder to fix, because although the Mormons once claimed, and once dominated, the entire Great Basin, and although a scattered Mormon population still extends as far as the east slope of the Sierra, most of western Nevada now belongs outside the empire and looks to Reno or San Francisco rather than to Salt Lake. The towns along the two transcontinental trails—the old Mormon Road through Las Vegas to Los Angeles, and the California Trail across the salt desert to Emigrant Pass—are partly Mormon yet. The agricultural areas of Nevada are fairly heavily Mormon, the mining region scarcely at all. It is more difficult, moreover, to tell a Mormon from a Gentile than it used to be. The western line is therefore tentative and fluid. But a compromise boundary might run from the Gila towns of Arizona northwestward to the junction of the Muddy and the Virgin (now under Lake Mead, behind the Boulder Dam), then curve northward to take in the eastern third of Nevada, and finally swing northeastward to enclose most of southern Idaho up to the Panhandle. All the boundaries are subject to question, and there is a twilight zone all around, as well as a large section of Arizona where the Mormons never got a foothold. Still, that rough oval will at least indicate the extent of Mormon culture.

It circumscribes a territory stretching from the thirty-third parallel to the forty-fourth, and from the western slope of the Rockies to an indeterminate line far out in the Great Basin. It includes all of Utah, most of southern Idaho, the southwestern corner of Wyoming, a strip of western Colorado, the northwestern corner of New Mexico, much of northern and central Arizona, and the eastern third of Nevada. Salt Lake City is somewhat north of the center, like a yolk in a hen's egg....

A more interesting part of the Mormon Country, topographically and socially, is that part which lies within, or rather virtually includes, what geologists call the Plateau Province. There the settlements are literally hewn out of the rock, founded with incredible labor and sustained against conditions that would have driven out a less persistent people after one year. Everywhere in the Mormon Country the proportion of tillable land to wasteland is extremely small. Three and three-tenths per cent, the average for Utah, is a high estimate for the Mormon Country as a whole. In the Plateau Province it can hardly be more than one per cent. The tiny oases huddle in their pockets in the rock, surrounded on all sides by as terrible and beautiful wasteland as the world can show, colored every color of the spectrum even to blue and green, sculptured by sandblast winds, fretted by meandering lines of cliffs hundreds of miles long and often several thousand feet high, carved and broken and split by canyons so deep and narrow that the rivers run in sunless depths and cannot be approached for miles. Man is an interloper in that country, not merely because he maintains a toehold only on sufferance, depending on the precarious and sometimes disastrous flow of desert rivers, but because everything he sees is a prophecy of his inconsequent destiny.

It is not merely the immensity and the loneliness and the emptiness of the land that bothers a man caught alone in it. The feeling is not the same that one gets on the great plains, where the sky is a bowl and the earth a disc and the eye is invited to notice the small things because the large ones are so characterless. In the Plateau Country the eye is not merely invited but compelled to notice the large things. From any point of vantage the view is likely to be open not with the twelve- or fifteen-mile radius of the plains, but with a radius that is often fifty and sometimes even seventy-five miles—and that is a long way to look, especially if there is nothing human in sight. The villages are hidden in the canyons and under the cliffs; there is nothing visible but the torn and slashed and windworn beauty of absolute wasteland. And the beauty is death. Where the grass and trees and bushes are stripped off and the world laid naked you can see the globe being torn down and rebuilt. You can see the death and prognosticate the birth of epochs. You can see the tiny clinging bits of debris that historical time has left. If you are a Mormon waiting for trump of the Last Days while you labor in building the Kingdom, you can be excused for expecting that those Last Days will come any time now. The world is dead and disintegrating before your eyes.

Nowhere in the world, probably, is the transitoriness of human habitation shown so outrageously. Nowhere is historical time pitted so helplessly and so obviously against the endless minutes of geological time. Almost anywhere in the Plateau Province, which stretches from southern Wyoming down across eastern Utah and western Colorado, and then fans out eastward and westward in Arizona and New Mexico, a man can walk into a canyon a block from his house and be face to face with two or three petrified minutes of eternity. That is worse, in some ways, than facing eternity itself, because eternity is a shadow without substance. Here is the residue of a few moments, geologically speaking. Here are thousands of feet of rock patiently deposited over millions of years, buckled up into the air with the slow finality of an express engine backing into an orange crate, and as patiently being worn away over other millions. In the Plateau Country you can read the rocks from Archaean to Quaternary, and see your own place in the ladder of an inhuman immortality. The Age of Man is there, a few hundreds or a few thousands of years old: Pueblo ruins in an arched cliff,

tiny granaries cached in the worn rock, Basket-maker burial cysts among
the crevices. That is the Age of Man—the relics of the Ho-ho-kim, the Old
People Who Left, about whom even the Indians know nothing but a name.
You can read it on down: the Age of Mammals in the Tertiary, the Age of
Reptiles in the Jurassic, the Age of Fish, the Age of Molluscs, the Age of
Nothing at All. It is all there from Basket-Maker to Trilobite in a few thou-
sand feet of rock that the wind even now is gnawing.

Here is your true Ozymandias. Look on my works, Ye Mighty, and
despair![1] Your destiny, as man, is to be a fossiliferous stratum in the crust
of earth; the land where Time is everything and nothing makes it plain. It
even makes plain how precarious is that petrified immortality of the fossil.
Let the land rise, as it has been doing, for a few more millions of years. Let
the wind blow against the faces of the cliffs, let cloudbursts roll mud and
boulders down the washes, and the Ho-ho-kim dwellings are gone, wiped
off like a mark sponged off a blackboard. Let stones break from the faces of
the cliffs through the centuries, let the cliffs retreat and retreat and retreat,
and the Age of Mammals is gone, stripped off, reduced to the dust from
which a new cycle can begin. Away go the Age of Reptiles and the Age of
Fish, away go Brontosaurus and Pteraspis and the shelled sea-worms. Many
of those layers of history are already gone from much of the Plateau Country. In places more than a vertical mile of them are gone. They survive clear
to the Eocene in the High Plateaus, fortuitously and temporarily, because
lava capped those tablelands and retarded the eraser. Shellac over a mark
on a blackboard and you can preserve it for a while, but not forever. Geology knows no such word as forever.

When the Great Basin was an island continent, the Plateau Province was
part of the ocean. The silt of rivers came down and was dropped evenly over
the depths. The sea filled in, the new deposits were lifted up and eroded,
sank again and had more sand and gravel and lime laid over the eroded surface. There were several risings and fallings before the movement ceased.
The water became brackish, and for a long time remained shallow, filling
in constantly with sediment and sinking as fast as it filled in. By the beginning of the Eocene period the sea had gone for good and the whole region

was one vast fresh-water lake, its bottom still sinking evenly to accommodate sediment coming down from the Wasatch and Uintah Mountains. At
the end of the Eocene the lake dried up gradually from the south, and the
land began to lift. But it lifted not in great folds, as it had lifted to form
the Cascades and the ancestral Rockies. The Plateau Province is an even-
tempered country. It had no need of catastrophe, it felt no call to buckle
the rock like soft leather. Evenly, slowly, the whole block of country rose,
shearing here and there to drop down another block between two uplifts.
The beds, for the most part, remained as horizontal as when they were laid
down. As the land rose, the surface water drained off down the estuary that
had formerly connected the lake with the sea. That drainage channel drew
tributaries to itself, forming a system of rivers, and started at once to cart
thousands of tons of soft Eocene sandstone in the Gulf of California.

The rivers are still there, and in substantially the same places. The rivers
are older than any of the local topographical features of the region—are
actually the prime movers in the carving of that topography. When the
climate began to dry up, the rivers cut down into their channels faster
than incidental erosion could break down the walls. The river valleys
became canyons with steep cliff-like sides. Floodwaters charged with sand
and gravel scoured the channels, ate the cliff sides and undermined them.
The cliffs fell slowly back and the wind got at them. Sand-bearing winds
chewed at their bases, undermined them again, chewed at the fallen talus
slopes and bore them away and went again after the solid rock.

Give that double process of corrasion and erosion millions of years, and
the topography of the country becomes credible and understandable, and
the cumulative effect becomes tremendous. The cliffs backed up, inch by
inch, from every main or tributary canyon. The level strata on their roofs,
still soft and easily eroded, were scoured by winds, swept by flash floods.
As steadily and inexorably as the land was formed it was destroyed again,
stripped clean, sent in red mud down the Little Colorado, the San Juan, the
Green, the Grand, the Escalante, the Paria, the Dirty Devil, the Virgin, into
the Colorado and down to the sea for the making of another country. In its
history the Colorado has built Imperial Valley on top of the sea bottom, cut
off the Salton Sea from its parent gulf, and until the Boulder Dam forced it
to drop its load higher up, was engaged in filling in the Gulf of California
like a child digging with a paddle on the beach.

If you looked for the Eocene Lake deposits around the Grand Canyon now you wouldn't find them. You wouldn't find the Trias or Jura. You wouldn't find the Cretaceous. You wouldn't find the Permian except in isolated buttes in the Kanab Desert miles back from the river—cameos of circumeroded stone, reliefs on a tomb, already beginning to be undecipherable. Thousands of feet of strata that once lay flat and solid over the whole Grand Canyon region both north and south are there no longer. They're at the bottom of the Gulf of California; your winter tomatoes from Imperial Valley have explored that lime with their roots.

But pretend for a moment that you are a bird (you'd have to be to do this) and are flying backward from the Grand Canyon, from the Kaibab Plateau, whose strata, like all the strata in this country, slope gently northward. You'll fly over solid Carboniferous limestone until you pass the Permian buttes in the Kanab Desert near Fredonia or Moccasin Springs. You'll come face to face with the retreating edges of the Jura-Trias at Kanab, fifty or sixty miles by airline from the canyon. That retreating edge forms the Vermilion Cliffs, the southern edge of the High Plateaus. Start multiplying (forget that you're a bird for a moment). Limit yourself to the area north of the canyon and multiply a mile of depth by sixty miles of width by the more-than-hundred miles east and west that this denudation covered, and you have a limited idea of how many cubic miles of solid rock such mild things as wind and rain can remove if you give them geological time to work in. Now you're a bird again. Fly ten miles up Kanab Canyon and you come to another tier of cliffs, the White Cliffs. Those are your Cretaceous shales. Rise above those and go fifteen miles more and the Pink Cliffs of the Eocene, capped with basalt, tell you that you are at the top of the ladder. These are the most recent and least eroded rocks in the region. Then perch and look back.

Step by step, cliff-line by cliff-line, the terraces break off to the Colorado. Layers of rock thousands of feet thick have come off as neatly as layers of paint before a scraper. The further you get back from the Grand Canyon the more recent the layer, until you meet the top in the Bryce Canyon formations of the Paunságunt Plateau. You stand and contemplate that vast wreckage, and the wind blows sand against your ankles and you yell and step back as if the wind were a mower blade.

Put it in terms of geological time, it is.

This was the country the Mormons settled, the country which, as Brigham Young with some reason hoped, no one else wanted. Its destiny was plain on its face, its contempt of man and his history and his theological immortality, his Millennium, his Heaven on Earth, was monumentally obvious. Its distances were terrifying, its cloudbursts catastrophic, its beauty flamboyant and bizarre and allied with death. Its droughts and its heat were withering. Almost more than the Great Basin deserts, it was a dead land. The ages lay dead in its brilliant strata, and the mud houses of the Ho-ho-kim rotted dryly in caves and gulches. In the teeth of that—perhaps because of that—it may have seemed close to God. It was Sanctuary, it was Refuge. Nobody else wanted it, nobody but a determined and God-supported people could live in it. Settle it then, in God's name, and build the Kingdom under the very eaves of that geological charnel-house.

NOTE

1. A reference to Percy Bysshe Shelley's poem "Ozymandias" (1818).

Part 2

Euro-American Explorers

Zion Canyon. Photograph by Charles R. Savage, ca. 1870. Savage took the earliest known photographs of Zion Canyon during a trip to southern Utah with Brigham Young. Courtesy of Church History Library, Salt Lake City, Utah.

7 | An Overland Trip to the Grand Cañon

JOHN WESLEY POWELL

Beginning with his legendary trip down Grand Canyon in 1869, John Wesley Powell and his team surveyed an enormous swath of the Colorado Plateau. In this excerpt he describes a daring journey his party made in 1872 down the East Fork of the Virgin River through Parunuweap Canyon to the mouth of Zion Canyon, which he called Mukuntuweap.

On the ninth of September[1] we made a fair start from the beautiful meadow at the head of the Kanab, and crossed the line of little hills at the head of the Rio Virgen,[2] and passed to the south by a pretty valley, and at ten o'clock came to the brink of a great geographic bench—a line of cliffs.[3] Behind us were cool springs, green meadows, and forest-clad slopes; below us, stretching to the south until the world was lost in blue haze, was a painted desert—not a desert plain, but a desert of rocks cut by deep gorges and relieved by towering cliffs and pinnacled rocks, naked rocks brilliant in the sunlight.

By a difficult trail, we made our way down the basaltic ledge, through which innumerable streams here gather into a little river running in a deep cañon. The river runs close to the foot of the cliffs on the left-hand side, and the trail passes along to the right. At noon we rested, and our animals grazed on the luxuriant grass.

After slow progress along a stony way, we camped at night under an overarching cliff, on the side of a beautiful glen or park, which is inclosed with high rocks on all sides except up and down the river. Here the river turns to the west, and our way properly was to the south, but we wished to explore the cañon that was below us. The Indians told us that the cañon narrowed gradually a short distance below, and that it would be impossible to take our animals much farther down the river. Early in the morning I went down to examine the head of this narrow part. After breakfast, having concluded to explore the cañon for a few miles on foot, we arranged that the main party should climb the cliff, and go around to a point eighteen or twenty miles below, at the foot of the cañon; three of us started on the exploration of the gorge called by the Indians Pa-ru-nu-weap or Roaring-Water Cañon. Between the little river and the foot of the walls was found a dense growth of willows, vines, and wild-rose bushes, and with great difficulty we made our way through this tangled mass. It is not a wide stream— only twenty or thirty feet across, in most places—shallow, but very swift. After spending some hours in breaking our way through the mass of vegetation, and climbing rocks here and there, it was determined to wade along the stream. In some places this was an easy task, but here and there we came to deep holes where we had to wade to our arm-pits. We soon reached places so narrow that the river filled the entire channel and compelled us to wade. In many places the bottom was a quicksand, into which we sank, and it was with great difficulty that we made progress. In some places the holes were so deep that we had to swim, and our little bundles of blankets and rations were fixed to a raft made of drift-wood and pushed before us. Now and then there was a little flood-plain, on which we could walk, and we crossed and re-crossed the stream and waded along the channel, where the water was so swift as almost to carry us from our feet; we were in danger every moment of being swept down, until night came on. We estimated we had traveled eight miles that day. We found a little patch of flood-plain on which there was a huge pile of drift-wood and a clump of box-elders, and near by a great stream bursting from the rocks.

Here we soon had a huge fire; our clothes were spread to dry; we made a cup of coffee, took out our bread and cheese and dried beef, and enjoyed a hearty supper.

The next morning we were wading again, sinking in the quicksands, swimming the deep waters, and making slow and painful progress, the waters still being swift and the bed of the stream rocky.

The day before, the cañon was 1,200 feet deep, but we found it steadily increasing in depth, and in many places exceedingly narrow—only twenty or thirty feet wide below, and in some places even narrower—for hundreds of feet overhead. There are places where the river, in sweeping past curves, has cut far under the rocks, but still preserves its narrow channel, so that there is an overhanging wall on one side, and an inclined wall on the other. In places a few hundred feet above, it becomes vertical again, and thus the view to the sky above is entirely closed. Everywhere this deep passage is dark and gloomy, and resounds with the noise of rapid waters. At noon we were in a cañon sixteen hundred feet deep, and we came to a fall where the walls were broken down, and the channel was beset by huge rocks, on which we obtained a foot-hold to reach a level two hundred below. Here the cañon was again wider, and we found a flood-plain along which we could walk, now on this and now on that side of the stream. Gradually the cañon widened; steep rapids, cascades, and cataracts were found along the river. We waded only when it was necessary to cross. We made progress with very great labor, having to climb over many piles of broken rocks.

Late in the afternoon we came to a little clearing in the valley where we saw signs of civilization, and by sundown arrived at the Mormon town of Schunesburg, where we met the train, and feasted on melons and grapes.

Our course for two days had been directly west through Pa-ru-nu-weap Cañon. Another stream comes down from the north and unites near Schunesburg with the main branch of the Rio Virgen. We determined to spend a day in the exploration of this stream.[4] The Indians call the cañon through which it runs Mu-koon-tu-weap, or Straight Cañon. Entering this, we were compelled to wade up stream; often the water filled the entire channel, and although we traveled many miles, we found no flood-plain, talus, or broken piles of rocks at the foot of the cliff. The walls have smooth, plain faces, and are everywhere very regular and vertical for a thousand feet or more, and then they seem to break back in shelving slopes to higher altitudes. Everywhere as we went along we found springs bursting out at the foot of the walls, and, passing these, the river above becoming steadily smaller, the great body of water which runs below bursts out from beneath this great bed of red sandstone; as we went up the cañon it came to be but a creek, and then a brook. On the western wall of the cañon stand some buttes and towers, and high, pinnacled rocks. Going up the cañon we gained glimpses of them here and there. After our trip through the cañons of the Colorado the year before, on our way from the mouth of the Virgen to Salt Lake City, we could see these buttes as conspicuous landmarks from a distance of sixty or seventy miles, away to the south-west. These tower-rocks are known as the Temples of the Virgen.

Having explored this cañon to its head, we returned to Schunesburg, arriving quite late at night.

Sitting in camp that evening, Chu-ar, the chief of the Kaibabbits,[5] told us one of the traditions of the tribes. Many years ago, he said, a great light was seen somewhere in this region by the Pa-ru-sha-pats, who lived to the south-west. They supposed it to be a signal kindled to warn them of the approach of the Navajos, who lived to the east beyond the Colorado River. Then other signal-fires were kindled on the Pine Valley Mountains, Santa Clara Mountains, and U-in-ka-ret Mountains, so that all the tribes of northern Arizona, southern Utah, southern Nevada, and southern California, were warned of the approaching danger; but when the Pa-ru-sha-pats came near they discovered that it was a fire on one of the great Temples, and then they knew that the fire was not kindled by men, for no human being had scaled the rocks. The Tu-mu-ur-ru-gwait-si-gaip, or Rock Rovers, had kindled a fire to deceive the people, and so this is called in the Indian language Rock Rovers' Land.

The next day, September 13th, we started very early, for we had a long day's travel before us. Our way was across the Rio Virgen to the south. Coming to the bank of the stream, we found a strange metamorphosis; the streams, as we had seen them above, ran in narrow channels, leaping and plunging over the rocks, raging and roaring in their course; but here they united, and spread in a thin sheet several hundred yards wide, and only a few inches deep; they were running over a bed of quicksand. Crossing the stream, our trail led up a narrow cañon, not very deep, and then among the hills of golden, red, and purple shales and marls—a region of bad lands. Climbing out of the valley of the Rio Virgen, we passed through a forest of dwarf cedars, and came out at the foot of the Vermilion Cliffs. We followed this Indian trail toward the east all day, and at night camped at a great spring, known to the Indians as "Yellow Rock Water," but to the Mormons as Pipe Spring.

NOTES

1. Though Powell wrote that the events described in this account occurred in 1870 during his preparations for the second voyage down the Colorado River, his article actually combines reports of different exploratory trips in the area. The descent of Parunuweap Canyon occurred on September 29 and 30, 1872, after the second Colorado River expedition. Donald Worster, *A River Running West: The Life of John Wesley Powell* (New York: Oxford University Press, 2001), 212.
2. That is, the headwaters of the East Fork of the Virgin, on the Markagunt Plateau.
3. The White Cliffs, west of the present-day Mt. Carmel Junction.
4. According to Steven V. Jones, who accompanied Powell on this trip, the party arrived at Shunesburg on the afternoon of September 30, 1872, and immediately departed southwest to meet their party at Kanab on October 2. Powell's description of Mukuntuweap, or Zion Canyon, may be based on accounts by other members of his expedition. "Journal of Stephen Vandiver Jones," ed. Herbert E. Gregory, *Utah Historical Quarterly* 16–17 (1948–1949): 159–62.
5. A name given the Kaibab Paiute band in northern Arizona.

8 | The Vermilion Cliffs, and Valley of the Virgen

CLARENCE E. DUTTON

*Clarence Dutton dedicated much of his life to exploring and doc-
umenting the geologic features of the American West. His* Tertiary
History of the Grand Cañon District, *with a massive companion
atlas illustrated by William Henry Holmes and Thomas Moran,
documents his explorations of the canyon country in 1879 and 1880
with equal measures of scientific description and breathless nature
writing. Here Dutton describes the approach to Zion Canyon from
the south.*

Late in the autumn of 1880 I rode along the base of the Vermilion Cliffs
from Kanab to the Virgen, having the esteemed companionship of
Mr. Holmes. We had spent the summer and most of the autumn among the
cones of the Uinkaret,[1] in the dreamy parks and forests of the Kaibab, and
in the solitudes of the intervening desert; and our sensibilities had been
somewhat overtasked by the scenery of the Grand Cañon. It seemed to us
that all grandeur and beauty thereafter beheld must be mentally projected
against the recollection of those scenes, and be dwarfed into commonplace
by the comparison; but as we moved onward the walls increased in altitude, in animation, and in power. At length the towers of Short Creek burst

into view, and, beyond, the great cliff in long perspective thrusting out into the desert plain its gables and spurs. The day was a rare one for this region. The mild, subtropical autumn was over, and just giving place to the first approaches of winter. A sullen storm had been gathering from the southwest, and the first rain for many months was falling, mingled with snow. Heavy clouds rolled up against the battlements, spreading their fleeces over turret and crest, and sending down curling flecks of white mist into the nooks and recesses between towers and buttresses. The next day was rarer still, with sunshine and storm battling for the mastery. Rolling masses of cumuli rose up into the blue to incomprehensible heights, their flanks and summits gleaming with sunlight, their nether surfaces above the desert as flat as a ceiling, and showing, not the dull neutral gray of the east, but a rosy tinge caught from the reflected red of rocks and soil. As they drifted rapidly against the great barrier, the currents from below flung upward to the summits, rolled the vaporous masses into vast whorls, wrapping them around the towers and crest-lines, and scattering torn shreds of mist along the rock-faces. As the day wore on the sunshine gained the advantage. From overhead the cloud-masses stubbornly withdrew, leaving a few broken ranks to maintain a feeble resistance. But far in the northwest, over the Colob, they rallied their black forces for a more desperate struggle, and answered with defiant flashes of lightning the incessant pour of sun-shafts.

Superlative cloud effects, common enough in other countries, are lamentably infrequent here; but, when they do come, their value is beyond measure. During the long, hot summer days, when the sun is high, the phenomenal features of the scenery are robbed of most of their grandeur, and cannot, or do not, wholly reveal to the observer the realities which render them so instructive and interesting. There are few middle tones of light and shade. The effects of foreshortening are excessive, almost beyond belief, and produce the strangest deceptions. Masses which are widely separated seem to be superposed or continuous. Lines and surfaces, which extend towards us at an acute angle with the radius of vision, are warped around until they seem to cross it at a right angle. Grand fronts, which ought to show depth and varying distance, become flat and are troubled with false perspective. Proportions which are full of grace and meaning are distorted and belied. During the midday hours the cliffs seem to wilt and droop as if retracting their grandeur to hide it from the merciless radiance of the sun whose very effulgence flouts them. Even the colors are ruined. The glaring face of the wall, where the light falls full upon it, wears a scorched, over-baked, discharged look; and where the dense black shadows are thrown— for there are no middle shades—the magical haze of the desert shines forth with a weird, metallic glow which has no color in it. But as the sun declines there comes a revival. The half-tones at length appear, bringing into relief the component masses; the amphitheaters recede into suggestive distances; the salients silently advance towards us; the distorted lines range themselves into true perspective; the deformed curves come back to their proper sweep; the angles grow clean and sharp; and the whole cliff arouses from lethargy and erects itself in grandeur and power as if conscious of its own majesty. Back also come the colors, and as the sun is about to sink they glow with an intense orange vermilion that seems to be an intrinsic luster emanating from the rocks themselves. But the great gala-days of the cliffs are those when sunshine and storm are waging an even battle; when the massive banks of clouds send their white diffuse light into the dark places and tone down the intense glare of the direct rays; when they roll over the summits in stately procession, wrapping them in vapor and revealing cloud-girt masses here and there through wide rifts. Then the truth appears and all deceptions are exposed. Their real grandeur, their true forms, and a just sense of their relations are at last fairly presented, so that the mind can grasp them. And they are very grand—even sublime. There is no need, as we look upon them, of fancy to heighten the picture, nor of metaphor to present it. The simple truth is quite enough. I never before had a realizing sense of a cliff 1,800 to 2,000 feet high. I think I have a definite and abiding one at present.

As we moved northward from Short Creek, we had frequent opportunities to admire these cliffs and buttes, with the conviction that they were revealed to us in their real magnitudes and in their true relations. They awakened an enthusiasm more vivid than we had anticipated, and one which the recollection of far grander scenes did not dispel. At length the trail descended into a shallow basin where a low ledge of sandstones, immediately upon the right, shut them out from view; but as we mounted the opposite rim a new scene, grander and more beautiful than before, suddenly broke upon us. The cliff again appeared, presenting the heavy sandstone member in a sheer wall nearly a thousand feet high, with a steep talus beneath it of eleven or twelve hundred feet more. Wide alcoves receded far back into the mass, and in their depths the clouds floated. Long, sharp spurs plunged swiftly down, thrusting their monstrous buttresses into the plain below, and sending up pinnacles and towers along the knife edges. But the controlling object was a great butte which sprang into view immediately before us, and which the salient of the wall had hitherto masked. Upon a pedestal two miles long and 1,000 feet high, richly decorated with horizontal moldings, rose four towers highly suggestive of cathedral architecture. Their altitude above the plain was estimated at about 1,800 feet. They were separated by vertical clefts made by the enlargement of the joints, and many smaller clefts extending from the summits to the pedestal carved the turrets into tapering buttresses, which gave a graceful aspiring effect with a remarkable definiteness to the forms. We named it Smithsonian Butte, and it was decided that a sketch should be made of it; but in a few moments the plan was abandoned or forgotten. For over a notch or saddle formed by a low isthmus which connected the butte with the principal mesa there sailed slowly and majestically into view, as we rode along, a wonderful object. Deeply moved, we paused a moment to contemplate it, and then abandoning the trail we rode rapidly towards the notch, beyond which it soon sank out of sight. In an hour's time we reached the crest of the isthmus, and in an instant there flashed before us a scene never to be forgotten. In coming time it will, I believe, take rank with a very small number of spectacles each of which will, in its own way, be regarded as the most exquisite of its kind which the world discloses. The scene before us was THE TEMPLES AND TOWERS OF THE VIRGEN.

At our feet the surface drops down by cliff and talus 1,200 feet upon a broad and rugged plan[e] cut by narrow cañons. The slopes, the winding ledges, the bosses of projecting rock, the naked, scanty soil, display colors which are truly amazing. Chocolate, maroon, purple, lavender, magenta, with broad bands of toned white, are laid in horizontal belts, strongly contrasting with each other, and the ever-varying slope of the surface cuts across them capriciously, so that the sharply defined belts wind about like the contours of a map. From right to left across the further foreground of the picture stretches the inner cañon of the Virgen, about 700 feet in depth, and here of considerable width. Its bottom is for the most part unseen, but in one place is disclosed by a turn in its course, showing the vivid green of vegetation. Across the cañon, and rather more than a mile and a half beyond it, stands the central and commanding object of the picture, the western temple, rising 4,000 feet above the river. Its glorious summit was the object we had seen an hour before, and now the matchless beauty and majesty of its vast mass is all before us. Yet it is only the central object of a mighty throng of structures wrought up to the same exalted style, and filling up the entire panorama. Right opposite us are the two principal forks of the Virgen, the Parúnuweap coming from the right or east, and the Mukúntuweap or Little Zion Valley, descending towards us from the north. The Parúnuweap is seen emerging on the extreme right through a stupendous gateway and chasm in the Triassic terrace, nearly 3,000 feet in depth. The further wall of this cañon, at the opening of the gateway, quickly swings northward at a right angle and becomes the eastern wall of Little Zion Valley. As it sweeps down the Parúnuweap it breaks into great pediments, covered all over with the richest carving. The effect is much like that which the architect of the Milan Cathedral appears to have designed, though here it is vividly suggested rather than fully realized—as an artist painting in the "broad style" suggests many things without actually drawing them. The sumptuous, bewildering, mazy effect is all there, but when we attempt to analyze it in detail it eludes us. The flank of the wall receding up the Mukúntuweap is for a mile or two similarly decorated, but soon breaks into new forms much more impressive and wonderful. A row of towers half a mile high is quarried out of the palisade, and stands well advanced from its face. There is an eloquence to their forms which stirs the imagination with a singular power, and kindles in the mind of the dullest observer a glowing response. Just behind them, rising a thousand feet higher, is the eastern temple, crowned with a cylindric dome of white sandstone; but since it is, in many respects, a repetition of the nearer western temple, we may turn our attention to the latter. Directly in front of us a complex group of white towers, springing from a central pile, mounts upwards to the clouds. Out of their midst, and high over all, rises a dome-like mass, which dominates the entire landscape. It is almost pure white, with brilliant streaks of carmine descending its vertical walls. At the summit it is truncated, and a flat tablet is laid upon the top, showing its edge of deep red. It is impossible to liken this object to any familiar shape, for it resembles none. Yet its shape is far from being indefinite; on the contrary, it has a definiteness and individuality which extort an exclamation of surprise when first beheld. There is no name provided for such an object, nor is it worth while to invent one. Call it a dome; not because it has the ordinary shape of such a structure, but because it performs the function of a dome.

The towers which surround it are of inferior mass and altitude, but each of them is a study of fine form and architectural effect. They are white above, and change to a strong, rich red below. Dome and towers are planted upon a substructure no less admirable. Its plan is indefinite, but its profiles are perfectly systematic. A curtain wall 1,400 feet high descends vertically from the eaves of the temples and is succeeded by a steep slope of ever-widening base courses leading down to the esplanade below. The curtain-wall is decorated with a lavish display of vertical moldings, and the ridges, eaves, and mitered angles are fretted with serrated cusps. This ornamentation is suggestive rather than precise, but it is none the less effective. It is repetitive, not symmetrical. But though exact symmetry is wanting, nature has here brought home to us the truth that symmetry is only one of an infinite range of devices by which beauty can be materialized.

And finer forms are in the quarry
Than ever Angelo evoked.[2]

Reverting to the twin temple across Little Zion Valley, its upper mass is a repetition of the one which crowns the western pile. It has the same elliptical contour, and a similar red tablet above. In its effect upon the imagination it is much the same. But from the point from which we first viewed them—and it is by far the best one accessible—it was too distant to be seen to the fullest advantage, and the western temple by its greater proximity overpowered its neighbor.

Nothing can exceed the wondrous beauty of Little Zion Valley, which separates the two temples and their respective groups of towers. Nor are these the only sublime structures which look down into its depths, for similar ones are seen on either hand along its receding vista until a turn in the course carries the valley out of sight. In its proportions it is about equal to Yo Semite, but in the nobility and beauty of the sculptures there is no comparison. It is Hyperion to a satyr. No wonder the fierce Mormon zealot, who named it, was reminded of the Great Zion, on which his fervid thoughts were bent—"of houses not built with hands, eternal in the heavens."[3]

From those highly wrought groups in the center of the picture the eye escapes to the westward along a mass of cliffs and buttes covered with the same profuse decoration as the walls of the temples and of the Parúnuweap. Their color is brilliant red. Much animation is imparted to this part of the scene by the wandering courses of the mural fronts which have little continuity and no definite trend. The Triassic terrace out of which they have been carved is cut into by broad amphitheaters and slashed in all directions by wide cañon valleys. The resulting escarpments stretch their courses in every direction, here fronting towards us, there averted; now receding behind a nearer mass, and again emerging from an unseen alcove. Far to the westward, twenty miles away, is seen the last palisade lifting its imposing front behind a mass of towers and domes to an altitude of probably near 3,000 feet and with a grandeur which the distance cannot dispel. Beyond it the scenery changes almost instantly, for it passes at once into the Great Basin, which, to this region, is as another world.

NOTES

1. South of Mt. Trumbull, on the North Rim of the Grand Canyon.
2. A near-quotation of these lines written in 1827 by Ralph Waldo Emerson: "And fairer forms are in the quarry / Than Angelo released," comparing Michelangelo's masterpieces to those of nature. Ralph Waldo Emerson, *Collected Poems and Translations* (New York: Library of America, 1994), 251.
3. A quotation of the New Testament (2 Corinthians 5:1).

The Temples and Towers of the Virgen. Engraving by William Henry Holmes, published in Clarence Dutton's *Tertiary History of the Grand Cañon District*, 1881.

9 | A New Valley of Wonders

FREDERICK S. DELLENBAUGH

Frederick Dellenbaugh was artist and topographer for John Wesley Powell's second expedition down the Colorado River. He went on to paint and write about the Colorado Plateau. This article, which describes in ornate prose his 1903 visit to Zion Canyon, reached a national audience in Scribner's Magazine *and contributed to national park designation. Dellenbaugh also exhibited his paintings of Zion at the 1904 World's Fair.*

Many years ago, while engaged with Major Powell and Professor Thompson[1] in their notable explorations of the Southwest, I had occasion to pass near to a locality dominated by a butte so gigantic that all its neighbors were dwarfed. Neither at that time nor when again at the threshold some years later, was I able personally to explore this splendid region; but a constant desire remained with me, and in 1903, twenty-seven years after my last glimpse of the vicinity, I found myself once more in "Dixie," as Southern Utah along the banks of the Virgin River is designated, with this Titanic mountain of bare rock, the Great Temple of the Virgin, lifting its opalescent shoulders alluringly against the eastern sky. Immediately behind the aggregation of enormous cliffs composing it was our ultimate destination, a marvellous valley, early named "Little Zion" by the Mormons who had settled near its lower end, and spoken of by the natives as Mukoontuweap, a valley practically unknown to the outer world, yet rivalling in beauty and grandeur even the Yosemite, the Yellowstone, and perhaps the Grand Canyon. So this monster butte became our beacon as our "prairie schooner," well laden with paint-boxes, photographic materials, and provender, held steadily on its course under fair May skies, steered skilfully by Brother Brigham, our Mormon pilot, its white sheeted top gleaming in the dazzling sunshine like the bold banner of a Crusader.

Brother Haproy, fresh from the shambles of Wall Street, a mere Lamb in this strange environment, alternated with me the privilege of conversing with Brig, in the pilot-house of the schooner, or of guiding the wayward nose of a youthful mare scarcely yet endowed with a sufficient abundance of horse sense to make riding an absolute delight. Thus we three went forth to our promised land. Close on our left lay the long blue line of the Pine Valley Mountains lifting their snow-streaked summits far above the wonderful labyrinth of many-colored cliffs and buttes and lava-beds threaded by our road, which, now rocky and dry, now sandy and dry, but ever dry, led continually up the deep basin of the river, a region scarcely less extraordinary than the valley of our destination. Except where water can be spread over the ground, the surface all through this country is so devoid of moisture that nothing but plants requiring a minimum is able to exist. Vegetation, therefore, is scattering, aggressive, threatening. At the same time one is surprised by its abundance, as well as by the richness of color and the profusion of exquisite blossoms in spring, the varieties of cacti especially being laden with flowers whose tender petals and soft beauty are a marvel in contrast to the parent stem as well as to the chaotic aridity of the environment. It seems as if a lion and a lamb were verily slumbering at our feet. And not only the cacti, but the "live oak" with its thorn-set leaf, the rabbit brush, the sage, the greasewood, and all the others have their blossoms, while in between, scattered thickly over the unfriendly earth, are multitudes of smaller flowering plants strange to all but the botanical traveller, and some of them, I fancy, still strange to him, yet as fascinating as the pampered products of a hot-house. But where water can be fed to the soil it becomes instantly prolific.

The Mormons being past-masters in irrigation, the rugged land contains a number of districts that, by contrast with the surroundings, rival the

Garden of Eden. Here grapes, peaches, almonds, figs, pomegranates, melons, etc., of choicest flavor are yielded in abundance. Every few miles the eye is surprised and gratified by the green fields and foliage of one of these bright oases, flowing, also, with milk and wine and honey. Nothing could be more refreshing than a sudden encounter with a broad green stretch of this kind after miles across arid wastes where one begins to imagine meadows, farms, and shady brooks to be mere phantasmagoria—when, lo! A magic turn of the road reveals a sweep of emerald with ditches of dashing water, plume-like poplars of Lombardy, fan-spreading cotton-woods, vineyards, roses, peach and apple orchards, fig-trees, and all the surroundings of comfortable country life. Again a turn, and the mellow beauty vanishes—not a drop of water then anywhere in sight.

Through such interesting, shifting scenery our schooner sailed on for several days, when Virgin City came in sight. As we approached this oasis we beheld the Great Temple, in full view from barren uplands, looming nearer and even nearer. At noon we heaved to our craft near the brink of a sharp canyon some five hundred feet deep, a mere gully amidst this extravagant topography, through which the waters escaping from the far up-country fume and fret, though without averting the harness; for the ever industrious Mormons have pushed into the depths and guided the stream by strategy to fields miles below. Around us in every direction tower incredible cliffs, buttes, pinnacles, gloriously painted, astonishingly sculptured, yet rendered insignificant by that masterpiece of Time, the Great Temple. Under the noonday sun it glows with an iridescence that intensifies its magnitude. The delicacy of the merging tints of red and white and creamy yellow, with tones of soft vermilion spread here and there athwart the white, like Alpenglow transfixed, is discouraging enough to the brush of the painter crouching in the shadow of the schooner. The foreground is gravelly desert sprinkled with the exquisite green of the sage-brush, inhabited, apparently, only by lizards, one large, active specimen resenting our intrusion by a series of angry hisses. Away below, sage-covered slopes extend to the distant green of Virgin City, overshadowed by the towering magnificence of the Great Temple, standing unique, sublime, adamantine. One hardly knows just how to think of it. Never before has such a naked mountain of rock entered into our minds! Without a shred of disguise its transcendent form rises preeminent. There is almost nothing to compare to it. Niagara has the beauty of energy; the Grand Canyon, of immensity; the Yellowstone, of singularity; the Yosemite, of altitude; the ocean, of power; this Great Temple, of eternity: "The Titan-fronted, blowy steeps / That cradled Time."[2] One feels here in sympathy with Childe Roland halting before the Dark Tower,[3] yet is uncertain whether, like him, to blow a blast of defiance or, like a Moslem at Mecca, to fall in prayerful homage.

Indeed, we are at last face to face with the Unattainable; no foot of man has ever touched the summit of this silent shrine, 7,500 feet above the level of the sea, 4,000 above the valley before us. Storm, night, the stars, the sun and moon, the elements, alone hold communion with that pristine crest. Under its shadow we may almost touch the latchstring of eternity; almost see ourselves in the dull mirror of Time. There comes a feeling that it ought to speak, to roar, to belch forth fire and brimstone, to give some sign of the throes of world-birth it has witnessed since these rocks were dyed in the antediluvian seas. But only the silence of the outer spheres encircles it; in all that wondrous expanse of magnificent precipices we hear no sound save our own voices and the whisper of the wind that comes and goes, breathing with the round of centuries.

In the morning we discover that the great butte, like a chameleon, has changed color. The rare opalescence has vanished; instead, the rock-mountain palpitates with a heavenly blue, as if metamorphosed to sapphire in a night. But the sun, mounting, darts shafts of light across the summit, the outlying pinnacles are set aflame; gradually the whole array of colors burns out again with all the intensity of yesternoon. To the left the white and red rock-domes of Colob Plateau stand luminous also, the color everywhere increasing in brilliancy as the sun falls, till the entire landscape appears kaleidoscopic, yet never harsh or crude. To eyes prejudiced by the soft blues and grays of a familiar Eastern United States or European district, this immense prodigality of color is startling, perhaps painful; it seems to the inflexible mind unwarranted, immodest, as if Nature had stripped and posed nude, unblushing, before humanity.

And the lavish display of color multiplies as we advance along the river, fording the stream occasionally, for in this whole region there are no bridges. At Grafton the poplar-studded fields present their welcome green, intensifying the radiance of the bounding rocks, the Great Temple ever rising supreme. The seven miles from Virgin City to Grafton have brought us more within its spell, yet, though no less overpowering, it now appears less mysterious, less Sphinx-like, less forbidding; the arrangement of the mighty precipices and resplendent colors is better seen, better understood.

The south flank immediately adjoining Grafton is more than a thousand feet lower than the main butte, yet its summit, which has been scaled from the opposite side, is some three thousand feet above the river, at least half this height being perpendicular and seamed by vertical lines of columnar projections from top to bottom. The face of this cliff, being slightly curved toward the south, forms an enormous sun-dial for the people of Grafton, the shadow marking the hour of high noon with considerable exactness. Once in a while, as if to strike the flight of the ages, a mass of rock breaks away and crashes in dust and thunder to the bottom.

Grafton has a situation that must some day make it famous, yet one dreads to think of this land being overrun by the ennuied tourist. But with an altitude of only 3,000 feet, a superb, dry climate, mild winters, magnificent environment, and a supply of delicious fruits, it cannot long remain unvisited if a railway ever is built within easy reach. The Mormons came here as early as 1861, but in 1867 the entire region had to be vacated on account of Indian troubles, and it was not till several years later that the settlers could return. Now there are twenty-three families, forming a total population of 115. Cliffs and buttes of all sizes, shapes, and colors enclose the valley. Up the cliff-wall to the south a road has been built. There is no way of getting out of the Virgin Valley without a climb of at least a thousand feet, and this is about the height the road at Grafton reaches. From the brink above, a startling vista opens up and down the valley, now seen to be in reality a wide, deep canyon, similar to the Grand Canyon, though on a smaller scale. It is perhaps four miles wide at top, with the bounding rocks broken into a multitude of fantastic buttes, crags, cliffs, towers, temples, pinnacles; and it is this extraordinary *variety of form* which makes the locality so attractive. Continuous straight, high canyon walls, while impressive, are apt to grow monotonous because of their regularity. Here every possible form of erosion seems to be represented.

The immediate flood-plain of the river is only about one-half mile wide, and green, cultivated fields gleam like gems wherever opportunity offers, the stream meandering through them in a mud ravine 900 feet wide, with vertical sides some ten feet high. At flood times the booming waters slash into the sides and sweep away acres of arable land, so that the fields are being constantly diminished in area. Wing dams[4] would afford protection, but the inhabitants are too few to undertake extensive works. This stream appears to me to be only the remnant of a once perennial torrent, the original sculptor of this valley in some past age when ice and snow on the high plateaus to the north afforded a bountiful reservoir. The whole country rises toward the north in a series of Cyclopean steps, and it is through these at right angles that the Mukoontuweap is cut, the Great Temple being but a remnant of the million billion tons of rock-strata which have been carried away by the rains and rivers through eons of time. In this long process of denudation there have doubtless been periods when corrosion was far more rapid than it is now, hence the deep canyons of this locality appear to be sawed down through a landscape which had already been brought to something of its present configuration before they reached their depth. The Virgin River is one of the conduits by which the floods from the High Plateaus of Southern Utah reach the sea, and in their flight they have carried along the incredible amount of denuded material which has been removed in the elaboration of these magnificent cliffs, and temples, and canyons. It has two main branches leading up into the heights of Colob and the Markagunt—the Mukoontuweap and the Paroonuweap, the former the more direct and monopolizing a greater area than the latter, which is compelled to share its waters with the Kanab Canyon, leading more speedily to the Colorado. Consequently the Mukoontuweap, or "Little Zion," is deeper and finer than its companion gorge. These two are, probably, the most extraordinary canyons, so far as width in relation to depth is concerned, in all the West. For a number of miles in each the walls, unbroken and vertical for 2,000 feet or more, approach to within twelve or fifteen feet of each other at bottom, and are very close at top, so that they are really merely deep, narrow gashes in the rocks, over-leaning at times to shut out the sky. Major Powell was probably the first white man to traverse these canyons, having gone through the Paroonuweap, at least, in 1872, on foot, of course. The enormous chasms are mainly cut through Triassic sandstone with a capping of the Jurassic, the latter extremely homogenous. Some of this upper stratum, which apparently has no defined separation from the underlying Triassic, is so soft on the surface that fragments of it crumble at a touch. It is the homogeneity of these rocks which has brought about the extraordinarily massive character of the unparalleled forms designated by the term "temple," a word that seems applicable, for they are not domes or pyramids alone, but often complex aggregations of giant precipices for which it is difficult to find a descriptive name.

Fording the river once more at Grafton, we pushed on up the valley, passing in about two miles the village of Rockville, just above which is the mouth of the valley we were particularly to examine; but instead of turning into it we went on up the Paroonuweap branch to a spot called Shoonesburg, once a village of perhaps fifteen families, but now, owing to the encroachments of the river on the fields, reduced to one, occupying a stone house on a naked hill above the group of deserted dwellings. Around, on every side, towered high broken cliffs, forbidding and desolate, making this as weird a location for a solitary family as could well be imagined. Desiring to pitch our camp where we would not be intruding, I mounted the barren, stony hill to make inquiries at the house, which finally stood before me bleak and mysterious like the abodes of the ogres in fairy-stories. The dreary appearance prepared me for a rather unpleasant reception. Hearing strains of music issuing from one portion, I went up to the door and knocked. I opened, expecting to be rather curtly met; but a handsome young fellow, playing a mandolin, most cheerfully said we were welcome to camp wherever we liked. A yard of one of the deserted cabins was selected for anchorage, and beside the tumble-down, half-log, half-adobe affair, long swept by the elements through every door and window, we halted the schooner. Near by, two large rosebushes in full bloom were reminders of the home life that once went on here. Some declare that there is no home life among the Mormons, but this does not agree with my own observations. Presently an old, old man,[5] neatly dressed as if for church, the day being Sunday, came to see us. He was the master of the bleak house on the bluff, and for forty years had watched the sun ride athwart these toppling rocks. I wondered if it now seemed to him as much like home as the fair New England meadows of his boyhood. The world here seems still in the making, and humanity scarcely sheltered from the blows of Nature's sledge.

Leaving the schooner anchored by the roses, we explored on horseback up the Paroonuweap Canyon as far as we could conveniently go, splashing back and forth across the stream and breaking through underbrush which at length, after about four miles, became so dense that the swift-flowing water full of bowlders was the only path open to us. We therefore turned about and reached our camp again just before dark. It is a beautiful gorge, but above Shoonesburg is less broken than below, and consequently not so interesting pictorially. Five or six miles above the point we reached is the mouth of the narrowest part, the deep gash in the strata before referred to. Sailing down from Shoonesburg we came about noon to the forks, and, fording both branches, stood at last ready to enter the Mukoontuweap, the Little Zion. At a solitary house I secured a specimen of the ancient pottery of the locality, dug from a grave. Pottery-making was extensively practised by the Indians who occupied all these valleys and canyons long ago. Those Indians who were living here when the whites first came belonged to the Pai Ute branch of the Shoshone stock. Just what their relationship to the pottery-makers was has not been determined. The Pai Utes have all been gathered into the neighborhood of Santa Clara, near St. George, so an Indian is a rarity on the upper Virgin.[6]

No sooner had we fairly swung into the entrance of the west-branch valley than we perceived its immense superiority in point of grandeur and coloring to all else save the Great Temple. The latter, however, is itself a part of the rare valley, for it forms the western gate-post, and is the forerunner of numerous other temples, some of them reaching up close to the altitude of its own mighty head. With the Great Temple on the one hand looming 4,000 feet, and on the other one of more than 2,000, the spectator is instantly enveloped in the maze of cliffs and color, a double line of majestic sculptures—domes, pyramids, pinnacles, temples, sweeping away to the north, dazzling with vermilion, orange, pink, and white—all scintillating in the burning sunlight with an intensity not comprehensible to those who have never had the good fortune to breathe this lambent air amidst the overwhelming profusion of color. And the splendor of all this exquisite Nature-painting is enhanced by the soft green of the cultivated fields and foliage of Springdale, the last settlement in this direction. The white summits of carved stone shine and shimmer like snow mantles against the sky, whose enchanting blue, flecked here and there by a drifting cloud, repeats on high the azure of the shadows, and gives the finishing touch to the panorama—to the opalescence of the valley. Yet with all this wonderful play of colors there is nothing garish or bizarre about this Opalescent Valley; sky and cliff and bottom-land are blended harmoniously into one picture.

The Great Temple, as it is approached from the west, at first appears ominous, forbidding, and we might expect the valley which it guards to offer a similar impression; but now the Temple from this point seems quite indifferent, in its attitude, while the Opalescent Valley itself opens wide and smiling, seductive as the realm of some Sleeping Beauty. But fairy-like though it is, we are sharply reminded by certain inward pangs that man cannot live by sight alone, and as we rumble along the single street of Springdale we look about eagerly for some propitious spot where to set a mid-day blaze in honor of Epicurus. Bishop Gifford[7] kindly placed his yard at our disposal, and into its capacious harbor our schooner sailed to a comfortable anchorage. A wide-spreading mulberry-tree threw its thick boughs above us, and from there we could peer out at the amazing back of the Great Temple, a hopeless wall of adamant. The highest point yet reached by the boldest mountaineer is easily distinguished from this spot. Some think there is a chance that one day the apex will be attained. If some reader wishes to vanquish this rock monster, the way for trial is plain. Springdale is the best starting-point, and the Mormons will treat him well. They are always agreeable and accommodating, and our stay in this beautiful valley was rendered more delightful by this fact. In an experience extending over a period of some thirty odd years, off and on, I have always found the Mormons kindly and helpful. The Indians being harmless anyhow, and gathered together at Santa Clara; there being no desperadoes in the country; and the Mormons themselves being always orderly, travel is perfectly safe and firearms are a useless burden. The laws prohibit the killing of game out of season, and, as the season for most animals is very short, a gun is useless also for hunting. Springdale vies with Grafton in the romantic quality of its location, and it is difficult to decide between them, though the views at the former place are even more unique. Climbing, as a sport, can be carried on here with an unlimited field.

Hundreds of summits have never been surmounted; scores of minor canyons have never felt the touch of a white man's foot. As for water, the visitor must not be fastidious. That of the river is wholesome enough, albeit rather gritty. Residents fill barrels in the early morning from the ditches which traverse every village, and allow the compound to settle. After a few hours it becomes palatable—at least so it seemed to me, though Brother Haproy thought otherwise. A few wells have been dug, but they have not always been superior in their product to the muddy fluid of the river. Swiftly it carries the mud along between the mighty rockforms, its tide a mixture in color of topaz and amethyst. It was well up now, and rolled down its gravelly bed with a vigor that betokened some trouble for our schooner, the way being no longer altogether dry, but, in view of the necessity of crossing some ten times between Springdale and the "Wire," and no bridges, quite the reverse. The Paroonuweap road had also been of this order, but we perceived from the greater volume here that our schooner might possibly ship a sea or two. However, some one had been as far as the Wire, only a day or two before, and the tide was reported at a possible stage, so we set sail with full confidence of reaching our destined port without serious difficulty. The frequent mention of this Wire in conversation made us curious to know about it. A wire was a strange thing to receive so much attention. Inquiry revealed that it was about seven miles further up the valley, the result of the cogitations of a Springdale genius, and quite an engineering feat in its way. A trail had been built at the point mentioned, up the cliff to the Colob Plateau, for the purpose of enabling the Springdale people to drive cattle for the summer to the heights, where there is good grazing. Immediately to the right of this trail is a well-nigh vertical cliff, about 3,000 feet up from its base. On top of this cliff, on the very brink, young Flanagan[8] constructed a windlass. Down below he built two others a distance apart. Around the three he succeeded in passing a series of wires forming a continuous cable. By revolving one of the drums the wire travels up or down, as the case may be, and any object attached ascends or descends at will. By this means supplies are sent up to men staying on the plateau, and various objects are passed both ways. On one occasion a wagon was taken up in parts; on another, a dog was treated to the aerial flight, tied in a basket. It was a week before the dog recovered fully, and since that time the vicinity of the Wire is a place he never visits.

The trail just to the left of the Wire is built along the lines of an old Indian path, formerly a precarious means of getting in or out of the upper end of the valley on foot; how precarious, may be judged by the fact that one of the last Indians attempting to traverse it slipped and was dashed to death down the precipices. Though now transformed into a horse-trail, it is still a *mauvais pas* enough, and when cattle crowd each other a carcass or two is the result at the foot of some wall. The drive for the season was to be made the day after our arrival at Springdale, and we were invited to accompany the expedition, but other affairs prevented our accepting. As one first approaches the Cliff of the Wire and searches for the trail one knows to be somewhere there, it seems impossible for man or beast to find an exit.

Two miles above the village we passed several houses, the final ones in this direction; henceforth we had the entire valley to ourselves; henceforth these mighty towers and temples reared their stupendous fronts for us alone; for us the river sent up its angry growl as if resenting our intrusion within this realm fit only for the Titan gods. Nearer came the domes and precipices, perpendicular for twice a thousand feet; closer came the great bowlders and bluffs by the river, till we were creeping along a roadway hewn out of the low hills by the Springdale people, who utilize some of the lands above. Without this no wagon could go farther. For a couple of miles the bottom is forbidding, the river roaring at our feet, the precipices leaping to the sky. Ahead are vistas of even greater pyramids with foreground of beating waters. These seem, indeed, to be balanced in the zenith. They are extraordinary, and though they have not the base-bulk of the Great Temple, they astound us by their beetling, towering character as much as did that giant butte. Words fail to express the sensations inspired by these excessive heights of naked rock. The river constantly forms an appropriate foreground, and at length as we near the upper end of this particular division, one of the most complete pictures of the whole valley unfolds before us. In the foreground are the chaotic masses of red rock through which the river tears its way; green cotton-woods and bushes then inject their note, leading on to a huge vermilion pyramid whose precipices cleave the sky in the May-day sun like a battle-axe, behind and above it rising the still, white rocks of the yet greater pyramids. A little farther on, the road leads out into bottom-lands again, where another phase of the valley begins. I mark four phases in all between the entrance and the upper chasm: the open phase as far as the beginning of the ravine, then the ravine, then the amphitheatre phase extending to the Cliff of the Wire, and finally the last narrowing phase from the Wire to the chasm.

Coming out of the head of the great ravine as upon the floor of another story, the magnificent series of pyramids on the left disclose their full majesty; the little river no longer frets amidst bowlders, but glides with a concentrated intensity. To the west opens a deep alcove, aiding to form here a huge amphitheatre. There are thick groves of cotton-woods in the wide, level bottoms; on the slopes of talus, cacti bloom gorgeously; there also are manzanita with its rich red stem and waxen leaf, sage-brush, and many other plants, cedars, piñons. The blue sky above again touches the right chord in the symphony. Up and down, east and west, extends the labyrinthian array of giant rock-forms so magnificently sculptured, so ravishingly tinted. Again we are impressed with the marvellous beauty of outline, as well as the infinite complication, of these Titanic buttes. It is doubtful if in this respect the valley has anywhere its equal. Not even the best part of the Grand Canyon offers a more varied spectacle. There is an isolation of each temple here that is rare, yet all are welded together in a superb ensemble.

A little farther on a particularly separated, enormous composition of naked rock—naked like all the others, except for a scattering of pine-trees on the extreme summits or along some precarious ledge—shot up on the left in the semblance of some Cyclopean organ, its flutings brought out by the waning sun—the Temple of Aeolus. The muddy river was much in our way, as we were forced to cross it often, and though it was not too stormy for our schooner, it yet flowed with determination and there was chance of soaking our cargo. Brig's masterful hand, however, carried it through every obstacle—waters, underbrush, driftwood—till at last we paused opposite the Cliff of the Wire, having crossed the stream only ten times. Being in advance, I hunted out the trail with my glass and pointed its position to the others when they came up. For a moment they ridiculed the statement, but a glance through the lenses proved my assertion. Night was drawing on. We found this point to be the head of easy navigation for schooners of our class, so we came to, pitched the tent, tied the horses to trees to prevent their departing from so unpropitious a spot, gave them a portion of the grain and lucern we had brought to keep them a day or two from starvation, and prepared generally for a bad night. The sky looked ugly. There was no use turning the horses out to graze, for the winter had been so severe the cattle usually herded here had consumed every blade of grass; even cottonwoods had been felled that the nutritious bark might prevent starvation. Judging from the appearance of the cattle we saw, the margin was very narrow. All about, and everywhere up and down the valley, the fallen trunks lay thick, often threatening to bar the schooner's progress altogether. They will furnish firewood for Springdale later. Cotton-woods are rapid growers, and all along the Virgin are cultivated in the villages for firewood; so the places of these that have been cut will soon be filled again.

Night and the rain fall down upon us together. The clouds sweep and whirl across the brows of the great cliffs, and the Cliff of the Wire multiplies its 3,000-foot verticality till it seems to be almost any height one chooses to imagine. The wind, the growling of the stream, the patter of the rain on the roof of the tent, all combine in a drowsy lullaby, and under our canvas we sleep undisturbed. When dawn crept shyly in, the opalescence was veiled by low-drifting clouds. The vast surfaces of bare rock had been soaked through the night, and now we saw shining cascades, quivering and feathery, dropping down from that upper world. These rain-cascades may be seen throughout the wondrous cliff-land of the Southwest, but those of the Mukoontuweap, and some I saw in the canyons of the Colorado, are the highest and most graceful that I remember. About noon, voices rang out from the upper air. But after all, the voices were not exactly angelic, and we knew it was some one descending the trail. A glass trained along the precipice discovered through the mist several small, moving, dark objects, distinguished as men and horses. They were of the party that had driven the Springdale cattle to the plateau. All day long, with one or two brief intermissions, the rain came down, and the clouds rolled among the summits of the cliffs. The air grew colder. Next morning found a thin layer of snow spread over the valley bottom, clinging to every available projection, and whitening the tops of the rock peaks. The horses, half starved and shivering, presented a sorry picture. For them the Opalescent Valley bore no charms. As the day grew older the storm broke, the heights came out in sun again, the snow at our level melted, and we saddled up and went on toward the head of the gorge, leaving the schooner and the tent to take care of each other. The valley so rapidly narrows above the Wire that it is properly a canyon. The walls shoot up sheer, after a talus of about 100 feet, and are from 2,000 to 2,500 feet in height, with occasional towers of the white sandstone still higher, seen through breaks in the red-wall bends. The color is deep red at bottom, with black streaks, merging into grayish white or whitish gray at the top. Every few hundred yards we forded the swift little river, the current sometimes making the horses feel rather wobbly under one as they slid across the stony bottom. Around one bend we saw, through a break in the cliff, into an alcove formed by the bend above, where a splendid fall five or six feet wide fell at least 800 feet, swaying in the wind. Ever narrower grew the canyon as we advanced, the vertical cliffs constantly approaching, till one felt like the prisoner of Tolfi, "in that rock-encircled dungeon which stood alone, and whose portals never opened twice upon a living captive."[9] The bottom was comparatively level, and at the Wire about 800 feet wide. This width fell to about forty at the point we finally reached, where farther advance was next to impossible at the stage of water prevailing. Finally, by plunging once more across the stream, now more concentrated, and back again to the east bank, I succeeded in dragging my horse along talus and through underbrush till I looked straight into the jaws of the narrowing chasm through which the river enters the valley. When Haproy and Brig came up, we concluded that the discomforts of progress onward at this stage of water outweighed advantages, and we decided to return. On the way back as in going up, we forded the stream ten or twelve times. Adding to this the ten crossings between the Wire and Springdale, it made a total of about forty fordings before we should again reach the settlement. Most of these fords could be avoided by a comparatively small amount of work necessary for a wagon to pass along the foot of an occasional talus, or through thickets of underbrush and cotton-woods. In the event of a sawmill being built on the high plateau, the people of the valley will construct the road. It is proposed to send the sawed lumber down on the Wire and haul it by wagon to Springdale.

Our horses now began to look gaunt and haggard from lack of feed. It was plain we could not linger at the Wire. Climbing the trail to view the wonders of the upper country, with its forests, wild-cats, cougars, mountain sheep, deer, and bear, was out of the question. We therefore reluctantly loaded the schooner again, put the helm hard aport, and went down with the current in the late afternoon. Never could the valley appear more resplendent than on that beautiful day as the sun streamed out of the West, sweeping the flanks of the precipices with a ruddy brilliance that intensified the gorgeous hues tenfold, while the shadow portions grew more sombre, fading at a distance into a rich cerulean bloom, broken by the dark green of cotton-wood groves. Surely it was a setting for a fairy-tale!

Just before the river, on the way down, breaks into the ravine, we made our camp on a piece of level bottom facing the grandeur of the mighty rock peaks of the Amphitheatre, and for a couple of days our eyes revelled once more in the play of color and grace of form abounding in this heart of the valley. Our enjoyment was enhanced by an opportunity we had through a passing rider of sending our famished horses down to Gifford's to be fed and sheltered. At night the solemn pyramids standing stark against the sky pointed vividly the terrific speed of the earth on its axis. We seemed to be watching the stars from a meteor express. Everything appeared to be shooting along at breakneck rate, till the mind felt dazed at the thought of such reckless whirling through space with these great sentinels of eternity.

It rends the heart to turn from the Amphitheatre, as any reader who may go there will testify; but nevertheless, with a firm resolution against these allurements, the schooner once more was directed toward Springdale, the restored horses pulling with a will, well spurred, no doubt, by recollections of the upper valley in the rear, as well as of oats a-plenty, ahead, down below. A charming day or two at the settlement, and we sadly turned our course toward the entrance to the valley. All too soon we passed beyond its giant gates, swung around the southern foot of the Great Temple, and arrived at Rockville, where for the last time we forded the river. With the help of an extra team, our schooner was towed up the long "dugway" surmounting the thousand feet of precipice that bind the valley immediately on the south, and on top of which our path lay off into Arizona, across broad plains. Mounting, ever mounting, the valley, the fields, diminish below; cliffs that seemed great melt away; others keep us company in their stead; while still others tower to touch the sky, with everywhere and always the Great Temple the chief note in the scale. At last we were on top, amidst a bewilderingly magnificent scene. The whole marvellous landscape circled around us now in one immense sweep, weird and wild to the last degree, with apparently no human life but ours within the vast radius of our vision. Mountain, canyon, cliff, pinnacle, valley, and temple stood forth, naked as in those first hours when lifted out of the enveloping seas; a wonderful, an appalling wilderness, of which Little Zion, the Opalescent Valley, is the heart and culmination. For hours, as we travelled, this all-pervading panorama, so varied and stupendous in outline and in color, threw its enchantment around us. Then nearer high cliffs veiled the Great Temple, its sky-swept crown of vermilion vanished, and with it all the kaleidoscopic region of Little Zion. Yet though the extraordinary cliff-land was gone, our schooner still coasted other cliffs of mighty outline and brilliant hue; still were we sailing through that wondrous "land of space and dreams."[10]

NOTES

1. Almon H. Thompson, John Wesley Powell's brother-in-law and his chief assistant during the second expedition down the Colorado River.
2. From Joaquin Miller, *The Ship in the Desert* (London: Chapman & Hall, 1875), 53, which gives the legend of a Spanish galleon somewhere in the Mojave Desert of Southern California.
3. Robert Browning, "Childe Roland to the Dark Tower Came" (1855), a poem titled after a line from Shakespeare's *King Lear*. Thomas Moran, another associate of John Wesley Powell and Dellenbaugh's fellow painter of the canyon country, completed a painting based on the poem in 1859.
4. Barriers built partway into a river to direct more of the current to the main channel.
5. Apparently Oliver Demille, who helped settle Shunesburg in 1861.
6. The 100-acre Shivwits reservation was established west of St. George in 1891.
7. Oliver D. Gifford, bishop of the Springdale LDS ward from 1894 to 1914.
8. David A. Flanigan; see chapter 19.
9. From William Mudford, "The Iron Shroud" (1830), which tells the story of a man imprisoned in an ever-shrinking chamber.
10. Another quotation from *The Ship in the Desert*.

Part 3

From Remote Outpost to Vacation Destination

George Fraser Jr. in the Zion Narrows. Photograph by Dave Rust, 1914. Courtesy of Church History Library, Salt Lake City, Utah.

10 | Journal, July 5–11, 1914

GEORGE C. FRASER

George Fraser and his son George Jr. visited Zion Canyon in 1914 during one of their sightseeing trips in the Colorado Plateau region. They were among the relatively few to visit Mukuntuweap National Monument at a time when unimproved roads made automobile transportation impossible beyond the town of Hurricane. Fraser's account includes vivid descriptions of the difficulties in reaching the remote canyon, his interactions with the local residents, and the spectacular view above Grafton—the same view that had enthralled Clarence Dutton more than thirty years earlier.

SUNDAY, JULY 5, 1914

Up 6:30 a.m.; temperature in car 62, clear; running through Sevier desert. High mountains on the east still showing snow; mud-holes in the desert and water standing in some depressions. Much of the surface bare, with growth of sage and low shrubs. Except for three large birds like crows and numerous gopher holes, we saw no signs of life. About half-way between Milford and Lund, George saw a Ford motor stuck in the mud, with a broken axle, and some horses being attached to pull it out. We subsequently learned that this car had been hired for our use to take us to Toquerville for $15, but the driver had gone to Milford to spend the Fourth, gotten drunk, and in the night ran himself into trouble.

Arrived Lund 9:38 on time. Grouchy young fellow named "Jim" greeted us with the inquiry as to whether we were the parties going to Toquerville and told us to hurry up and get our luggage on the automobile. I demurred and inquired for Doolittle[1] and found him. He pacified Jim for a few minutes and we went into Doolittle's storeroom, changed our clothes, packed the stuff we were not going to take and threw into the duffle bags what we thought we needed, all in a great hurry, under repeated urgings and threats from Jim, who backed up his own insistence with messages from an old lady that was in a hurry to get to Cedar City.

Lund is in the midst of the desert and most unattractive. Manderfield[2] said the less time we spent in Lund the better we would like it, which completely describes the place.

Left Lund 10:40 in a Cadillac motor. In the back seat was an elderly man, his wife and a silent person. On the front seat an old lady, a girl of about 22, named Edna, and Jim, the driver. George and I on the little seats in the middle. Our luggage and everybody else's strapped on the running board or anywhere it would hold.

Jim announced that he had been in Milford to spend the Fourth and had not gone to bed all night and was very tired. Edna kept him awake as long as she stayed with us. She went most of the way across the desert and was dropped at a dry farm operated as an experiment by a Nebraska man. In every depression the recent rains had made havoc with the road. We ran through many puddles and mudholes and in places had to leave the road altogether, which, after all, did not make much difference.

Our course lay about southeast to a gap in the hills near Iron springs, where we struck the road from Modena to Cedar. Across Cedar Valley we looked up the canyon of Coal Creek to the high Markagunt Plateau and vaguely, through the misty atmosphere, could descry the vermilion, white and pink of the outcropping rocks terraced in accordance with the several formations.

After Edna got out, Jim told us to beat him over the head if we saw him going to sleep.

Distance Lund to Cedar City 35 miles. Arrived 1 p.m.

We were taken to a hotel and told to eat lunch, after which Jim would call for us. Hot, filthy dirty and lunch vile. Had to work hard not to eat flies.

Two Harvard men at hotel. They were part of a party of six who planned to hunt for 2½ months with Uncle Jim Owens[3] on the high plateaus in an effort to capture alive a cougar. The larger of the Harvard men very fresh. Came from Groton and turned out to be the same fellow that irritated Alter on the Kaibab last year.[4] He had blood-poisoning in his foot and was compelled to lay up. His friend was keeping him company.

While in the middle of lunch the owner of the automobile, B. F. Knell, a large man with a black mustache and loud voice and an aroma of whiskey, burst in and told me he would not take us to Toquerville. He asked what arrangements had been made. I told him Doolittle had arranged with Jim to take us to Toquerville for $20. Knell refused to go beyond Belleview. Considerable argument ensued. Finally Knell got the manager of the telephone office to open up the wire (telephone service is suspended most of Sunday) and we got Doolittle. A compromise was ultimately effected, whereby Knell agreed to take us within 2½ miles of Toquerville, and arranged with Anderson,[5] who had a ranch there, to take us into Toquerville for $2. Left Cedar City 2:45 p.m. Sun out and hot. Knell drove. Jim was sent to bed.

Followed south down the valley along Shirtz Creek, crossing numerous side canyons. Beginning south of where we entered Cedar Valley the Pine Valley mountains rise steadily in height. They form the dominant feature of the landscape until the sheer face of Hurricane Cliff comes into view.

The road was substantially level for the first 12 or 13 miles and everything went well enough. Then we got into the basalt. The valley narrowed and the road ran along the mountain on the east side over a gorge cut by the river. It was winding, with a steep fall of 60–75 feet on the right and descended at a fairly heavy grade. Knell tried to put on the brake and it would not hold. He asked me to take the wheel while he pulled the brake with both hands, which, of course, had no result, as the brake was entirely burnt out. George, sitting behind, took direction of affairs and instructed Knell how to brake with his engine so that we negotiated this stretch of road in safety. A few miles further down, after passing Belleview, another steep down grade was encountered. Here Knell lost his head, turned white, broke out in a cold sweat and said "Boys, she's off." George was sitting in the front seat and tried to get Knell to put the engine in low speed, but Knell was too frightened to do anything. I urged George to jump, but we all stayed in the car, except one of the bags, which fell off and was run over. We ended by running into a dry wash at the bottom of the descent, going part way up the other side and settling back again. Right here Anderson met us.

We paid Knell and sent him about his business. This was at 5:40 p.m.

Anderson had a two-seated buggy with the back seat out and the rear filled up with apricots and peaches. George got out a shotgun and killed two cotton-tails on the way down to Toquerville. Distance 2½ miles. Arrived Toquerville 6:30.

We were taken to the house of Mrs. Naegle, on the northerly edge of town. About the house is a vegetable garden and numerous fruit trees. Mrs. Naegle is a widow. She was married before to a man named Klineman, and her daughter, age about 25, lives with her. Miss Klineman taught school at Enterprise last winter. She played the piano for us very well during supper.

Mrs. Naegle's husband was the son of one of the original settlers, a German, who built a large stone house at Toquerville, back in the 50's. He had seven wives, the only survivor of whom we saw living across the street from Mrs. Naegle.

Naegle's principal occupation was making wine. He made about 2500 gallons a year. He constructed large cellars to keep it in. The old house is now deserted.

Toquerville lies about two miles north of the Virgin River, on the southerly slope of a basalt flow running across the Hurricane Valley. Its water comes from a spring a mile and a half away bursting from the mountainside. It has the best water in the whole Dixie country and plenty of it. The water flows from the spring to the town in an open ditch and is carried through the town in deep gutters. To get a drink of water for cooking purposes, you walk into the street, stand on a board bridging the gutter, and help yourself. Its name is of Indian derivation, "Toquer" meaning black and indicating the color of the rock thereabouts. Its soil is wonderfully fertile.

We had fresh figs, apricots, cherries, peaches, tomatoes, and various kinds of vegetables. In addition they grow quantities of almonds and grapes. Roses bloom for nine months in the year.

We found D. D. Rust[6] waiting for us and spent part of the evening planning out the trip. To bed about 9:30, G. C. F., Jr. and Rust sleeping on cots on the porch and I in a room.

MONDAY, JULY 6, 1914

Up 5:45 a.m., temp. 66, temp. of water in the ditch 58. Miss Klineman tried hard to get us some Dixie wine or at least grape juice, but none was to be had. The wine industry flourished until about three years ago, when a temperance wave struck Dixie, since which time very little wine has been made and none is to be had except on the quiet.

Last night Rust had arranged with a Mr. Duffin to drive us to Hurricane at 6 o'clock. He turned up at 7 and we left at 7:15. Rust had with him two horses and saddles. Duffin provided a side-spring buggy, with one seat, and we filled the back with our luggage and supplies.

From Toquerville we proceeded generally east of south, over a rough road, steep in places, and along a creek. For about four miles and until reaching La Verkin Creek, the way was over lava. There seemed to be flows of different ages, the youngest evidently very recent, because I saw a contact by the road where lava lay over river gravel and had baked the upper surface.

8:15 a.m. arrived at La Verkin, four miles from Toquerville. A small town with little land under cultivation. Floods in the Virgin have created havoc with the old farms. There was growing some grain, many peaches and apricots and grapes. Got some ripe apples here.

La Verkin Creek and the Virgin both flow in deep canyons. We forded the former and crossed the latter on a good iron bridge right by the Hot Sulphur Spring. This spring rises on the south bank of the Virgin, about 25 feet above the river in a limestone. It deposits sinter and a green fungus grows where the waters flow, creating a bright stream of color. Temp. of spring 104 degrees. Sulphurous odor apparent 200 yards away. Taste bitter.

9:20 arrived at Hurricane. While Rust shopped, Duffin drove us one mile to the west, to foot of a volcanic cone. We had to walk up. Arrived at the top at 10:15. Temp. in the sun 117; shade 99. There is a distinct crater at the summit, which is worn off toward the north. Duffin has been familiar with this mountain since the early 70's and he called attention to the obscuring, within that time, of the basalt at the summit. Beside the cone we were on, there were three others in the immediate vicinity, one of them with an even more distinct crater than that we inspected. There was every evidence of recency of volcanic action. I found a perfect volcanic bomb and the ground was covered with pumice, scoriae and clinkers.[7]

Returning from the volcano, arrived at Hurricane 11:50. Hotel kept by Mrs. Ira Bradshaw of English parentage. Husband soft-looking and has reputation of taking things easy. Conspicuous on the parlor table was a large and handsome book, entitled "The Curse of Drink." Except for this, the entire parlor was filled with a patchwork quilt spread out on a frame. Mrs. Bradshaw said she was not expecting any boarders so she had arranged to do a quilting. Soon after lunch one of the neighbors came in to help quilt. House clean; lunch very good. Great many flies, but the house screened, so the dining-room was comfortable. Temp. in the house, 2 p.m., 88; in wagon, 3 p.m., 96. Lots of fruit and fresh vegetables.

We had expected to hire another team at Hurricane, but Duffin wanted to go with us, in spite of the fact that he had no luggage and had not even brought his coat. So we loaded supplies and started at 3 p.m., retracing our steps across the bridge over the Virgin by the Sulphur Spring and to La Verkin.

Near La Verkin we turned northeast, ascended a steep and very rough hill and followed along its side above the canyon of the Virgin River to Virgin City. From the crest of the hill above La Verkin had fine view up the Virgin, showing the towers. Approaching the crossing of North Creek, fine view to the north over the permian and trias, with white beehive shaped peaks of the jura in the distance.

Virgin City is poor, with little land under cultivation. The houses in the town are surrounded by fruit trees. I asked the privilege of purchasing some apricots of the lady who kept the post office. She instructed me to climb an apricot tree and gave me a basket, which I filled. In the meanwhile, she gathered some apples and presented us with all the fruit, and some water thrown in.

The Virgin water is so muddy it must be allowed to settle before being put to household use. As far as possible rain water is preserved, but precipitation here is so slight that there is not a great supply from this source. Each householder consequently takes water from the river in barrels and allows the mud to settle before drawing off the top for drinking and culinary purposes.

From Virgin City we continued up the valley, mostly along the north bank of the river, but several times fording the stream, to Grafton (formerly

Wheeler). The last five miles of the way the road was very rough and ran under cliffs of basalt, showing in places fine columnar structure. Camped at Rockville under a tree at river's edge. Barometer showed rise of 550 feet from Hurricane. Cooked supper; slept on the ground; to bed 10 p.m. Thirty miles today.

TUESDAY, JULY 7, 1914

Up 4:15; temp. 10 p.m. to 4:30 a.m., minimum 66, maximum 72. Strong breeze; comfortable night. Rust developed sore throat. Told of tendency to quinsy and scared us; doctored him with Dioxogen.[8]

Rockville lies about 1½ miles to the west of the forks of the Virgin. The peaches here were especially fine and we saw many mulberry trees. The berries are used as hog feed. Years ago silk worms were raised, but the market for the silk is so poor it does not pay now. Between Rockville and Springdale we skirted the permian slopes forming the base from which rose in dignified majesty the Western Temple of the Virgin, disrespectfully (even if with some degree of verisimilitude) dubbed the Steamboat.

Arrived Springdale 8:45. Stopped at store kept by J. J. Ruesch, native of St. Galleri Switzerland, here since 1874. Has forgotten most of his German. Here met a party of Salt Lake school teachers—five women and three men, one of the latter McNeisch, Princeton, '97. These people knew the Alters and had heard of our coming. Their outfit consisted of two riding horses, a big pioneer's wagon driven by Jim Emmett and a buggy driven by a young man. Jim Emmett formerly lived at Lee's Ferry. He is a pioneer. He was driven out of Lee's Ferry by the Grand Canyon Cattle Company people, with whose superintendent he had quarreled. The two men had guns out for each other for some time. Emmett was accused of stealing cattle up in that country and of various irregularities, with what justice I could not learn.

Near Springdale numerous black thorny locusts; flowers—roses, daisies, poppies and single carnations. Lunched by the river, just below Crawfords, near a ford. Bathed in the river, temp. 68. Just as we were going in [,] a wagon-load of women crossed ford. Rust saved the day by covering us with horse blankets.

Fine view up amphitheater running back of the Steamboat. White sandstone walls are discolored by the dripping from the red cap of the mountain, which supports rich vegetation of large yellow pine and Douglas fir trees. This presents the finest view we have seen yet. The Crawfords have fine apricots and peaches. We bought some eggs from them. The river is rapid, carrying gray mud.

Left Crawfords 1:30, arrived at camp, 1½ miles above foot of cableway, 5 p.m. Up 525 feet from Springdale and 900 feet from Rockville. Temp. 5 p.m., 84.

Whole afternoon followed up deep canyon with precipitous walls in most places and the bottom not to exceed half or possibly three-quarters of a mile at its widest points. At cable tramway valley bends toward west for a little way and then north again. We camped in a widening of the valley, between two narrow gateways. Here the walls are so high that at 5 o'clock the entire valley bottom was in the shade. After supper climbed over talus at foot of westerly wall of canyon. Clouds obscured the moon. To bed 9 o'clock, when the stars began to come out and breeze arose from the north.

WEDNESDAY, JULY 8, 1914

At 2:45 a.m. clear with very bright, nearly full, moon. Up 5 a.m. River down perceptibly since last night. At 7 a.m. started on horseback; rode about a mile and a half up canyon; left horses 7:40. After ten minutes' walking on dry land we had to ford the river and from this point were almost continuously in the water until our return.

About a mile and a half above where we left the horses, the canyon closed in so that the stream filled the entire bottom and it continued practically this way as far as we went. It was impossible to swim against the current and we had to wade over the rocks, chest deep. About a mile above this point we struck a side canyon of equal depth and narrowness with Zion Canyon, coming in from the southeast. The water was very muddy, of gray color. Rust guessed and afterward confirmed that this was the Orderville Gulch. Up to this point there had been no sun to warm us. The canyon was in places less than 20 feet wide. The walls looked to be 1000, perhaps 1500 feet high, rising sheer and in several places concave, so that the sky overhead was obscured. We were cold from the water and very wet. Here we found some drift-wood, built a fire, took off our clothes, dried them on the rocks and warmed ourselves in the sun. About two miles above where we left the horses, the trias seemed to dip under. From there on we were in the cross-bedded sandstone. The finest and most striking cliffs of this appear on the side walls of the Orderville Gulch.

At 1 p.m. we started up Orderville Gulch and followed it until 2:45. Our progress was slow because of the roughness of the walking and although there was not a great deal of water in the stream, we kept pretty wet. We encountered three waterfalls, one of them 20 feet high, which we had to climb. The Orderville Gulch Canyon is narrower than the Zion Canyon and apparently equally deep. In five places—perhaps more—the sky is shut out overhead. We estimated that we walked 2½ to 3 miles up this canyon. Left for return down canyon 2:50; arrived lunch place 3:55; ate remains of lunch and left 4:30 and followed up Zion Canyon until 4:55. The sky was overcast, a few drops of rain fell, and we heard the rumblings of thunder. The canyon was as dark as an hour after sunset. Overhanging walls obscured the sky. Reluctantly we turned back and hurried down the canyon as fast as we could, reaching the horses at 6:25 and arriving at camp at 7:10. We estimated that we walked and waded up Zion 5 miles and up Orderville Gulch 2½ miles, a total of 15 miles, plus 3 miles more on horseback from and to the camp.

While the day was hard and fatiguing and at times we suffered from the cold, none of us were any the worse for it. As a matter of precaution we each took two grains of quinine and some raw whiskey before supper....

SATURDAY, JULY 11, 1914

A cloudless night; moon still up at sunrise. Up 6:15; cool. Heavy dew during the night for the first time. Somewhat troubled by flies and mosquitoes, owing to the proximity of the corral.

Ascended hill to west; fine view down Virgin Valley and up Shunesburg Creek. Left camp 8:30. Took Rust's two horses and Maude out of Duffin's team. Rode up Parunuweap eight miles until 11:20. Brilliant sun overhead. Horses could go no further. Instead of the sheer cliffs characteristic of Zion Valley, the Parunuweap is bounded by steep naked slopes, save for the bush-covered talus, and the valley bottom is relatively wide. Though tempted to proceed up the creek to a waterfall that lies about four miles beyond where we stopped, the heat and fatigue and the difficulty of treading the under-brush made us turn back. Left on return 1 p.m., arrived in camp, riding hard, 3 p.m. George, riding bareback, had his saddle blanket slip and fall off. Took bath in Shunesburg Creek. Very hot sun. A little relief around two o'clock when it clouded over and a few drops of rain fell.

Shunesburg was one of the first places settled in the upper Virgin Valley. Its grave yard contains the remains of many of the old settlers; old timers are buried there even now. Outside of the corral and the alfalfa fields about it, the only sign of habitation is a great stone house standing on the hill slope south of the Virgin. This was built by the original DeMills prior to 1874. It is in three sections, each with a door, the center for the old man and two wings for each of his wives.

Left Shunesburg about 4. Arrived Rockville, six miles, about 5:30. Found eight young men in two groups sitting in the road outside the post office, playing High-Low Jack and waiting for the mail.

Arrived Grafton, via the same road we took on the trip up, 6:30 p.m. Camped in the center of town on the basketball field of the schoolhouse. George and I did not dismount, but proceeded at once up the cliff to the south of Grafton over a new road lately constructed. Rise from Grafton to summit of this hill 800 feet by barometer. On the way up, overtaken by a shower, but before this struck us, stopped and photographed panorama of the towers of the Virgin. As we ascended the hill, the shower left us and passed over the Virgin Valley to the north; to the southeast in the direction of Short Creek another shower appeared, creating a rain-bow. As we neared the summit, the rain-bow spread and arched completely over the Virgin Valley to the east of us. Soon a double rain-bow appeared, the outside bow not quite complete, but the inside one rising at the north from the summit of the Steamboat, and ending at the south in and near the head of a side canyon coming into the Virgin Valley from the south. To the west the Pine Valley Mtns. stood up as a high wall and to the east the entire upper Virgin Valley was spread before us with all the temples brought out in sharp relief by the light of the setting sun; the colors of the rocks of every shade, from the light shales at the base of the permian through the choco-late at the summit, the vermilion cliffs above and the brilliant white of the jura, capped and streaked by the gypsiferous layers above, were accentuated and changed chameleon-like, as the sun moved down, and finally its light reflected from the clouds struck them. In the maze of color and sculpture, interest in and appreciation of details was lost. We were not tempted to have recourse to our glasses. This view was a picture framed by nature in the rain-bow, that only disappeared when the sun's rays passed. Whether this view was more beautiful than any other I have ever seen is not subject to determination; it is, however, one of a very few to be remembered as the most magnificent.

We lingered on the summit until dusk had well set in, and reached camp after dark—about 9:15. Three men living in Grafton sat about while we had supper, and gave us considerable information.

Grafton was formerly called "Wheeler," and as such appears on the old maps.

To bed 10:30.

NOTES

1. Local businessman H. J. Doolittle, who made travel arrangements for the Frasers.
2. Union Pacific agent J. H. Manderfield.
3. A Forest Service ranger serving in the Kaibab Forest north of the Grand Canyon.
4. J. Cecil Alter of Salt Lake City published an account of his visit to the North Rim in the *Salt Lake Tribune*. Fraser read the account and corresponded with Alter while planning his trip.
5. Probably Frank Anderson, son of Peter Anderson, who owned a ranch at the junction of the Arrowhead Trail (now I-15) and the road to Toquerville and Hurricane.
6. Fraser had contracted with Kanab resident David D. Rust to be their guide and photographer.
7. A volcanic bomb is a rock formed from lava that was ejected from an erupting volcano and that cooled before hitting the ground.
8. Tonsillitis or perhaps strep throat. "Dioxogen" was a preparation of hydrogen peroxide, an antiseptic. (Footnote in original publication.)

11 | The Canyon Sublime

Mukuntuweap So Named

Frederick Vining Fisher

*Methodist minister Frederick Vining Fisher visited Zion Canyon
from Ogden, Utah, in 1916 and took photographs for a traveling lec-
ture he was developing to promote the scenic wonders of the West.
During his visit, he and two companions from Springdale played a
game giving the various features of the canyon a name, and many
of the names they invented are still used today. In this article in the
local newspaper, he recounts his visit.*

Editor *Washington County News*

Dear Sir:—Before I leave southern Utah tomorrow after our trip of
one month, which has covered 636 miles in auto and "White Tops"[1] and
in which I have lectured 12 times and taken 370 views of this wonderful
land, I want to fulfil my promise and write you of Little Zion, the "Canyon Sublime."

On this trip I have stood with you at Tuweap and seen the Giant Gorge
of the Grand Canyon in its mighty majesty, faithfully followed McCormick's Ford tracks,[2] rode through the sweep of the beautiful Kiabab forest, gazed from Bright Angel on the Grand Canyon's grandest realm, seen
the stretch of the desert from Pipe Springs, the Emerald Valley from Hurricane Hill, bathed in La Verkin's hot springs, drank from the Blue Spring
on Cedar mountain, ate Apostle Ivins'[3] trout breakfasts in the crisp air of

9000 feet by Panguitch lake, gazed at sunset on the most glorious color city in the world, the City of Ten Thousand Castles which we call the Cedar Breaks, and from Mammoth Ridge 9942 feet above the sea seen the world of Utah from Nevada's mountains, Old Baldy's summit and Dixie's vales on one side and the Cedar Mountain's autumn clad glory, the Vermillion Cliffs of Kanab and the reach of the Kiabab on the other, America's greatest long distance view but—Little Zion is the climax of all.

I would I had time to tell of Claud Hirschi's[4] "white top," sturdy team companionable "Tip" and his own splendid self or of Mrs. Dennett's good meals at Rockville, of the camp in the canyon, of the nervous departure of Mr. Bingham up the long narrow gorge on foot mid-stream for views and his dramatic return with cloths for neckwear after an involuntary bath of himself and camera in the upper river, of the sunrise over the Temples of the Virgin, the sunsets in the "Court of Many Waters" and the wild storm in the "Court of the Ages" where the cliffs echoed the pealing thunder and the sun transfigured the falling rain, but I forbear all this to simply, plainly, briefly, characterize Little Zion.

I called Little Zion "The Canyon Sublime." It is all that and more. Mr. Dennett of Rockville who speaks Pah Ute says the name of inner Mukuntuweap means "The land or home of God," and that no Indian will sleep in it and that they always sacrifice to it. How fitting the name: "The home of God," or Zion; both well express this canyon which is not wonderland like the Yellowstone, nor beautiful like the Yosemite, nor a scene of awe like the Grand Canyon but which is the most stately, dignified, impressive temple in the world.

Little Zion is no place for a tourist resort but a place of pilgrimage for poets, patriots, artists, dreamers, and worshippers, only folks who pray have any right to go there.

It is not a canyon so much as a series of nine majestic great inner courts stretching for seven miles from the wonderful portals whose guardians are the Temples of the Virgin and seen best from the Gifford[5] place at Springdale to the "Voice of the Waters" at the "Gates of Eternity" where the famous gorge reaches away twelve miles more to Crystal Spring on Cedar mountain. Each of these courts grow smaller and more impressive as one passes through them and on to court after court through the narrow passes that connect them.

We named them in order, the "Court of the Wind," the "Court of the Sun," the "Court of the Patriarchs," the "Great Amphitheatre," the "Court of Music," the "Court of Poets," the "Court of Many Waters," the "Court of Ages," and the "Voices of the Waters."

Leaving Springdale one enters the "Court of the Wind" between the temples of the Virgin. We named it that for there the wind never ceases to blow. The "Temple of the Sun," the only lofty peak in the canyon on which the sun shines from sunrise to sunset—with companion peaks—mark the ["]court of the Sun," while the Temples of Abraham, Isaac, and Jacob overshadow the "Court of the Patriarchs." From there one enters the glorious great Amphitheatre which I called the "Court of God." Leaving that the pass of the canyon leads where a great organ is one side of the Court and a sounding board on the other so we call that the "Court of Music." Homer, Milton, Shakespeare all loom high in the "Court of Poets." The Cave of Everlasting Rain, the Falls of Pak, the brawl of the clear water, all distinguish the "Court of Many Waters" where the cable is.

But it is beyond that in the solemn silence of the great walled "Court of the Ages" on one site of which looms the "Great White Throne" and on the other the "Royal Towers" and beyond which the falling waters never cease and the "Gates of Eternity" open and the strange, weird winding gorge opens that one feels at last the sublimity, glory, and power of Little Zion.

If the Yosemite is Goldsmith's Dream Incarnate, if the Yellowstone Milton's Paradise Lost, and the Grand Canyon Dante's Inferno, then Little Zion is the Revelation of St. John, the Apocalypse of God, the New Jerusalem let down from the skies; the Mukuntuweap, the Home of God, aye, Little Zion, the image of the Eternal Zion whose builder and maker is God.

NOTES

1. That is, by covered wagon.
2. George McCormick, a mining prospector and rancher on the North Rim in the early 1900s.
3. Anthony W. Ivins, southern Utah native and member of the LDS Church's Quorum of the Twelve Apostles.
4. Rockville resident with whom Fisher named the various features of Zion Canyon.
5. Oliver D. Gifford.

12 | Zion Canyon

Utah's New Wonderland

HOWARD S. NICHOLS

This 1917 pamphlet, sponsored by the Los Angeles & Salt Lake Railroad, painted Zion Canyon in awe-inspiring prose, while reassuring potential visitors that the canyon, though remote and still little known, offered the comforts and amenities of civilization, including the first-class service of a "Wylie Camp."

Zion Canyon, stupendous in depth and overpowering in its peaceful magnificence of beauty, was not known to the public until 1917.

Some intrepid Mormon pioneers explored it in 1861, but as it lay hidden far away in the mighty mountains of southwestern Utah, close to Arizona and Nevada, few outsiders heard of it during the next fifty-six years.

Then all at once through vigorous and concerted action by the United States government, the State of Utah, Washington County and the Los Angeles & Salt Lake Railroad (Salt Lake Route) this extraordinary region was made known and made accessible to the world. It is expected that Congress will decide to preserve its pristine splendor and make the entire district Zion National Park. U.S. engineers made a most substantial automobile road inside its boundaries, and this was connected with a similar state and county highway to Lund station on the railway, through the efforts of former Governor William Spry. The Salt Lake Route put in effect a satisfying schedule for travelers; an excellent motor stage line began operation; and the famous Wylie-Way camping service, known to all Yellowstone National Park visitors, was established in Zion Canyon by W. W. Wylie.

Thus, five and one-half decades after its romantic discovery, this secreted territory was suddenly and simultaneously disclosed to and put within reach of the American people.

A new type of country in contour and climate, is found in this southwestern corner of Utah and adjacent parts of Arizona and Nevada. It is strange and attractive. It suggests a cross between two types: between the warm plateau region of Central Mexico in the Sierra Madres, and our Rocky Mountains. It has some of the bold beauties of the Rockies combined oddly with certain southern airs and graces. There is no repellant harshness here and you feel a friendly attitude even in towering cliffs. You gaze on canyon gateways of such spacious hospitality that your imagination leaps again as in boyhood fancies and Arabian Nights dreams of travel in foreign climes.

Brigham Young, great colonist and President of the Mormon Church, long ago gave the name of Little Zion to this channel of the Rio Virgin, because of its startling profundity, amazing beauty of coloring, rock walls, towering domes and vegetation, and its surpassing peace which suggested to him a Heaven on earth.[1] There is, indeed, a most pleasing tranquility in the entire region, which soothes the nerves and satisfies the eye.

The tremendous hush of this deep canyon, however, was too much for the superstitious Indians of early days and although they sometimes made daylight hunting raids into it after deer, bear, and bison, they never camped or spent a night within the vast gorge. Nor could the friendly Mormon settlers with whom in later years the Red Men traded freely, ever persuade any one of them to sleep in the canyon. The inducements offered of a white man's cabin, bed, and peculiarly good food, were useless. The Indians always left before sundown, gravely explaining that Mukuntuweap was a place of Great Spirits, who would punish in the night all intruders.[2] But today, weary of city clamor and smoke, civilized men and women find this prodigious cleft in the wilderness, clean, quiet, and most refreshing.

The newly opened land of beauty and rest is now comfortably accessible. By the modern magic of transportation combining a great railroad, automobiles, and good roads, Zion Canyon has been brought within easy reach of all. Yesterday it was forty-eight hours of hard teaming from the railroad; today it is but six hours of interesting scenic motoring from the platforms of the swift transcontinental caravans of the Salt Lake Route.

You leave the train at Lund after breakfast in the morning, and step into a big high-powered machine for a smooth spin over the good new county highway to Cedar City. The plateau lies beneath you level as a floor. On the right rise Table Buttes against the western sky, and in succession you see Iron Mountains, Granite Peak, and Cedar Valley.

Cedar City, pretty foothill town of 3,000 happy people, has an air of thrift and a good hotel where you enjoy a remarkably satisfying luncheon. The handsome buildings of the Utah Agricultural College branch, the fine schools, and swarms of automobiles here surprise you. You roll away in the machine again. The dark green cedars enrich the charms of the landscape. Many of them are so perfectly symmetrical that they seem to have been trimmed by other hands than those of Dame Nature.

Hamilton's Fort, with its thick stone walls shows how the Mormon pioneers at times had to assemble for protection against the Indian hordes. Mt. Henry, miles away, scratches the sky. Kanarraville, tiny hamlet, waves a greeting as you flit by. Dixie National Forest with its sylvan wealth is on the right.

The Great Pine Valley Mountains stretch their mighty heads toward the Heavens. Bellevue town, and Toquerville with its four yearly crops of luscious figs, bask in the sunshine as you slip past in your big car. The thoughtful guide points out to you on the right the famous Silver Reef Mine, known all over the west, and the Hurricane Fault, familiar to geologists in all lands as the greatest fault known in the whole world. This most startling formation has attracted mining engineers and mineralogists from nearly every geological institute in America.

The total length of Hurricane Fault is more than 200 miles; wherever seen it forms an important topographic feature, and it finally disappears

under floods of lava in the Tushar Range. It represents a terrific displacement of the earth's surface and an upheaval beyond comprehension.

In fact the entire region is of absorbing interest to scientists and laymen
because of its natural wonders. Cliffs fling their unassailable heights into
the clouds and gorges yawn prodigiously.

It is a land of magnificent distances and glorious vistas. Wherever the eye
looks, there is a scene worthy of a great artist. Craters of extinct volcanoes
are numerous. The White Buttes catch your eye on the left. Red Bluffs further on swell upward like prodigious terracotta sculptures. La Verkin creek
winds serpentine-like among the hills. The views suggest some enchanted
land of imagination.

Rockville is a lusty little town of stone houses and log cabins in a narrow valley. Grandly the rock walls rise above the homes of the sturdy pioneers. The pears, strawberries, peaches, and other fruits and vegetables of
this region are most delicious.

Luther Burbank, the wizard of modern agricultural science, as far back as
1907, said of this Dixie County's fruit exhibit at the great Sacramento California Fair:

"In all my life I have never seen such a magnificent display of peaches."

Throughout the ages, floods of melted snows and rains slowly wore into
the earth's surface these terrific chasms of the Southwestern states: Zion
Canyon, Grand Canyon of the Colorado river, Yellowstone Canyon, and
others in this territory. Innumerable frosts chiseled them. The indefatiga-
ble winds, too, were their sculptors. Today weird formations catch the eye.
Contrasting hues in stone challenge the painter to imitate them. Cliffs and
pinnacles change colors in shifting light as if by magic.

At dawn Zion Canyon seems ghostly, veiled in dim mystery, vaguely
promising strange splendors. Presently the rising sun shoots shafts of rich
light into dark hidden gulches and giant rock clefts, producing supernatural beauties of shadowed angels and splendid splotches of gold on grim old
walls. The superstitious Indians who would not spend a night in the canyon, furthermore would never even enter it until the sun was high in the
heavens, until these mysterious effects of light and shade were gone. Then

they hunted hard and fast in the narrow defiles and hastily retraced their steps into the open country.

It is in the full light of midday, however, that the real proportions, magnitude, and charm of Zion Canyon are revealed. Immersed in light, illumined to its uttermost recesses, its majesty and immensity are unforgettable.

You drive in ease on the floor of the canyon and look up to ascertain its depth instead of looking down, which is a novelty of sensation in itself.

Beside you a green cliff rises 3,000 feet sheer, cutting the sky so far away that huge pines look like ferns on the distant edge of the precipice. A pink pinnacle of sand-stone glows in the sunlight like the tower of a palace in a city of dreams. Beyond looms a purple rim 9,400 feet high. The Zion river here sings a triumphant song as it sweeps on to join the Colorado river nearby in the Grand Canyon of Arizona. You see gray fortresses with fronts fretted and seamed by ages into a marvelous maze of intricate lines, and figures suggesting Egyptian hieroglyphics or Aztec inscriptions, but you know that only the hand of Time could do such work. Further on rises a monstrous overwhelming pile of stone, so colossal that the tall poplars at its base look like a tiny hedge beside a mansion. You enter a silent sunlit amphitheatre vast enough to hold a dozen Roman Coliseums and yet you do not feel lost or lonely. Its beauty makes you gasp at first; then comes the feeling that the delightful place belongs as much to you as to anyone, that Nature made it to be enjoyed, and you explore its innumerable charms of color and form.

There stands West Temple, a magnificent mass of time-defying rock. Here is the Chieftain, a titanic Indian profile so amazingly perfect even to its feather headdress that you are surprised to see a stone face which really is a face.

The Great White Throne is tremendously impressive as your glance rises more than a mile to it through the pellucid air. The steel cable swinging dizzily aloft from the bottom of the largest amphitheatre to the canyon rim, is used by the settlers to lower lumber from the plateau mill. Sometimes men perform the hair-raising feat of sliding down the 4,000-foot strand. This sight is guaranteed to thrill the most blasé of all beholders.

On a smooth level raised spot near the river commanding fine views in all directions, stands the first of the welcome Wylie-Way camps with its cheerful air of thorough comfort and permanence. Complete to the smallest detail with every arrangement in its effect for the ease, health, and pleasure of guests, this royally good camp is the product of thirty-five years of experience in Yellowstone National Park.

Mr. and Mrs. Wylie personally selected the site in February, 1917, after days of careful exploration and investigation. Mrs. Wylie in her humorously wise way says that most people like to camp but do not like to "rough it," so the Wylie-Way provides no cots but the best beds that can be bought, excellent meals, jolly camp fires morning and evening, intelligent camp help, and an atmosphere of frankness and friendliness which travelers appreciate. The tents are sanitary, have sound board floors, stout frames, windows, and doors, and are substantially erected in every particular. Small stoves stand ready to furnish warmth if needed. Hot and cold water and excellent service are provided. It is camping de luxe.

In this fertile well-watered district where nestle the little farms and orchards of the Mormon pioneers at the entrance to the canyon, the Wylies found an abundance of fruit, vegetables, milk, butter, poultry, and live stock with which to supply the camps. And it is nice to have fresh growing things to eat in season even when sightseeing in a land of wonders.

From the happy Wylie-Way camp you may contemplate at leisure an inspiring panorama; table rocks level as a floor to the very brink of 2,000-foot precipices, gray slopes richly marked with dark green cedars forming a primitive park which would make a landscape architect envious, monumental pillars, gently rounded cones, vast spires with fluted sides, minarets, and stout rugged towers rising from dark shadowed canyon sides into the sunlight of the glorious heights.

The musical murmur of the Rio Virgin comes softly to you, birds sing in the trees, a refreshing breeze tempers the genial warmth of the friendly sun, and reclining comfortably in your steamer chair you absorb the peace of Little Zion.

The sunset, its paint brush dripping with glory, strikes the great gorge. A transformation begins; gray walls become amethyst, blue ridges deepen to royal purple, vast domes catching fire blaze against the turquoise sky, and snowy cloud-masses aloft turn into flush pink. The rims of East Temple and other temples gleam like mighty opals: fire red, steel blue, water-green, and glistening drab. The stream at the bottom of the gorge changes from crystal to smoky topaz and sometimes borrowing gleams reflected from cliffs and clouds above, runs in a glorious crimson flood like a river of blood.

Soaring eagles seek their lofty nests in the crags. Shadows deepen, lengthen. The mauves, pinks, grays, and scarlets fade from the sky and are succeeded by a cool blue. Stars begin to faintly twinkle. Camp fires are lighted at the comfortable Wylie camps and the serene splendor of the night descends upon Zion Canyon.

The cliff dwellings and hieroglyphics of the Ancients, found in Parunuweap Canyon, near Shonesburg, will appeal to those who are interested in the extinct races of men which inhabited this region long ago. A month might be well spent visiting the many places of interest.

NOTES

1.   On the origins of the name "Zion," see the introduction to this volume.
2.   Challenging this popular idea about his people's relationship to Zion Canyon, Southern Paiute Clifford Jake stated,

> Zion still has a lot of good spirits in it. Grand Canyon too. Song in the water, song in that rock wall; got some voice down there, some medicine mens....In Hurricane, there's a hole there where the wind comes from, old people knew about it. We called it Nurricon, "Wind House." Pah Tempe Hot Springs—all Paiute Indians know that's a very sacred special place the Creator put there. Paiutes come from all direction, soak for aches, sores. Have to pay for it first, talk to the water, give a token, maybe find a beautiful, really good rock for a donation for the water....Weeping Rock, very sacred place, have to pay to drink from that place too. Afraid of Zion? Rumors you're talkin' about now. The Indians had gardens up the canyon.

> William Logan Hebner, *Southern Paiute: A Portrait* (Logan: Utah State University Press, 2010), 73.

13 | Zion Canyon and the Colob Plateau

LeRoy Jeffers

In this article, published in Scientific American, *outdoor adventurer and writer LeRoy Jeffers takes readers beyond the typical tourist destinations of Zion Canyon to vistas high above the canyon floor and into the rugged Kolob Plateau (which had been added to the national monument just a year before). Jeffers wrote just months before Zion was made a national park, at a time when corners and canyons remained unmapped and unexplored.*

Although a hundred miles distant from the nearest railway, the Zion National Monument in southern Utah is destined to be visited by an increasingly large number of travellers. Leaving the Los Angeles and Salt Lake Railway at Lund, one may travel by auto across the desert to Zion Canyon, by way of Cedar City. On every hand is sage brush, greasewood, rabbit brush, and shad scale, while the prickly pear livens the landscape with its bright magenta flowers. Jack rabbits and prairie dogs run to cover as we pass; and, with the increasing heat, the air gathers whirls of dust that rise in columns for five or six hundred feet above the floor of the desert, and travel rapidly along for a mile or two. Volcanic mountain ranges purple in the distance, or loom with deceiving reality in mirage. If one is fortunate he may see a phantom city, with its buildings and steeples, seeming to lie but twenty miles across the desert sands. We cross a ridge of almost pure iron that is dotted with cedars, while another is composed of black, contorted volcanic rock. In the foot hills are great flocks of dirty brown sheep which give Lund importance as a shipping point for wool.

Near Cedar City there are glimpses of red and yellow walls, while beyond we follow for miles beneath the yellow-gray and slate-colored cliffs of the Hurricane fault, the greatest of all known faults in the world. On the right are the little known Pine Valley mountains, while beyond on the road to St. George is a brilliant patch of cherry-red sand, an unmistakable landmark which is seen from the far distant heights of the Colob Plateau. Near Toquerville is a cluster of black, volcanic cones; while, above the village, lines of varicolored buttes rise one upon another in imposing array.

After a very steep ascent, there opens before us a glorious view of temples and buttes aglow with marvelous coloring in the setting sun. Towering above is the Great Temple of the Virgin, locally known as Steamboat Mountain, 7,650 feet, the highest in the region. From the banks of the winding, treacherous Rio Virgin, slopes of green lead to a desolate desert region extending to the base of the red cliffs, which are dotted here and there with pine and cedar. Then follow vertical walls of gray and white, streaked with color from a vermilion butte which crowns the mountain like the upper deck of a steamboat. Its brilliant walls are topped by a rich green forest of pines, the whole making an unforgetable combination of form and color. Looking upward toward the Colob Plateau we see the most curious red and white domes; while, across the river, the temples of Smithsonian Butte are painted with soft reds and browns.

We pass Grafton, Rockville, and Springdale, curious old Mormon settlements of stone and adobe, on the banks of the Virgin and of the North Fork near its entrance to Zion Canyon. Tall poplars line the streets, through which there flow streams diverted from the river, life-giving and purifying alike for man and beast. A new era dawned for the valley with the summer of 1917 when it was first opened to automobiles, and fruit and produce were in increasing demand. So important are the scenic wonders of this little known region that, in the spring of 1918, the President increased the size of the Monument reservation from 15,840 to 76,800 acres.

Near Springdale we have an unequalled view of the Great Temple with its sublime precipice of 2,900 feet. Beyond, a canyon on the right is spanned by a natural bridge in process of formation; while, on the opposite side, the fantastic Towers of the Virgin astonish us with their unusual architecture, and their vivid hues of red, of orange, and of white. From a climber's point of view, few of the sandstone walls of the valley are attractive during the heat of summer. Circuitous routes are necessary to reach the summits of these tremendous cliffs and Yosemite-like domes, almost none of which have been ascended. Viewing the Great Temple from all sides, one finds it promising only from Springdale, and, on one of the warmest days known to the region, I found myself far up its heated cliffs. Here was a magnificent view of the valley, painted in richest browns and reds and enlivened by bright green along the river. Far across the intervening heights were the upper reaches of the Parunuweap, and distant purple capes and headlands leading to the Grand Canyon of the Colorado. An insufficient supply of water finally forced my retreat to the river.

By far the finest effects in Zion Canyon are seen at sunset and at sunrise. Then the great sandstone walls which surround one glow with the most exquisite and unusual colors, and one lingers long in worshipful silence. Brown and red are the cliffs, while above they are cherry and white; elsewhere there are magenta spaces, and layers of smooth, fresh chocolate seeming as if they were but newly cut. Where streams have fallen, the cliffs are seamed with black. But most beautiful of all are the rosy pinks which liven the walls, or mingle delicately with the white. More rarely there are golden-yellows crowning the white, and completing a color harmony of which one never tires.

Awakened in the cool of the morning by the sweet voices of birds, one may gaze upward a couple of thousand feet from the Wylie Camp to the summit of a tree-fringed precipice that seems almost to overhang one. Proceeding up the valley one is continually impressed with the amazing architecture and sculpturing of the canyon walls and giant buttes. The beauty of the Gothic cathedral is on every hand. Here are immense amphitheatres with colossal buttresses; vast dome-shaped mountains recessed with crypts where the rock has shelled off; and innumerable towers and spires shimmering in pink and in purple. Giant bosses of colored rock overhang royal arches, and temples and colonnades are on every hand. On the face of one great cliff is a rectangular doorway, probably 50 feet in height, which resembles the entrance to an Egyptian tomb. One magnificent butte, standing far out in the canyon, rises to nearly the height of the surrounding walls, and is called Angel's Landing; another with fluted columns is named the Great Organ; while still another with wonderful walls of white tipped with sunset yellow is known as El Gobernador.[1]

The eye is never weary, for the varied greens of the canyon floor offer pleasing contrast to its brilliant walls, and the base of one great cliff is embroidered with vines and yellow columbines. At Cable Mountain are two 2,700-foot wires which bring down lumber into the valley from the forest on the summit. Until recently one might make a rapid and rather thrilling ascent of the mountain by clinging to the sling on which the timber is secured. One of the most comprehensive views of the region from above is at Hick's Point, which is reached by climbing out of the canyon from the base of Cable Mountain. On the ascent one passes through a narrow gorge with overhanging walls of great height, and afterward views a mountain of cross-bedded sandstone laid out like figures on a cake. I have forced my way up several summits in the wild unmapped country east of the canyon rim, finding ample exercise, but no water.

At Raspberry Bend the river loops between precipitous walls and great domes. These are ever varied, for below are 2,000 feet of bright red Triassic sandstone, while above there is almost the same thickness of white Jurassic sandstone. This in turn is often topped with pink or blood-red layers. One finds surprisingly little talus at the base of the cliffs, for the rushing river has long since taken it away. Down the face of a 2,000-foot cliff a tiny waterfall glistens white in the sunlight. Pausing on little ledges, and then leaping 1,000 feet in the wind, it is torn to ribbands, and reaches the valley in colored mist. Now and then an eagle sails away toward the distant heights. Following up the stream on horseback between walls over 2,000 feet high that rapidly narrow until the river is but a few feet across, we were finally turned back by the depth and swiftness of the current, against which the horses were unable to proceed.

To the west of Zion Canyon, and over 3,000 feet above it, lies the Colob Plateau. Probably visited as yet by less than a score of travellers, it will eventually attract many who seek the finest canyon scenery that Nature has to offer. When I am asked to compare one mountain with another I seldom comply. So with our National Parks and Monuments, each is different, making its own appeal to the lover of the beautiful and the grand in nature. But when I seek the mountains for my vacation, I do not feel it has really commenced until I am in the midst of their highest and wildest scenery. That which satisfies must equal or surpass the finest with which I am acquainted. Consequently I classify scenery according to the grandeur of its appeal as primary or secondary. I do not attempt to compare Zion Canyon, and those seen from the Colob Plateau, with the Grand Canyon of the Colorado. They are dissimilar in scale, but they are each of primary appeal. Studying either one does not deaden the charm of the other.

From the floor of Zion Canyon to the extremity of Horse Pasture Plateau, which overlooks it on the west, is a trip of 35 to 40 miles over some of the roughest roads and sheep trails to be found in the mountains. Most of the way is decidedly up hill, and one has time to enjoy the distant view of pink and vermillion cliffs and purple mountains. The sandstone of the Lower Colob is very unusual in appearance, in some places resembling a multitude of red beehives. Nearby a 1,000-foot cone, dotted with trees, reminds one of a dish of strawberry ice cream. We climbed the heights above the canyon of Coal Pits Wash, forcing our horses for miles up the most inhospitable walls and through continuously resisting undergrowth. We also visited Le Verkin Canyon, riding through Hop Valley with its brown walls and sandy floor. The view at the junction with the canyon is remarkable, the lower gorge of Le Verkin being brown, while the upper walls and domes are vermillion. Nothing could be more striking than this intense color against a bright blue sky with white clouds. At the head of the canyon are Le Verkin Breaks, where great tree-covered masses of earth have slid downward from the upper slopes.

It was a long, hard climb to the Upper Colob, but eventually we came to miles of quaking aspens and to the welcome waters of Blue Spring. Here were vast flocks of sheep which pasture on the plateau, and annihilate for years all the natural beauty of the forest. In order to obtain a comprehensive view of the region, we climbed a distant mountain that overlooks the deep and narrow cleft of the North Fork of the Virgin. On the way we saw white and pink sego lilies, and great fields of dandelion and larkspur, gleaming like cloth of gold embroidered with blue; while, in the distance, was the rich color of the Pink Cliffs.

From the Blue Spring it is a steep descent through aspen, yellow pine, and manzanita to the long point called Horse Pasture. Before reaching Potato Hollow we skirted the head of a symmetrically rounded side canyon, from whose depths rises a Yosemite-like dome. Here we watched the softened colors of the sunset indescribably blending with the painted landscape. In the morning we followed the rim of the plateau for some hours to its farthest extremity above Zion Canyon. It was rough work on horseback forcing our way through oak and manzanita, but we found a fine grove of yellow pine, and everywhere were the deep magenta, yellow, pink, and white blossoms of the prickly pear. On the way were wonderful views of an immense canyon located well to the west of Zion Canyon. It has been referred to as the Great West Canyon, and through it flows North Creek, one of the forks of the Virgin. No one is known to have penetrated its many miles of splendid scenery or to have climbed any of the remarkable buttes that rise with it. Accompanying us was a famous cougar hunter who was born on the Colob, and who intends some day to find a way down the sheer cliffs that guard this virgin canyon. The whole Colob region, as well as that of Zion Canyon, is as yet unmapped, in detail. Great West Canyon has marvellously colored slopes and side canyons, and from the rim, one may look down on a rolling sea of white sandstone brilliantly streaked with pink. Its isolated buttes have vertical walls of vermillion, while their summits are covered with acres of trees. In the wall of one great butte is a tremendous archway, hollowed out like a cave. The view from the final point of Horse Pasture is rugged in the extreme. Great temples and buttes of varied architecture and coloring are isolated by narrow V-shaped canyons, while a couple of miles below in the distance, we get a glimpse of the green floor of Zion Canyon.

After a rough journey back to the river, we left in the quiet of the evening just as the full moon appeared above the mystical towers and temples of the Virgin.

NOTE

1. The Great White Throne.

14 | Zion National Park
with Some Reminiscences
Fifty Years Later

A. KARL LARSON

Karl Larson was a preeminent chronicler of southwestern Utah, or Utah's "Dixie." In this excerpt from an article published in Utah Historical Quarterly *in commemoration of the fiftieth anniversary of Zion National Park, he recounts from a local perspective his first encounter with the canyon, the dedication of the park, and the day the president of the United States came for a visit.*

Now I wish to reminisce a little on my own early experiences in Zion Canyon. They will recall, to a good many people at least, the events of nostalgic years past.

My first acquaintance with the park goes back more than fifty years. A hard land in which to make ends meet, Dixie had no industry to absorb its young men and women nearing maturity. If employment were found, it was in the mines or on the range caring for cattle, sheep, and goats. In the spring of 1918 I received an offer of a job to herd sheep in the wilds of Orderville Gulch among the breaks of the east watershed of Zion Canyon. My Uncle Joseph (Jode) Covington telephoned me at the store in Washington that he would meet me in Zion Canyon at the foot of Cable Mountain at 2:00 p.m. on a day late in May. My brother Eldon accompanied me on the journey to bring my horse home. We stayed at Hurricane the first night with Uncle Jode's wife, Aunt Bergetta, and early in the morning struck out for Zion, arriving there a few minutes before the appointed hour. There were still evidences of recent farming on the flat where the lodge now stands; dried cornstalks in irrigation rows gave mute proof of not long-distant cultivation. The Wylie Way Camp had just been established, but there seemed little evidence of activity that I can remember. We ate the sandwiches Aunt Bergetta had thoughtfully provided, and as we finished we heard Uncle Jode's "hallo" up on the trail. He was walking; he had left the horses at the sawmill at the brink of Cable Mountain because it was safer for a novice to travel that trail on foot.

I said good-bye to Eldon and began the long, hard climb to the sawmill. The sun was low when we reached the summit. We made it to a ranch at dark, where we spent the night. Bright and early the next day we continued through very rough country to the sheep camp deep in Orderville Gulch, where we arrived in time for breakfast.

Fate apparently did not intend me for a sheepherder. My own cooking, after nearly a month, was more than my outraged stomach could bear. On top of this I had an attack of dysentery that I thought would finish me. The boss could not leave the sheep, so he asked if I could find my way to the sawmill, while he rode to Orderville, after corraling the animals, to seek a herder. I was more than willing to try. At Jolley's Ranch I obtained some good homemade bread and fresh milk from a sympathetic housewife, who offered to let me stay for a day or two to regain my strength. The new food seemed to settle my upset digestion, so after about an hour's rest I proceeded on my way, reaching the sawmill about 4 o'clock in the afternoon. No one was there, so I began the long walk down the trail, rocky and sandy by turns. The constant travel downhill was wearing on my already tired feet and legs, and by the time I reached the bottom I was worn out.

A cold bath in the Virgin restored my flagging strength and drooping spirits, and I decided I could make it to Springdale. The canyon was beautiful with a deep soft haze that had settled over its brilliantly colored cliffs and side canyons, but these were not calculated to excite my better nature. I was wondering where I could spend the night. At that moment my appreciation for the marvels of Zion was akin to that of my father, who two years earlier had gone to Zion for a load of lumber brought to the canyon floor by the fabulous cable. Mother remarked that she had heard that the canyon was beautiful; how about it? My father replied with understatement characteristic of him: just a lot of big cliffs and rocks; nothing to get excited about.

At the cable's framework I paused briefly to view that marvel of man's ingenuity in the face of seemingly insurmountable odds. It was years later that I learned of David A. Flanigan's attempts to construct with baling wire a device for lowering lumber cut from the forested area back of the sawmill at the top of the great cliff. Faced with defeat after several fruitless trials, he went back into the vast solitude of the canyon to think, to try to learn what mistakes had brought him only failure.... Flanigan here received the inspiration to try once more. He was successful, and millions of feet of lumber were brought to the canyon floor where the freighter's wagon took it to all parts of Dixie.[1]

It was dusk by the time I had covered the weary miles to Springdale. I bought some cheese and crackers at the store, then located a small half-finished haystack on which I hoped to stretch my aching limbs for the night. But my better judgment led me to ask the householder for permission, and he, kind soul, offered me a bed which I gratefully accepted. Next day, footsore and weary, I hiked to Hurricane, where I called the store in Washington—it had the only telephone in town—and asked the proprietor to have my folks send Eldon with a horse to bring me the rest of the way home.

Such were the circumstances of my first acquaintance with Zion Canyon. Two years and three months later I was there again under far more pleasant circumstances, on September 15, 1920, to witness the dedication of the new park by National Park Service Director Stephen T. Mather. I was there by virtue of membership in Earl J. Bleak's Dixie College Band, otherwise I could not have been present. The place was crowded with dignitaries on a national, state, and local level, not to mention the authorities of the Mormon church. Then, of course, there were many of the inhabitants of the nearby towns of Washington, Iron, and Kane counties. Nearly a thousand people collected for the event. It was a crowded Model T. Ford I rode in. No baggage was allowed except one quilt each and our instruments. We wore our band uniforms consisting of navy blue coats and caps trimmed in fancy white braid and brass buttons, which were well covered with dust from the trip that lasted about four hours from St. George to Zion. There were the inevitable delays to pour water into the steaming radiator and to clean fouled spark plugs. We arrived late in the afternoon, dusted ourselves off, tuned our instruments, and got in a few marches before the Cedar City Band made its appearance. It was a matter of pride with us that we be the first band to play against that magnificent backdrop of canyon walls. It was a small group, only fourteen in number and lacked the best balance in the world. School had not yet started, and it was a group brought together to play at the Fruit Festival and Rodeo which preceded stake quarterly conference prior to school's opening. What we lacked in number and finesse we made up in enthusiasm.

President Heber J. Grant of the First Presidency was there representing Governor Simon Bamberger. Stake President Edward H. Snow and his counselors, Thomas P. Cottam and George F. Whitehead, together with an assortment of high councilmen, bishops, mayors, county commissioners, and lesser lights made up the rank and file of the crowd. I ran into jolly Uncle John Covington from Orderville, who had brought his troop of boy scouts down the Cable Mountain Trail to be at the dedication. It was perhaps the biggest day in Utah's Dixie since the dedication of the St. George Temple over forty-three years earlier.

Director Stephen T. Mather was present and with him Reed Smoot, Utah's perennial United States Senator, flanked by Mayor C. Clarence Neslen of Salt Lake City and a large number of the city's Chamber of Commerce, with Union Pacific Railroad bigwigs and camera men from Paramount, National, and Pathe motion pictures to make newsreels of the great event. Altogether it was a gathering of official brass—religious, civic, and business—the like of which had never been assembled in Washington County.

That evening after we had eaten in the Wylie Way's dining room, there was an impromptu program with the two bands each trying to outdo the other. The Ariel Quartette from Salt Lake City captivated the large crowd with its rendition of "Oh, by Jingo," and other popular songs, while a

Stephen Mather, director of the National Park Service, addresses the crowd at the dedication of Zion National Park, September 15, 1920. Photographer unknown. Courtesy of Special Collections, Sherratt Library, Southern Utah University.

member of the Salt Lake group moved everybody to convulsions with his humorous readings, especially when he essayed the role of the Sanpete Swede. A dance followed in the Wylie dining room with the Cedar City Band furnishing the music. It was so crowded—the room was not large—that dancing was no great exhilaration.

It was now late and we had to think of a place to sleep. My brother Eldon and I shared two quilts—one under and one over—on a bed of oak leaves. Before long the canyon breeze had us shivering; the ground sloped, and we spent much of the night inching back uphill to stay on the quilt. The night was miserable. Daylight revealed other forms lying nearby; I saw Sheridan Ballard shivering in his quilt with feet braced against two oak saplings to keep him from sliding downhill. Everyone agreed it had been a rough night out, but a good breakfast from the Wylie kitchen dispelled our gloom, after which we tuned our instruments and waited for the dedication.

At 11:30 the program got underway, with Director Mather presiding. Richard R. Lyman offered the invocation. Thereafter followed ten speakers, most of them stressing the theme of good roads. They included Senator Smoot, Mayor Neslen, former Governor William Spry, President Grant, D. S. Spencer, W. S. Bassenger, and a Mr. Comstock—these latter three were railroad representatives—Dr. C. G. Plummer, W. G. Wylie, and Joseph S. Snow. The talks were interlarded with musical numbers from the two bands and the Ariel Quartette. Director Mather then dedicated the park in these words:

> This day we shall long remember. Today is the christening day of a most wondrous child born of God and Nature—a child of such ethereal beauty that man stands enthralled in her presence. Born but yesterday—the yesterday of Nature when man was not, it yet remains for man this day to be thy godfather, to keep and cherish thee forever as one of the beauteous things of the earth and to christen thee—Zion National Park.[2]

Then with the bands leading, the crowd sang the "Star Spangled Banner" and the event was history.

I may have gone to Zion sometime during the next two years, but if so, memory does not record it. But I was there again in June 1923 when the President of the United States, Warren G. Harding, honored the newly created park with a visit. In spite of dirt roads, Zion had quite a few tourists, whose enthusiasm soon made the Dixie people feel that in Zion they had a resource that eventually would yield rich dividends.

Schools in Washington County had been out for some time, and to get a band together posed a problem. Earl J. Bleak hustled around to secure a semblance of an organization. I had just completed my first year of teaching at Hurricane and was waiting for summer school on Mt. Timpanogos to begin, so Mr. Bleak invited me to join his skeleton group with my slide trombone. We were to go to Zion the day before the President arrived in order that no slip or accident would mar our getting there. Even so we almost failed to make the grand celebration.

For transportation of the band members and their instruments Mr. Bleak had secured the services of Mr. Chauncey Macfarlane and his Ford ton truck. He had just had it overhauled, and it was as tight as a Dixie pioneer musician after serenading town on the Twenty-Fourth of July.[3] We planned to leave early in order to arrive at the park well before sundown. Alas! Macfarlane's Freight did not get away from St. George until noon, and the hour it consumed in covering the five miles to Washington, where it picked up my brother Eldon and me at one o'clock boded ill for a speedy arrival at Zion. The Ford heated up to steaming point almost immediately following the replenishment of radiator water, and at every town—Harrisburg (almost a ghost), Leeds, Anderson's Junction, Toquerville, Virgin, Rockville, and Springdale—we poured water into this thirsty iron monster; and on the long stretches between villages we fed it sparingly from canteen and water bag.

Much of the way was uphill, and on the more pronounced grades like the Washington Black Ridge, Cotton Wood Hill at Harrisburg, and the notorious LaVerkin Hill we literally "put our shoulders to the wheel." I swear we pushed that piece of reluctance up every hill between St. George and Zion. Night overtook us somewhere before we reached Virgin, and we continued pushing in the bright moonlight. It was one o'clock in the morning when, completely exhausted, we reached the neighborhood of

Wylie's Camp. Hungry and footsore, we spread our one quilt on the flat and fell into the troubled sleep of exhaustion, too tired to complain of the cold fresh breeze that swept down from the Narrows.

Morning brought a change in our spirits. We ate our food, then piled into the Ford, seemingly no worse from its grueling experience of yesterday, and back we went to the park entrance to await the President's caravan. We made the cliffs reverberate while we waited; as soon as we finished a march, the four members of the Springdale-Rockville Martial Band immediately took over. Three of them, John Dennett and Oliver and Freeborn Gifford were the remnants of Edward P. Duzette's Martial Band of pioneer days. They played as men inspired, rolling their rhythms with an enthusiasm beyond description. Finally someone shouted, "They're coming!" and we fell to with all the spirit we could muster. The car in which the President and Mrs. Harding were riding stopped just as we finished. He leaned out, waved to us, and said pleasantly, "That's fine! I used to play in the band myself." The martial band then began its stirring routine, and when they finished, Mr. Harding said with deep sincerity, "I've never heard better drumming in my life!" He spoke a few words of appreciation to Duzette's veterans, then the caravan moved on its way to the Wylie Camp. While he rested and had lunch inside, the bands played and a chorus from St. George and Dixie College, led by Professor Joseph W. McAllister, sang "Build Thee More Stately Mansions," "O Ye Mountains High," "Utah, We Love Thee," "Pilgrims' Chorus," and the "Star Spangled Banner." When finally the President came out, a handsome figure of a man, he graciously stood for some time shaking hands with several hundred people who waited in line to greet him. Afterward he was whisked away for a horseback ride to the Narrows, and riding with some trepidation he disappeared with a group of horsemen from our sight. For the ride he discarded coat, collar, and tie and placed a large blue bandana around his neck.

The news of his death shortly afterward, followed by the scandals involving his administration and his own personal life, saddened me greatly, as I am sure it did all those who saw and met him in Zion National Park that bright day in June. The President had been most grateful and friendly to the people of Washington County; he had made them feel that he cared about them, especially at Toquerville where he addressed a large crowd including a number of pioneers, among whom was Elizabeth Steele Stapley, the first white child born in Utah (August 9, 1847).

> It takes courage…to leave peaceful homes and lead out into the wilderness.…It is a great pleasure…to meet you people of the south, to see your great county and what you have done. It must be a great satisfaction to you pioneers to have made the wilderness blossom… and this must be your reward. Surely God had a purpose when he prompted these pioneers, and I have reverent regard for them…no place in America can offer a finer company of Americans than I see before me now.[4]

I have been to Zion many times since those memorable days of its dedication and the President's visit. I never go there without recalling with satisfaction my participation in those thrilling events, and without thinking that no pilgrimage to Zion can ever compare with those two days of unforgettable memory.

NOTES

1. Flanigan's account of constructing the cable is found in chapter 19.
2. "Zion Park Dedicated," *Washington County News*, September 16, 1920, 1.
3. Pioneer Day, a Utah state holiday commemorating the arrival of the first Mormon pioneers in the Salt Lake Valley on July 24, 1847.
4. "A Great Day for Utah's Dixie," *Washington County News*, June 28, 1923, 1.

15 | All Aboard for Zion

HENRY IRVING DODGE

In sharp contrast to earlier visitors to Zion, who encountered rough roads and campsites, tourists by the mid-1920s were treated to a smooth car ride of three hours after a night's stay in the luxurious El Escalante Hotel at the end of the rail line in Cedar City, Utah, and then enjoyed the modern conveniences of a park lodge. The following article, taken from a 1926 promotional brochure by Union Pacific, extols the wonders of the canyon and lists prices for the modern conveniences now found there. The author, Henry Irving Dodge, was well known at the time for his novel Skinner's Dress Suit.

Once upon a time the good Lord said: "Men have been doing foolish things—trying to interpret me. I'll give them a hint. I'll make something graceful, dignified for them to follow. For I love the beautiful."

Then the good Lord—obviously the use of the pronoun here is impertinent—made Zion Canyon.

"Sublime," observed the good Lord, "but not enough." Again the good Lord picked up His chisel, gouged out the earth, and fashioned the Grand Canyon.

Again the good Lord contemplated His handiwork: "Too magnificent, too thunderous, too gloomy, too somber, too terrifying. I'll give them something in lighter vein, fanciful—for I love the fanciful."

So the good Lord swung His chisel into the earth again and gouged out a great bowl—Bryce Canyon. Giving free rein to His fancy, the good Lord fashioned in this bowl all kinds of figures and on its walls He etched almost everything that was ever made as if recording the history of all creation—from then to now. But more of this later.

One said to me, "Go to Zion Canyon for the spiritual influence of it. If you are threatened with the effect—without cause—superstition—atheism—go there. Go there, and while you're there for the good Lord's sake, keep still. Don't try to describe it. Just contemplate. Humbly, joyously contemplate."

Said another, "If you want to look into Heaven, go into Zion Canyon and look upward; if you want to look into Hell, stand on the edge of the Grand Canyon and look down."

In a way this is true, for you dwell in the bottom of Zion and look up where the chaste, granite figures point into the sky. At the Grand, you stand on the rim and look down—down into a red inferno. That's the way it struck me. From the bottom of Zion, you look up and worship and appeal, but you draw back from the edge of the Grand Canyon in terror.

So much has been written of the vast and awful splendors of the Grand Canyon of the Colorado, that the sublime beauty of Zion has been overlooked.

After visiting Zion, Bryce, Grand, Cedar Breaks, my loyalty for my first love—Zion—is unshaken.

I had heard that the three great canyons were wholly different. I confess I didn't see how that could be. But I soon found that they were different in every respect but the coloring—and, perhaps, they were different even in the coloring.

What can one do when he has but a week in which to view the major canyons? The digestive organs of his imagination are clogged. He is fortunate if he can, in the retrospect, keep them even hazily distinct and separate. There are smaller, or better, less magnificent canyons—subordinate canyons to be visited which one never hears of. And any of these "little fellows," if it were the only one of its kind extant, would be worth going around the world to see.

Verily, on reaching Bryce Canyon, after standing subdued in wonder on the North Rim of the Grand, one wouldn't have given it a second glance if its distinctly different beauty did not enchant one. I can't explain. I can only say, "Go and see for yourself."

As for describing the scenery with my feeble pen, I can only say that no one would have the impudence to attempt it but a college girl or a patent lawyer, whose business it is to describe everything, but whose stuff no one ever reads.

The experience of Kipling is consoling. The noted Englishman was standing on the bank of the Columbia River—notebook and pencil in hand.

"What yer doin'?" said a native, approaching.

"Trying to write a description of it."

"Bub, yer better put up yer pencil and paper because it just simply can't be done."

I was told that Kipling said later, when writing about the Yellowstone, "I don't expect anybody to believe this." If I were gifted enough to convey even a suggestion of the wonders of the canyons, I'd repeat the later words of Kipling.[1]

The college girl, unless the good Lord should guide her hand, would tell you of her reactions to the scene. But you would not get anything of what the scene was. The patent lawyer or the civil engineer would give you the facts and figures, geometrical descriptions. But, oh, what's the use! I doubt even if a Poe would attempt it.

I can only say that the many colored photographs I have seen are not a whit exaggerated in color—and of course, not in form. This I know. For this I have seen with my own eyes. I can't even do as the college girl would do for I can't tell you how I reacted to the scene. I don't think I reacted at all. I was wonder-stricken, that's all—plumb wonder-stricken. I utterly failed at first to take in the beauty of it. But my spiritual eyes gradually opened as we progressed into Zion Canyon. For the approach into this wonderland is gradual.

We left Cedar City, southwestern Utah, a night's train ride from Salt Lake City, about nine o'clock in the morning. Traveling by a great, smooth-riding automobile bus over a fine road and through moderately pictur-esque scenery, and all keyed-up for the first sight of the canyon, we made the sixty-two-mile trip to Zion National Park in a little more than three hours.

Nature is the greatest of all dramatists. She never perpetrates an anticlimax unless man meddles with her work. The approach to Zion is no exception. The scenery up to a certain point had been progressively beautiful. Suddenly we rounded a curve and entered at the rear of a vast amphitheatre. Away in front of us was the stage. We approached as if we would enter upon it. Here is the setting. Mark well the metaphors. "The Watchman"—a mountain on the east—guards well the approach. Having passed this guardian in safety, we laid our propitional offerings upon the "Altar of Sacrifice," a slender, flat-topped pinnacle of ivory, stained red, it seemed, with the blood of martyrs. We next passed "Bridge Mountain"—on the east—and entered into Zion proper. However, we found other rites and ceremonies to perform before entering the Sublime Presence. We passed the "Court of the Three Patriarchs," pausing a moment to contemplate their magnificence. Again we did homage—devout and reverent contemplation—at the "Temple of the Sun," whose summit catches the first glimmer of the rising sun and reflects the last glories of the same.

We proceeded at leisure through the main court to the base of "El Gobernador, the Great White Throne," whereon the foot of man has never trod. While worshiping here the rustle of the angel's wings on "Angel's Landing" (in front of the Throne) and the chimes of the "Great Organ" (at its side) may be heard (in fancy) in the sighing of the wind through the trees and the gurgling and swishing of the river as it wends its way over the stones. Remember these great forms are not mountains as we always think of mountains but colossal pinnacles of ivory, it would seem, varicolored and with naked sides—some like loaves of bread standing on end. Zion Canyon is a group or cluster of these—an intimate family group, one might say. A museum of the Gods—a garden of heavenly spectres.

In reverent mood, you may proceed to the "Temple of Sinawava" and worship in your own untrammeled way; then on to the "Mountain of Mystery" and work your own charms trying to unfold Nature's secrets concerning it. Thus endeth the metaphor.

The mountain—or, rather, pinnacle—top plateaus have never been explored. There is no way to climb those smooth perpendicular sides that reach up three thousand feet from the floor of the canyon. No one knows what living things obtain up there. One presumes they are only birds and insects whose sanctuary has not yet been violated by the airplane.

What makes Zion the Temple is that in it you're always looking up. With most other canyons you're always looking down, and one never associates looking down with worship. Let any man stand there in those beautiful silences and declare there is no God and he's got more courage than I have. Or he is a bigger fool.

Zion is my first and only love among the canyons. The others fascinate me but I don't love them. They are marvelous beyond the conception of man. But there is a chaste sweetness, a spiritual warmth to Zion that the others haven't got. It's a sanctuary of the soul. There's a certain intimacy to it. You feel toward it as you would toward your mother. That's because you're so close to it—not worshiping at a distance. You feel like petting it, running your hands over the smooth sides of its images. You couldn't do that with the Grand Canyon....

Another writer—he must have been a painter or a geologist or a civil engineer—courageously adventures the following:

A "Yosemite Valley done in oils" comes close to a description of the principal features of Zion National Park. This gorgeous valley has about the same dimensions as the famous Yosemite Valley. Extraordinary as are the sandstone forms, the color is what most amazes. The deep red of the "Vermilion Cliff" is the prevailing tint. Two-thirds of the way up the marvelous walls and temples are painted gorgeous reds; above the reds they rise in startling white. The "Vermilion Cliff" rests upon three hundred and fifty feet of even a more insistent red relieved by mauve and purple shale. That in turn rests upon a hundred feet of other variegated strata. Through these successive layers of sand and shales and limestones, colored like a Roman sash, glowing in the sun like a rainbow, the Mukuntuweap River has cut its amazing valley. The entrance is between two gigantic stone masses of complicated architectural proportions which are named the West Temple and the Watchman. The latter is seen from a foreground of river. From a stairway of many colors it springs abruptly twenty-five hundred feet. Its body is a brilliant red. The West Temple, which rises directly opposite and a mile and one-half back from the rim, is over a thousand feet higher.[2]

Hal G. Evarts, also using the architectural metaphor, writes in the *Saturday Evening Post*:

> It seemed that we gazed out across some vast oriental city that stretched away for a dozen miles. Scores of gaudy mosques and tinted towers, striped citadels topped off by flat-roof gardens rose in countless tiers from this congested, painted metropolis....And the coloring! Imagine a tremendous city of spires and turrets...its buildings catching every dazzling reflection of the sunset....There were soft apricot and salmon tints, vague pinks and creams; lemon blending into deepest orange...with here and there a haunting suggestion of pale mauve. Brilliant red spires stood beside domes of ivory white. In many of these fairy structures the stratifications pitched so abruptly as to lend a spiralling barber-pole effect.[3]

Here are some useful facts:

An excellent road has been completed from the Park entrance to the Temple of Sinawava, some seven and one-half miles. Twenty-six miles of trails, so well maintained as to be usable at all seasons of the year, lead to the most important points in the Park. One may journey on horseback from the floor of the canyon to the East and West Rims. The West Rim trail begins at the foot of Angel's Landing, is tunneled along a ledge of the wall for two hundred feet into a deep flower-filled gorge, then zigzags up nearly to the level of the top of Angel's Landing. The other trail leads from the foot of Cable Mountain up to the East Rim.

Zion Lodge, a delightful hostelry, consisting of a main central building and a large number of square, two-bedroom cottages, nestles under the towering East Wall between the Mountain of the Sun and the Great White Throne. Here one may be accommodated for five and one-half dollars a day—room and board. Or you may get your breakfast for a dollar, your luncheon for a dollar twenty-five, dinner for one dollar and one-half, and may occupy one of the excellent bedrooms for a dollar seventy-five a night. The meals are excellent and so are the sleeping accommodations.

An attractive free public camp-ground has been established about half a mile from Zion Lodge in the shadow of the Great White Throne for motorists having their own camping equipment. Shade trees and pure water are available. So, one may sleep in his own bed, get his meals at the Lodge, or do anything else he darn pleases.

Also, one may hire horses and guides with which to nose about the Park or mount its almost precipitous sides. The rates for these are very reasonable—something like a dollar an hour for a horse. If you like to make the journey to the Rim, which may take you a day and for which you will require a guide, it will cost you ten dollars for the round trip. If there are two of you, it will be seven fifty each, or five dollars apiece if there are three. This includes everything—guide, luncheon, and horses.

NOTES

1. In 1889, before *The Jungle Book* and *Just So Stories* made him a household name, Rudyard Kipling traversed the United States en route to England from his native British India. He wrote of his experiences in *American Notes* (1891) and *From Sea to Sea and Other Sketches, Letters of Travel* (1899).
2. This is a close paraphrase of Robert Sterling Yard, *Glimpses of Our National Parks*, 3rd ed. (Washington, DC: Government Printing Office, 1920), 67.
3. Hal G. Evarts, "Desert Playgrounds," *Saturday Evening Post*, February 17, 1923, 7.

16 | The Great White Throne

Has It Ever Been Climbed?

Angus M. Woodbury

Angus Woodbury spent several summers as Zion National Park's first interpretive ranger. In June 1927 he was part of a search party that rescued William H. Evans, a daredevil climber who inaugurated rock climbing in the canyon with his attempt to scale the Great White Throne.

"Did you hear about the man climbing the Great White Throne?" the Superintendent asked me.

"No! When did that happen?" I rejoined.

"They say a fellow went up to try it yesterday and didn't come back."

"Of course he didn't get up?"

"I don't know. They report seeing a fire on the Throne last night."

"Lightning," I answered, thinking of the recent thunder storms.

"Well, let's go up to the camp ground and investigate."

As we went, my mind reverted to an attempt I had once made to climb that majestic monolith—the Great White Throne. I reviewed the details of that trip—how I had, with others, gone entirely around that gigantic rock and studied with an experienced eye every possible nook and cranny on all four faces. It was clearly impossible on the west and north faces where those vertical cliffs towered 2,500 feet from the canyon floor. Nor was it possible on the east side where another vertical wall 1,200 feet high overlooked the beautiful Hidden Canyon. On the south side, in the rear of the Throne—there was a possibility. The wall there was only a thousand feet high and it was not a vertical wall—merely a steep slope. But surely no one would be fool-hardy enough to climb such a slope! A loosened foot-hold might be a prelude to a free slide to the bottom.

Arriving at the camp ground, we soon found people who had seen the fires the night before. Standing at the foot of that majestic wall rising a sheer 2,500 feet above us, they pointed out as nearly as possible the location of the fires.

"We saw fires in two places," one man said. "First, it was on top at the left; later, it seemed to be over by the big arch, and one time, it looked like a fire falling through the arch. We thought it was a fire ball like you see in Yosemite and didn't pay much attention to it."[1]

Knowing that the arch was several hundred feet below the top and that above it was a narrow shelf that would effectively stop any embers that fell from the top, I discounted the testimony and thought that, it being dark, they had not accurately located the fires.

We located the climber's partner and learned the story. His name was Evans and he was a great mountain climber. He was absolutely fearless and took no thought whatever of danger. Mountain slopes and precipices had an irresistible appeal, drawing him like a magnet. An unclimbed mountain was, to him, like bait to a hungry bear.

As soon as he heard that the Great White Throne had not been scaled, he could not rest until he made the attempt. The two had spent several days in the Park and Evans had spent much of the time studying the Throne from many angles. Two days before, he had reconnoitered the north face, but came back before noon. The following day, he had been up on the East Rim trail, spending much of his time studying the Throne. Then he had started out with the avowed purpose of scaling the height. He carried with him a short rope and a small canteen of water, but no food, saying that he would probably be late that night and might not be back until the next day. If he reached the top, as the fires indicated, he ought to be returning here by noon.

Excitement reigned. Rangers had gone out hunting his tracks, expecting to meet him or hear from him any minute. If he did not return by noon, then it would be time for action.

The rangers returned by noon and reported no word from him. They had, however, found his tracks and knew which route he had taken. His silence was ominous! If he were alive and unharmed, he could, in all probability, have heard us shouting, so the probability was that something had happened. We must start an immediate search for him.

A consultation followed. The consensus of opinion placed him in the canyon at the south rear of the Throne where the lone possibility of climbing it lay. But that canyon was 1,500 feet above us at the top of precipitous walls. How to get to it was the question.

Ruesch[2] was for taking horses around the East Rim trail and coming back over the plateau from the rear. A good suggestion if we had more time. I was for taking his tracks above the Grotto and around to the foot of the Throne, the shortest and quickest way, but there was one bad place we dared not climb without a ladder.

"We can soon make a ladder," said Ruesch. And so it was agreed.

When the ladder was ready, willing hands carried it up the angular slope through the heavy brush to the foot of the bad ledge. It was on a narrow shelf on which there was just room enough to stand. Below was a steep slope leading down to the top of a vertical cliff 300 feet high. Carefully, very carefully, the ladder was raised into position. The foot was not solid. We picked a hold for it to rest in. Dalton stood behind and helped hold it in place. Russell held the foot to keep it from slipping.[3]

Cautiously, I started up the ladder. Near the top I hesitated. Dalton was shaking in his shoes.

"For God's sake, man, do be careful," from Russell.

And: "I wouldn't go up that damn thing for ten thousand dollars," from Ruesch.

The 16 feet of ladder was not long enough and I knew it. I could not climb over a hump just above its top. I stood there pondering. Far below, on the road near the camp ground a group of people were anxiously watching, among them our congressman. At the foot of the ladder were a group of veteran mountaineers deprecating the attempt. Somewhere on the mountain-side above a young man was probably writhing in agony if no worse fate had befallen him. Something must be done!

A dramatic moment! I could not go forward and I could not admit defeat! If there were only a rope fastened from above, anyone could climb it. We knew by his tracks that Evans had gone this way without any help, but no one in the group was willing to take the unwarranted risks that he had taken. I looked carefully for possibilities. Over on the left, was a crevice—a crack in the rock full of possibilities—if one could only get to it. If the ladder were laid down and used as a bridge, I could make it.

I slowly descended. We lowered the ladder across to the foot of the crevice. Carefully, cautiously, I walked across whereas Evans had blithely stepped around a sloping rock upon which a slipping foot would have meant sudden death. I climbed up through the crack, fastened the rope and dropped one end down over the ladder which had in the meantime been replaced. Gifford[4] came up with the aid of the rope and we were then ready for the hunt.

Following Evans' tracks, we hurried on into the canyon above the Grotto. His tracks continued on up the bottom apparently leading into a blind canyon. We decided not to follow them but to go directly over to the foot of the Throne, the shortest way possible and pick up his tracks over there. We climbed over the hogsback on the left and dropped down into the next deep gorge. The exit was not so easy. Scaling some precarious ledges, crannies, and crevices, we reached the top of the next ridge and soon made our way over to the foot of the Throne.

We skirted the foot where Evans should have gone up. No signs and no tracks could we find. We tested the slope to see if it were possible to climb it. Walking up some distance, we found it easy to ascend but dangerous coming back down. Skirting the foot in the opposite direction still looking for tracks, we soon came out on the ledge above the camp ground and signalled "No luck."

We were puzzled. A man could not disappear without leaving tracks. If he did not get to the Throne, where could he be? Looking back into the canyon where we had left Evans' tracks, we could see the blind canyon into which he had gone. To us, it seemed that a human could not possibly climb out of it. We had taken the only other alternative route and were positive that he had not come out that way. The inference was that since his tracks led into a blind canyon, he must still be there. Our hope then lay in following his tracks till we found him.

It was nearly dark when we had returned to the point where we had left his tracks, and knowing that we could do nothing in the ledges in the darkness, we went down for the night. We reached the foot of the ladder in safety, but the darkness had become so intense that we could not find our way down for fear of the ledges below us. Russell came up with a flashlight and led us down. The crowd at the foot were anxiously waiting for word that we had not to give.

Tired and weary, I tossed on my couch all night long, thinking of the possibilities of a lad alone in the mountains and trying to solve the riddle of his strange disappearance. Had we missed his tracks? Had he strayed and got lost? Had he fallen and injured himself? Was he still in that blind canyon? Or had he reached the Throne as the fires seemed to indicate? We would find an answer on the morrow.

By dawn, I was up getting ready for a new day's hunt. Ruesch, Russell, and Gifford took horses up the East Rim trail planning to come back over the plateau above looking for his tracks. Shieffer and I planned to follow his tracks up through that blind canyon. We climbed the ladder in safety and took his tracks up the canyon. Near the head, we encountered a snow-drift (June 29) protected by the mighty cliffs above. Just beyond, the canyon narrowed to a vertical slit—a chimney—300 feet high and just wide enough to admit a human body.

Above the slit and underneath the overhanging cliff, a buzzard was soaring around. Knowing the carrion-eating habits of the bird, horrid pictures of ugly possibilities flashed through our minds. It was imperative that we go on, up through that slit where Evans' tracks led, much as we hated to do so.

With back against one wall and feet braced against the other, we wriggled our way up through that chimney-like slit in the cliffs. On top, the climbing was worse than ever. Expecting to find the end of our search at any minute, we continued along his tracks upward, ever upward. The buzzard was gone and his story was a lie—we knew when we reached the open slope at the head of the canyon. But here, the danger of slipping and rolling was so great that even Shieffer balked.

"Well Woodbury, there's no sense in one of us going over the edge and I'm not going any farther."

While debating what to do, we hea[r]d the horsemen yell from above indicating important information but we could not understand clearly what they said. Inferring that they had found his tracks on top of the plateau, we felt that there would be no further use for us to continue. We retreated down through the slit to the bottom of the canyon and climbed out on the ridge that I had crossed the day before.

Just across the next deep box canyon, a quarter mile distant, the horsemen were waiting for us to appear. We could easily hear them. Russell shouted:

"We found his tracks where they came out of the canyon and followed them around the plateau to the edge of the canyon behind the Throne. There, they dropped off into the head of the canyon where it's awful steep and rough." It was the worst place he could have chosen to get into the canyon.

"He must be over in that canyon where we were hunting for him yesterday. He can't be any other place," I said. "You had better go in and see."

"Alright," returned Russell. "You wait there until we come back."

And right glad we were to do so. A chance to rest was welcome news after our heavy exertions of the morning.

A half-hour later, about 3 o'clock, he came back and shouted, "We've found him and he's alive. Come over as quick as you can."

Before leaving, we went down to the ledge overlooking the Grotto and gave the signal that he had been found—three yells in succession. The superintendent below getting the message telegraphed to the nation that he had been found.

It took us just an hour to cross that deep gorge a quarter-mile across. In the meantime, Ruesch, Russell, and Gifford had made a stretcher and carried him out of the brush where they had found him at the foot of the Throne about 50 yards beyond where we searched for him the day before.

And when we came to him, what a sight! Clothes nearly gone; lacerated, bruised, and sandpapered; his face a mass of sores; one eye swelled shut; but apparently no bones broken. Undoubtedly delirious, he talked to us but there was no coherence to his speech. He could tell us nothing about his trip.

With four men hold of the stretchers—the fifth man taking turns—we carried him out of that thousand-foot canyon.

We did the best we could, but whenever a limb or a bush scrubbed a sore spot, he swore as only a true sailor can.

Reaching the top at 5 p. m., we put him on one of the horses and with a man on behind to hold him in place, we rode around the plateau and down the East Rim trail. Arriving at the foot of the trail at 10 p. m., many willing hands were ready to transfer him to a waiting ambulance which took him to the Lodge, where three doctors were ready to care for him.

At the end of two weeks, they took him home to Pasadena, where he spent many weeks convalescing in the hospital. While in Zion, he regained but a few lucid moments during the entire two weeks stay.

Did he reach the top? It is an open question. During his lucid moments in Zion, it was possible to pry out a few details of his trip, and after his return home, further details filtered back to us. It has thus been possible to piece together the outlines of his story.

He thinks he reached the top about dark, built a fire, and the wind blew embers down onto the shelf above the arch, where a new fire started. He climbed down to put it out and in doing so knocked embers down through the arch. Finding shelter on top in a small cave, he stayed there all night. On the rock he carved his name and a warning to other fools who made the trip. At daylight, he started down. At one point along the way, he attempted to slide from one bush to the next, but missed it and remembered nothing more. His watch stopped about 5 o'clock and he was found the next day at 3 p. m.—34 hours later. One of the doctors stated that it was a good thing—the delay in finding him—as the rest gave him a better chance for recovery from brain concussion.

"Did he get to the top?" exclaimed a skeptic. "I'm not sold on the idea. When someone else goes up there and finds his name carved on the rock, then I'll believe it. Until then no one can make me believe that he did not fall going up!"

NOTES

1.   From 1872 until the late 1960s, the owners of the Glacier Point Hotel at Yosemite National Park staged a popular nightly display called the "Yosemite firefall." Hot embers were dumped from bonfires placed at the top of Glacier

Point, simulating a waterfall made of fire. Stanford Demars, *The Tourist in Yosemite, 1855–1985* (Salt Lake City: University of Utah Press, 1991).

2. Walter Ruesch, first custodian of Mukuntuweap National Monument and first superintendent of Zion National Park.
3. Harold Russell served as a park ranger beginning in 1920.
4. Barney Gifford (Woodbury diary, June 28, 1927, J. Willard Marriott Library, University of Utah).

17 | Letters

EVERETT RUESS

Everett Ruess spent four years wandering the canyonlands of the Colorado Plateau before disappearing in 1934, at the age of twenty. Ruess, who wrote nature poetry and made linoleum cuts for prints of the canyon scenery, stayed several weeks in Zion Canyon, most of the time spent recovering from a severe reaction to poison ivy. In these two letters, he writes of his misfortunes and musings in the canyon. Also included here is a poem he began composing while at Zion.

August 18 [1931]
Zion National Park, Utah

Dear Father and Mother and Waldo,[1]

Yesterday I reached Zion Canyon, the ninth day out from the North Rim. We came about 130 miles, traveling half the day and retiring during the hot part.

The first few days were spent in the Kaibab Forest, among aspens, firs, and pines, with deer and white-tailed squirrels. I lightened the load by disposing of the Dutch oven and some other things for a meal and some provisions. I did not take the main traveled road, but took a road which had not been used for so long that it was almost obscured. Then I came through

Fredonia to Kanab where I bought some foods I had been craving. Next I was out in the real deserts once more, camping in a sandy hollow, with the crescent moon low in the sky.

Yesterday morning I tracked the burro to his lair before sunrise, but as soon as I unhobbled him he galloped away and I had to chase him for a mile, then drive him down and finally caught him. I had difficulty in making him go through the mile-long tunnel on the Zion-Mount Carmel highway. He only had his picture taken six times on this trip, but that was because we did not follow the main road.

Zion Canyon is all I had hoped it would be. I am not actually in the park, but half a mile below it in the canyon, camped under maple trees by the Mukuntuweap River. There is no fodder for the burro farther up, but here there is a field of alfalfa for him. I went to Zion Lodge last night for the mail, and had to walk the four miles back.

I am enclosing some maple seeds. I did have some porcupine quills, but they've disappeared.

Love from Everett

August 27–28 [1931]
Zion National Park, Utah

Dear Bill,[2]

For six days I've been suffering from the semi-annual poison ivy case—my sufferings are far from over. For two days I couldn't tell whether I was dead or alive. I writhed and twisted in the heat, with swarms of ants and flies crawling over me, while the poison oozed and crusted on my face and arms and back. I ate nothing—there was nothing to do but suffer philosophically.

Yesterday morning I managed to pry my lips far enough apart to insert food. I thought my eyes would swell shut, but not so. Even now, they are mere slits in the puffed flesh.

You may remember that last year I took antitoxin injections and bounced happily off on my vacation—within a few days I was suffering it again with dull resignation. One chap says to use saltwater, another gasoline, another claims tomato juice is a sure cure. Nothing I used in times past alleviated the raging perceptibly. Most of the dope sold is stuff you paste on your face until you are a worse mess than before. I was just recovering from a dose of poison oak when I started this trip.

I get it every time, but I refuse to be driven out of the woods. My face is on fire as I write, and I managed to make a painting at dawn of a peak that has fascinated me. I'll have to repeat it when I'm well, then send the best version to you.

My friends have been few because I'm a freakish person and few share my interests. My solitary tramps have been made alone because I couldn't find anyone congenial—you know it's better to go alone than with a person one wearies of soon. I've done things alone chiefly because I never found people who cared about the things I've cared for enough to suffer the attendant hardships. But a true companion halves the misery and doubles the joys.

It is true that I can be happy alone and many times I've felt relieved to be in solitude. I look forward to my trip tomorrow because it will take me into the solitude again.[3] But a real friend is not an intrusion.

I've been scraping along one way and another. I told my family not to send money but they've sent some. The park is adding territory, and farmers have to move. I helped one tear down his house, but got sick with the heat and then poison ivy. I'd rather starve than exert myself physically for wages, anyhow. I make it a rule not to be concerned about filthy lucre until after I'm broke.

While I was sick I could hear the squeak and bang of boards being pounded and nails being pulled. The farmer here is a Mormon, bishop of this district. His three daughters are named Velate, Merle, and Leda. He with his wife lived on this spot for twenty-five years.[4] The government is going to remove all traces of habitation, allowing the green fields to go barren and the fruit orchards to die for want of water. Some park employees had flowers in their gardens but the architect made them pull them out because they weren't in harmony.

I'm truly glad you enjoy the picture—as I told you once before, an artist can't paint for himself alone—he must find someone else who thinks his stuff is good.

On this whole trip I haven't met anyone who really cared for art—not even the few tourist artists I met.

I started a poem the day before I sickened—here are the first four lines:

I have been one who loved the wilderness
Swaggered and softly crept between the mountain peaks
I listened along to the sea's brave music;
I sang my songs above the shriek of desert winds.

Evert

[...]

Wilderness Song

I have been one who loved the wilderness:
Swaggered and softly crept between the mountain peaks;
I listened long to the sea's brave music;
I sang my songs above the shriek of desert winds.

On canyon trails when warm night winds were blowing,
Blowing, and sighing gently through the star-tipped pines,
Musing, I walked behind my placid burro,
While water rushed and broke on pointed rocks below.

I have known a green sea's heaving; I have loved
Red rocks and twisted trees and cloudless turquoise skies,
Slow sunny clouds, and red sand blowing.
I have felt the rain and slept behind the waterfall.

In cool sweet grasses I have lain and heard
The ghostly murmur of regretful winds
In aspen glades, where rustling silver leaves
Whisper wild sorrows to the green-gold solitudes.

I have watched the shadowed clouds pile high;
Singing I rode to meet the splendid, shouting storm

And fought its fury till the hidden sun
Foundered in darkness, and the lightning heard my song.

Say that I starved; that I was lost and weary;
That I was burned and blinded by the desert sun;
Footsore, thirsty, sick with strange diseases;
Lonely and wet and cold, but that I have kept my dream!

Always I shall be one who loves the wilderness:
Swaggers and softly creeps between the mountain peaks;
I shall listen long to the sea's brave music;
I shall sing my song above the shriek of desert winds.

NOTES

1. Everett's older brother (1909–2007).
2. Bill Jacobs, a friend from high school.
3. From Zion Canyon, Ruess traveled to the North Rim of the Grand Canyon.
4. Daniel and Sarah Crawford, whose farm on Oak Creek became part of Zion National Park and whose son is included among the interviewees in chapter 29.

18 | Amid the Mighty Walls of Zion

Lewis F. Clark

In the summer of 1953 Lewis Clark, who later became president of the Sierra Club, descended the Zion Narrows from Chamberlain's Ranch on assignment for National Geographic. *The marvels he described and the accompanying twenty-five color photographs introduced more than two million readers to Zion National Park.*

"Let's go through the Narrows of the Virgin River this summer," wrote my brother Nate. He enclosed photographs which he had made on a brief scouting trip earlier in the year. His letter breathed enthusiasm.

We had long dreamed of such a trip into the wilds of southwestern Utah's Zion National Park. Here the North Fork of the Virgin River has been chief actor in one of those geological dramas which were responsible for so many of our country's miracles-in-stone.

NATURE'S WALL STREET 2,000 FEET DEEP

Eons ago, when the land started to rise from the sea, a stream meandered gently southward. As the land rose, the stream cut slowly but inevitably into the underlying rocks. Like an endless belt of sandpaper, grit-bearing water scoured its way through layer after layer of sandstone until it dug a fantastic, sheer-walled canyon.

Today, with a fall 10 times that of the Colorado in Grand Canyon National

Park, the Virgin River tumbles along a channel that reaches a depth of 2,000 feet; at the bottom it is little wider than many a city street.

We knew that the canyon of the Virgin River Narrows, like the colorful gorges of the Colorado River, is spectacular and awe-inspiring. How impressive it really is we were to learn by splashing along its gravelly bed and stopping repeatedly to look at the walls towering higher and higher above us. The chasms carved by the Virgin River are probably unrivaled for their dramatic combination of depth and narrowness.

Visitors to 148-square-mile Zion National Park, which cradles the Virgin River for part of its course, number in the hundreds of thousands each year, yet only a few are known to have penetrated all the way through the Narrows.

Perhaps the earliest was Grove Karl Gilbert, surveyor, map maker, and Trustee of the National Geographic Society from 1890 to 1905. In 1872 he traversed the North Fork from a point near its head to its junction with the East Fork. Mukuntuweap and Parunuweap, the Indians called these branches of the river.

The miles of canyon floor, in places only 20 feet wide between sheer walls sunk almost a half mile into the sandstone, he named the Narrows. He described the entire course of the North Fork as "the most wonderful defile it has been my fortune to behold."[1]

We believed a trip through the Narrows would take the better part of two long days. Summer would give more hours for travel and the best light for photography. Dry weather would simplify our camping gear.

Zion National Park has two dry periods, early summer and late fall. Between them comes a thunderstorm season, with occasional wild flash floods. We hoped that the first week in July would still be in the so-called dry period, and chose the long July 4th week end for our adventure.

Our equipment had to be lightweight, and waterproof in case we had to swim. Single-thickness wool blankets sewed into mummy-case bags, food for two days in the gorge, movie and still cameras and film, all were fitted into waterproof plastic bags.

In Zion, as in many other national parks, those who would go climbing or exploring beyond the trails are required to register at park headquarters. Rangers can then advise parties regarding safety precautions, and may dissuade leaders from unwise trips. They also know where to start looking if visitors fail to return as planned.

RANGERS AT FIRST SAID NO

The first reaction of Zion's chief ranger was that we should not make the trip. From early July through August, he told us, travel in the Narrows is inadvisable because of the threat of flash floods. The thunderstorm season was imminent.

His views, admittedly reasonable, were an abrupt setback to us. Yet we were optimistic that the dry spell would continue. We talked for an hour and a half, going over the perils of the journey and possible alternative trips.

Meanwhile, park officials realized that our leaders were experienced and that we had given much thought to the adequacy of our preparations and equipment.

Finally it was agreed that our party would drive to the plateau land near the head of the gorge and make a decision next morning on the basis of weather prospects on the spot.

Not far beyond the east gateway to the park we turned north off the Mount Carmel Highway onto a gravel road. Light clouds in the west produced a beautiful sunset, but made us wonder about the weather. "Red sky at night is the sailor's delight," goes the jingle. It was really orange, but we tried to see rosy hues.

Chamberlain's Ranch was supposed to be only 30 miles from the highway. Our county road humped up and down for an interminable distance. We finally camped a few miles from the ranch. The night air was nippy, and we sat close to the campfire as we reviewed plans for the next day before turning in.

There is a time in the gray dawn when one can't tell whether the sky is clear or overcast. The stars had been bright earlier; now they were gone. I heard others stirring and decided it was time to start a breakfast fire. Soon we could see that there were no clouds—a good omen.

URANIUM PROSPECTOR HAD BEEN THERE

At the Chamberlain Ranch we talked with the owner and with a uranium prospector who drove by. He told of going down into the gorge several times. Their assurances strengthened our decision to try it.

We drove through a ford and followed a tortuous road. At its end a prospector's cabin stood on the edge of a flat that had been a meadow before the meandering stream had cut its banks and lowered the water table. We were then two miles east of the park boundary, and ready to start.

The three girls in the party were to drive one of our cars back to Zion Canyon—a trip with its own arduous aspects. They agreed to meet us about 4 o'clock the next afternoon at the south end of the Narrows in Zion Canyon; we nine men would try the river.

To their shouts of "Good Luck!" we strode off toward the stream. According to our map we had about 12 miles of water-grade route between us and our goal. This would take us through the gradually deepening upper gorge and between the towering walls of the Narrows to the Temple of Sinawava.

The broad, open valley contains a series of meadows and sandy flats through which the stream meanders. On either side pine-clad ridges lay under a sparkling sky. Soon the valley narrowed. There were occasional little cliffs as we splashed from one side of the creek to the other, sometimes wading midstream.

Heights increased as the creek bed dropped steadily. Through the woods we glimpsed a huge vermilion precipice. Awed, we gazed up to red sandstone, the source of the colorful stain streaks on the lower panels of the walls.

Periodically we counted heads. At one time half the party was missed; after a wait they came into sight around a bend. One man dangled a headless rattlesnake. The advance group had passed a sloping bank when Jonnie Serna, always alert for living things, saw the coiled snake and caught it with a forked stick. In the noise of the rushing water the snake's rattling had not been audible.

From then on we were careful to watch beside our steps as well as ahead.

DETOUR VIA A NATURAL STAIRWAY

By now the walls of the gorge were hundreds of feet high. Low waterfalls were easily passed or detoured at this stage. Then came one that was a problem. The narrow stream plunged past smooth rocks into a foaming pool of unknown depth. We hesitated to dive or jump. Then I remembered a remark of the park naturalist, and searched through the trees and thorny brush against the cliff on the left bank. There it was—a cleft barely two feet wide in a massive rock. Once through this, we descended a narrow natural staircase to the shallow end of the pool below the falls.

At an occasional break caused by an entering side stream, we tried to locate our position on the map. It was as baffling as a jigsaw puzzle. The main tributary streams were dry, and their narrow gorges were similar to the irregularities of the canyon walls.

The gorge became narrower. In places we felt as if the very walls were closing in on us. We watched for possible escape ledges where we could climb to a point beyond what appeared to be the high-water mark. We had heard rumors of gorge waters rising 100 feet in 10 minutes.

Some say you can smell the musty downdraft ahead of a flood. There are reports of floods in other canyons in the park, and photographs of a wall of water plunging down like a wave crest. The thought that we could be trapped never quite left our minds.

In Dark Cliff passage the walls rose sheer and smooth, like the hull of a ship in dry dock. Cavern Passage was evidently cut through harder rock, overhanging and twisted. As we looked up, no sky was visible.

Abruptly the cavern opened out into a hall which looked deceptively simple. But along the shallow side of the stream we stepped into quick-sand. Fortunately, by wading into deeper water we found firm bottom.

Farther on the walls parted again, and we passed into a natural temple. Sculptured cliffs with hues of buff, red, orange, and amethyst rose above us.

Through another portal on our right a clear and wider stream flowed along the far edge of the sandy floor. The bed was filled with round stones, many bluish gray. This was Deep Creek.

Just beyond the confluence the enlarged stream entered a narrow gorge and disappeared around a bend. As we looked up, the Y-shaped sky pattern of the cliff tops suggested a name, Upsilon Temple.

Several hours of sunshine remained on the open country above, but the light was already fading in the canyon. We selected a campsite on a rocky bar in Deep Creek, several hundred yards above its junction with the main stream. On an escape ledge we cached our cameras and extra food. Soon the pungent smoke from a driftwood fire gave promise of supper on the way.

IDYLL IN A SANDSTONE WORLD

From a sandy couch I gazed straight up to three pine trees silhouetted against a deep-violet sky. The glow of the fire grew dimmer.

On my left, to the north, the stars disappeared behind thin clouds. Could it be raining in Cedar Breaks? I heard a roaring sound. The cool air was as fresh as ever. The sound grew louder, like distant thunder or a great waterfall.

Then I saw winking lights. It was a plane. Relaxed now, I watched the moonlight patiently revealing the upper walls of the chasm with a soft light. Then I dozed.

The next time my eyes opened the sky was paling. A fire blazed and the doubts of night were forgotten. Two ambitious lads accepted challenges and took a dip in the cool dark pool, then galloped over for hot coffee. We resealed our sleeping bags in their plastic covers and tied extra clothing and film in waterproof bags.

Before the sun had touched the stream we were on our way again.

The canyon had looked forbidding in the evening shadow; now it beckoned with sunshine and a bright sky.

Although many of the intermittent tributaries enter the river in hanging valleys, from which their occasional waters leap as cascades and clear falls into the main canyon, Kolob Creek enters with quiet dignity at mainstream level. Beyond, at Amphitheater Temple, a beautiful green meadow was filled with grasses and wild flowers. Tall pines stood against the omnipresent cliffs.

AVALANCHE TORE LIMBS FROM PINES

Downstream we had to climb over the debris of a fresh-looking avalanche. Tons of rock of all sizes had poured through a notch high in the cliff. Branches had been torn from pines by the hurtling boulders. Over all lay a blanket of fine rock dust.

Noon came before we realized it. We made a rite of lunch. Over a natural dam of logs and huge boulders the main stream plunged into an alluring pool, bounded on the far side by irregular cliffs and on the near side by rocks on a sandy beach. A cold spring, partly hidden by spreading ferns, seeped from the east wall. We dived and swam like dolphins, and then lay on warm rocks while the hot sun dried our bodies and soaked into relaxed muscles.

This fantastic canyon carved deep into the Navajo sandstone of Jurassic time must have been millions of years in the making—yet the thought of it reminded us of more miles of canyon between us and our destination. Spurred by our schedule, we shouldered packs and began the sloshing tramp again.

Suddenly, as we rounded a turn, the walls closed in. Here were the real Narrows. As far as we could see, water filled the gorge from side to side, save for an occasional gravel bar. The walls, generally about 20 feet apart, loomed vertically many hundreds of feet. High up, they receded slightly and continued to soar in a series of ledges.

As we reached the end of the first stretch and made a slight turn, the chasm continued in the same manner in another long passage with no escape ledges. Often the walls overhung the stream 15 feet or so above low water. In places we couldn't see even a patch of sky by which to judge whether the weather was still favorable.

At one point I heard a low gurgling—mysterious and ominous. After a search, I found its source, a spring higher than my head, pouring into a dark pool.

Around a bend the chasm widened, but each side was blocked by immense rocks fallen from the heights. The only way was through the pool, which was too deep to wade. Putting cameras and wrist watches into plastic bags, we plunged into the water. The packs buoyed us surprisingly well. Two of the "frogmen" simply floated their packs, towing them like barges.

MAKING FRIENDS WITH WATER OUZELS

We were surprised to find several water ouzels, seemingly unconcerned at our approach. Whether through fear or lack of it, one of these small slate-gray birds sat quietly on a branch while we petted it. Another was gently picked up and carried a quarter of a mile. It seemed not frightened but merely curious when placed on the branch of a tree. Endearing birds of spray and foam, water ouzels "fly under water" in search of food.

Many times we seemed to be splashing through high, vaulted tunnels and passages where, for 40 or 50 minutes of travel, we saw no possibility of climbing off the bottom if the waters should rise.

In some places, we had heard, one can see the stars in midday. We didn't see them; perhaps we didn't look in the right places, or a growing overcast hid them.

Although the riverbed was mostly round stones, from the size of a man's head down to gravel, the going was fairly secure with the aid of our walking sticks. As we stopped for a moment to take the sand from our shoes, welcome sunbeams slanted down from the notch of steep and rocky Imlay Canyon.

Again the walls closed in. The water became deeper, though not because the stream was rising. The course was more winding. We were traveling a narrow tunnel whose eerie walls echoed and re-echoed our voices.

Then we entered another stone chamber, with flaring rock buttresses on either side. Feeling that we were threading our way between the feet of giant pachyderms, we called it Elephant Temple.

This point, at the junction of Orderville Canyon, was as far as Nate had come upstream on his scouting trip in May. This tributary enters at mainstream level through an even narrower slot from the east; one can touch its walls with outstretched hands.

Where the river makes an almost closed horseshoe bend, we glimpsed the Mountain of Mystery jutting skyward. Then the canyon widened, and on the gravelly shore we saw horseshoe tracks and a gum wrapper. Civilization was near.

At last, seven great bends beyond Orderville Canyon, we heard voices. Across the river were the girls. They had walked up beyond the end of the trail that leads from the loop road in the Temple of Sinawava. We were weary but filled with satisfaction at having achieved our goal.

As we emerged dripping from the river at the trail's end, a group of park visitors looked toward the Narrows from which we had come and listened to the ranger tell of the hazards which lurked there.

That night it rained lightly.

Several weeks later we heard that a flash flood had inundated the whole canyon at the Temple of Sinawava. The river's volume increased 50 times, most of the rise occurring within about 15 minutes. How I would like to have seen the turbulent gorge then—from a safe perch!

NOTE

1. George M. Wheeler et al., *Report upon Geographical and Geological Explorations and Surveys West of the One Hundredth Meridian* (Washington, DC: Government Printing Office, 1875), 3:77.

Part 4

Human Constructions

Upper cable works, ca. 1912. Stereograph by William R. Crawford. Courtesy of Special Collections, Sherratt Library, Southern Utah University.

19 | Story of Zion Cable

DAVID A. FLANIGAN

In 1901, after months of trial and error, David Flanigan successfully installed a wire and pulley system from what is now called Cable Mountain on the east rim of Zion Canyon to the valley floor 2,000 feet below. The cable works operated for more than two decades, giving the settlers of the upper Virgin River access to millions of board feet of lumber. Here Flanigan recounts the story of the cable's construction and the physical and spiritual struggle he endured to make his vision a reality.

At the request of friends I relate a few memories in connection with the "Zion Tram" or "The Wire," as it was known, in Zion canyon. The so-called "wire" was regarded as a mystery by many who were more or less familiar with its wonderful performance. The story of the "wire" has never been told and perhaps the details never will be told.[1]

The story of the "wire" had its beginning with a remark which Brigham Young was purported to have made at Rockville some sixty years ago. Whatever it was that Brigham Young really said in this connection it was believed by the pioneers to have been a prophesy [prophecy].[2]

The pioneers of Utah believed that Utah was one of the choice spots of the earth, that it was the will of God that this vastly rich storehouse of natural resources be developed and that Brigham Young had been appointed by God to lay the foundation for such development.

The pioneers of "Dixie" shared in this general belief in regard to Utah but they also believed that "Dixie" was one of the very choice spots of Utah. When asked to give a reason for this belief, some have said, "Brother Brigham said so, now get around that if you can." Some have tried to explain. Some have said: "Wait, perhaps some day you'll understand."

My parents were pioneers of "Dixie" and I believed as the pioneers believed. I believed when Brigham Young prophesied, pertaining to things material, that he expected some one to prepare for action.

Previous to 1902, I had thoroughly explored Zion canyon in the hope of finding some natural channel through which timber could be removed into the canyon. This work was begun in 1889 and was continued whenever I could spare a few days at a time for the purpose. Finally I decided that perhaps a tramway would be the most logical means of obtaining this lumber which Brigham Young was purported to have promised the people of "Dixie."

Being unable to buy a cable alone I suggested to a number of men that we unite our efforts and make the experiment. The suggestion was declined. I decided to buy some cheap wire and make a cable. In the spring of 1902 I bought about seven hundred pounds of common bailing wire for this purpose. When my father and members of his family found that I was going ahead, alone if necessary, they gave me all the support they could.

One hundred pounds of this wire was carried to the top and lowered. More wire was drawn up by a windless [windlass]. I had availed myself of all the information I could get on tramways in general, but so far as I could determine, nothing had ever been designed to suit this location. Failure after failure was made. Wire was lost in the course of the experiment. Finally I was compelled to admit that my theories had been fairly well proven out and the results were far from satisfactory. I had lost faith. I had failed.

Perhaps my state of mind caused me to take undue note of jokes and light remarks. I may have expected support and encouragement which had not been given. I believe I felt that those who had supported and encouraged me were disappointed, for after all what had I done to merit support and encouragement? I was trying to accomplish something which was considered impossible, considering the means with which I had to work. Opinion throughout the country was divided as to whether the distance was not too great for the very best of steel cable to operate successfully. A careful study of all the tramways of which I could learn from mining journals and other sources failed to give me any encouragement.

I wanted to be alone. I was in Zion. Food had been forgotten. It was night and very dark. There was bitterness in my heart. I thought of what we call the "Dark Age" when every shadow was supposed to conceal an evil spirit. Was not this a "Dark Age" also? I thought of the race of people who had given to this place the name, which means "In Thy presence I weep." Why did they weep? I thought of the thousands of millions of people who had lived and died on the earth since this great stone monument was placed here. Who placed it here? For what had all these people lived and died?

I looked between these mighty walls of stone thousands of feet high, at these brilliant suns which we call stars, thousands, perhaps millions of them. I wondered if they were giving light to other worlds and other struggling races. If so, for what were these races struggling? What was the meaning of this vast scheme of things? What was one weak mortal in the presence of all this?

I tried to pray. But—had I not prayed and worked for fifteen years for this one thing which had not been granted? Perhaps I didn't know how to pray, or work. I began to wonder if I really knew anything, or if I ever had known anything.

Then I wept, for I was overcome by the power of God. By that simple, sober, careful process of reasoning which God had given me and which I had not properly used and developed. I had been trying very hard to think and had just begun to understand. My great physical strength which had been a matter of comment throughout the country had been broken in an effort to develop false theories and ideas pertaining to details which had been arrived at after hasty and thoughtless consideration.

Why had a primitive race said "In Thy presence I weep"? Perhaps because, "Thy presence" inspired thought and with thought came regret, remorse, and suffering.

But it is well for man to think, and when he fails to think he is required to suffer, for when man violates the natural law, the same natural law, which is the law of God, exacts a penalty from which there is no escape. I now resolved to give myself over, as completely as possible to careful, concentrated thought, for I was now convinced that this was the power of God, and that the ability of man to accomplish things worth while was measured by his ability to properly develop this power of thought which God has given him.

I was now thankful for every condition which had combined to bring me into this mighty thought-inspiring solitude, this place called "Zion," where the stars shine bright by day and brighter by night. Where the "Ages" represented by monuments of stone are assembled for review, that they may inspire from time to time a passing race. Where one receives the impression that all things are recorded, and that in eternity will be found a careful record of what one thought and did while on the earth. Where earthly achievements and thoughtless, indefinite desires appear as things not worth while, if they are to be charged to our eternal account; where simple, silent thought comes to be regarded as the highest and most perfect expression of prayer; where man learns to fear God, to pray to God; to rely on God; to question and discount the judgment of men; to be slow to accept the opinions of his fellow men and slow to accept his own hasty and thoughtless conclusions. Where man learns to stand without the support of his fellow men when he feels that he is right; where hope and faith in the universal scheme of things is inspired; where man is made to feel that if he is anything, he is the humble servant of God. And finally, where a careful review, if an attempt to explain something about Zion, is followed by a feeling of regret, for here, one may look, listen, see, hear, feel, and think, and live a thousand years in a day. And why should one expect, or be expected to explain.

We were discussing a wire, a very small, weak, inferior wire, but this was destined to become a great wire and these were the elements which were to make it great. This wire was so very small and weak it could not do the work I had planned for it unless it was permitted to work in strict conformance with the natural law. It had no great strength to be thrown away in misdirected effort.

I went back to the work with renewed hope and energy and finally succeeded in designing the tram so as to work in accordance with the natural law. I had come close to this design long before, but it took much careful thought to perfect the final details. The capacity of this wire tram was more than one thousand feet of lumber per hour. Many hundreds of thousands of pounds of lumber and other material was transported by means of this wire tram and the wire was still in good condition. One-half of this so-called "wire" was five-ply. One-half was three-ply. The five-ply was somewhat smaller than the ordinary le[a]d pencil. The five-ply carried the load and the three-ply guided the load into Zion canyon thousands of feet below.

In addition to one million pounds, or more [,] of lumber and other material which was transported by means of this wire tram, the wire was also useful in helping to determine the relative size of the two cables for the best results, and for developing a practical design for this extraordinary location which did not permit of any supports except at top and bottom and for which no precedent had been found when the great distance was taken into consideration. There were many elements to be considered during the experiment and the wire was very convenient material with which to prove out and perfect the various details.

Finally, the design having been developed and proven out, roads having been built, a steam saw mill moved and placed in operation near the tram, and the wonderful, almost unbelievable performance of the wires having removed the elements of doubt as to whether or not the tram could be made a success, men could now be found who were willing to replace the wire with heavier cable, and they were in no danger of having their reputation or credit impaired by making an investment which would not meet with the approval of conservative men.

In the year 1907 the wire was replaced with heavier cable and the way provided whereby the people of Dixie were to receive many millions of feet of lumber which the pioneers said Brigham Young had promised them.

NOTES

1. In 1926, Flanigan published a more detailed account of constructing the cable in a pamphlet titled *The Outstanding Wonder of Zion Canyon*. A copy may be found in the Zion National Park archives.
2. David Flanigan's brother William remembered Brigham Young prophesying that lumber would be brought down the canyon walls "like a hawk flying." Quoted in Dena S. Markoff et al., *The Outstanding Wonder: Zion Canyon's Cable Mountain Draw Works* (Springdale, UT: Zion Natural History Association, 1978), 5.

20 | Zion Park Lodge

CHRISTINE BARNES

The original lodge in Zion National Park was designed by Gilbert Stanley Underwood and built by the Utah Parks Company to accommodate the tourists brought to the park by railroad and shuttle bus. Situated far up the North Fork of the Virgin River in full view of the canyon's most iconic rock formations, the lodge opened in 1924. Architectural historian Christine Barnes here tells the lodge's story, including how it was ravaged by fire in 1966 and rebuilt within months.

As the 20th century began, the southern environs of Utah and its panoramas of shifting colors and eroded landscape had been overlooked in America's quest for Western adventure. By 1905, the South Rim of the Grand Canyon had a bustling tourist trade that was a boon to the Santa Fe Railway. Now, the possibility of promoting tourism in the colorful canyons of southern Utah seemed to have potential for the state, federal government, and Union Pacific railroad.

The stunning region still was virtually inaccessible. Native peoples had hunted game and gathered wild plants and seeds, later building pueblos and planting crops. Fur trappers and traders blazed the Old Spanish Trail, which followed a portion of the Virgin River. By the time John Wesley Powell arrived in 1872 as part of [the] western survey conducted by the U.S. Geological Survey, Mormon settlers were there to greet him. Having pushed south of Salt Lake City pursuing cotton-growing land in Utah's "Dixie," they had settled in Zion Canyon, establishing the town of Springdale in 1862. Powell chose Mukuntuweap, "straight river," as the canyon's name. The Mormon community found "Zion" more fitting.

Farming was a struggle, but there was no denying the splendor of the setting. When talk came of the area becoming part of a national monument, the Mormon settlers agreed. In 1909, Mukuntuweap National Monument was established, and that same year the Utah State Road Commission began constructing a highway system to unlock the beauty of southern Utah.

As with other scenic destinations in America, it would be a railroad that first transported the public to these spectacular destinations. The Union Pacific's Los Angeles/Salt Lake City main line stopped at Lund, Utah, north of the monument, where a few hardy tourists left the comfort of their Pullman cars and boarded coaches for the country that would later be called "A Colorful Kingdom of Scenic Splendor." The "Kingdom's" accommodations consisted of campsites at the mouth of Zion Canyon, the North Rim of the Grand Canyon (operated by the Wylie brothers), and on the rim of Bryce Canyon. Even with primitive shelter and rocky roads, the touring public was enthralled by this remarkable country.

Horace Albright, acting superintendent of the National Park Service, began transforming the region into a group of national parks and monuments. As Stephen Mather's right-hand man in charge during one of Mather's illnesses, Albright first looked over the southern Utah canyonlands' national park potential in 1917. The fledgling National Park Service had its hands full with developing Yellowstone, Yosemite, and Mount Rainier national parks, but Mather agreed that national park status was the only way to assure preservation of the divine landscapes that included Zion and Bryce canyons. Mukuntuweap National Monument was renamed Zion National Monument in 1918. In 1919, Zion National Monument came into the national park fold.

"They, Albright and Mather, both knew that if people didn't visit these places, they wouldn't value these places," explained Tom Haraden, assistant chief naturalist at Zion National Park. "They were the right people for the right time, and that doesn't happen very often. If they weren't doing what they did when they did it, we wouldn't have what we have today."

With few funds to develop park tourist facilities, Mather turned to the Union Pacific railroad. The UP system saw potential in extending railroad lines into the little known and commercially untouched portion of Utah. Not only would the lines open up the spectacular red and white canyons of Zion and pink limestone formations of Bryce to tourism, they also would provide transportation lines for agricultural products, coal, and ore from the region.

In late 1922, the Union Pacific outlined a five-million-dollar plan that included constructing a new road from Lund to Cedar City, and creating lodging for the Cedar City, Zion, and Bryce sites and a smaller facility at Cedar Breaks (made a national monument in 1933). The UP would later include Grand Canyon Lodge on the North Rim and the Kaibab Forest in what it called the "Loop Tour" to "The most colorful vacation region on earth!" via motor coaches.

Once the UP settled on the tour concept, challenges for completing the project were huge. Road access to the parks, forests, and monuments was miserable, and the water situation unreliable. After securing concession contracts to the parks and monument areas and confirmation that the roads would be improved, the UP constructed a branch rail line from Lund to Cedar City, where a new depot was built; in 1923, they opened El Escalante Hotel in Cedar City, the "Gateway to the Utah Parks."

Stephen Mather, aware of the railway's obvious domination of the development, required that a separate company be formed to manage the operation. Utah Parks Company (UPC), a railroad subsidiary, was established for appearance's sake.

The first major construction was Zion Park Lodge. Initially, the plan was to build at the site of the Wylie Camp.[1] Instead, a spot with a spectacular canyon view, and better airflow and motor coach access, was selected along the north fork of the Virgin River. The decision still is appreciated eighty years later.

Three miles into the canyon, leafy trees against Zion Canyon's wall frame the lodge. A towering cottonwood now anchors the two-acre carpet of sloping lawn.

Carl Croft was born in Canyon Country, and began working for Utah Parks Company after college in 1948: "Sitting in front of the lodge on the beautiful lawn you are part of the canyon; it is part of you. You don't have to leave the lawn to see the canyon at Zion. You don't find that every place."

A railroad architect drafted the first lodge plans. Neither Mather nor Daniel Hull, landscape architect for the national parks, found the symmetrical design in keeping with the setting. Hull had another architect in mind for the job. He suggested to his friend and colleague Gilbert Stanley Underwood that he apply for the job. According to Underwood's biographer, Joyce Zaitlin, Underwood was summoned to UP's Omaha headquarters to discuss the job in May of 1923. He was hired with little fanfare and sent to survey Zion and Bryce, where he did sketches. Here the young architect had an opportunity to apply principles from his Harvard education to the natural setting.

Underwood's first Zion Lodge drawing with a main lobby and spanning guestroom wings was rejected. Instead, Mather envisioned something less obtrusive. With the national parks on the brink of an influx of private car travel, Mather also wanted accommodations that would serve more than affluent rail travelers. Underwood's later attempts included the main lodge with surrounding Standard and Deluxe Cabins, a plan that was implemented in all of Underwood's work for the Utah Parks Company. Thus began a fruitful relationship between Underwood and both the Union Pacific and the National Park Service.

In 1924, a dining pavilion at Cedar Breaks and Zion Lodge opened. An extravagant celebration kicked off the 1925 season with government dignitaries and Union Pacific officials on hand to welcome visitors to Zion Park Lodge and the lodge at Bryce Canyon.

Additions and cabins were constructed on Zion and Bryce between 1926 and 1929. In 1928, Grand Canyon Lodge was completed on the North Rim of the Grand Canyon. Underwood was responsible for all of the work. With each plan, Underwood refined his approach to rustic architecture. He drew from the Arts and Crafts style that influenced the National Park Service, and developed elements that he would repeat throughout his career. Each successive stone and timber lodge became more dramatic while still reflecting its individual park.

"I think that Underwood was one of those cornerstones in the development of NPS rustic architecture. To build structures that are secondary to the landscape, something we should keep in mind today. To make sure

Zion Lodge, 1938. Photographer unknown. Courtesy of Special Collections, Sherratt Library, Southern Utah University.

these structures lie lightly on the land," observed Jack Burns who, as Zion's cultural resources specialist, oversees preservation issues for the NPS.

At Zion, the first floor of the two-story main lodge had a lobby and bathroom facilities, an office, and store. The second level had a kitchen and dining room, and took advantage of the setting with a large balcony off the dining area.

Built of exposed frame construction, the balcony was supported by four large native sandstone columns reflecting the vertical lines of the park. Here was the beginning of the architect's making native stone the crux of his park designs. Centered behind the columns were full-length, multipaned windows on each level. Wood tongue-and-groove siding covered the exterior. A kidney-shaped swimming pool and two rustic bathhouses, designed by Underwood, were added later.

Built to last the length of UP's concession contract of twenty years, Zion Lodge weathered well. When Carl Croft began maintenance work at Zion twenty-some years after its opening, the 4x4 posts and tongue and groove on the inside were still in good shape.

Ten duplex Deluxe Cabins (1927) and five fourplex Deluxe Cabins (1929) randomly set along a pathway complemented the rustic design of the main lodge. Native stone fireplaces, chimneys, and foundations, and exposed milled framing, gable roofs, and front porches, were in keeping with NPS philosophy and the atmosphere of the park. The Deluxe Cabins also featured the luxury of hot and cold running water. Cabins were furnished with a day bed, a rollaway bed, rockers or armchairs, wicker writing desks, and dressers with mirrors, wrought-iron lamps, and tightly woven rugs. Simple standard cabins rounded out the guest accommodations.

Native sandstone was quarried within the park and at a site near Springdale during various stages of construction. Timber was another matter. At the turn of the 20th century David Flanigan had decided it would be much easier to cut timber on the rim above Zion and lower it to the canyon floor than to spend a week or two hauling it from the Kaibab Forest. After a few years of trial and error, he perfected a pulley system that made just such a plan reality. Flanigan purchased an existing sawmill and moved it to Stave Spring where the logs were milled before being lowered to the canyon floor, a trip of two-and-a-half minutes. The last major use of the cable system was in 1924, when it ferried lumber to build Zion Lodge.

Zion and the Canyon Country were ready to be "discovered" with the help of the Union Pacific's crack copy writers who created a marketing blitz promoting the "Colorful, Colossal, Sublime" sights with three-, four-, or five-day Grand Circle tours.

Touring cars picked up rail passengers and were ready to roll. As the cars approached Zion, the sunroofs were peeled back, the women tied on their kerchiefs, and everyone stared up at the wonders rising around them. Access to Zion was dramatically improved with the 1930 completion of the Zion–Mount Carmel Highway and mile-long tunnel that connected Zion more easily to Bryce and Grand Canyon national parks. With the improvements, visitorship skyrocketed from under 4,000 people in 1920 (prior to the lodge opening) to 55,000 in 1930 when facilities were in place along with a state-of-the-art road.

A visit to Zion, as with the other Canyon Country parks, was enhanced with ranger-led nature walks, horseback rides, campfire sing-alongs, and skits performed by summer employees, mostly students who worked double duty as maids, cooks, and bellmen. Visiting the Utah parks became a patriotic "Out West" experience. As with other national parks, one of the most loved traditions was the "sing-away" wherein employees gathered to greet and say goodbye to guests. Groups of visitors, the women usually dressed in billowing skirts and pearls, and men in natty casual attire, waved goodbye as they motored away.

It's not difficult to find someone who recalls past days at Zion National Park. There is a passion that draws each generation back. Judi Rozelle works as the NPS concession management analyst at Zion. "My grandfather Walter Ruesch was the first acting superintendent in 1919. My grandparents lived in the park before it was the park," she recalled. "My mother was assistant head housekeeper in 1949. I learned to swim at the old pool that used to be in front of the lodge. I took naps on the linen shelves and ate in the employee dining room. I have such a strong attachment; I was only four years old and I can remember walking on the path behind the old lodge."

Memories of the historic Zion Lodge now are just that. On January 28, 1966, the lodge burned.

"I was at the office in Cedar City. I got a call," recalled Carl Croft, then manager of facility maintenance for the UPC. "My crew burned it down. It was an accident—doing some repair work. A remodeling project where we were putting in new flooring and getting the old vinyl floor covering up.

"The railroad crew fought the fire as best they could until the park service got there with their pumper and their crew and knocked it down in pretty fair order."

All that was left was the stone fireplace, pillars, and some of the kitchen equipment.

Executives at the railroad's Omaha headquarters decided to rebuild. "They had their own architect and in a few days they had preliminary drawings and in a couple of weeks they had the conceptual drawings," said Croft. "A couple of weeks later eight to ten truck loads rolled up, and in one hundred and eight days it was up and we were ready for business."

What had been built in those 108 days was a simple two-story utilitarian building with little appeal and none of the design and planning that went into earlier park architecture. "It was hideous," summed up Judi Rozelle. In 1992 a reconstruction effort added some of the original lodge's appearance to the new building, and included stone pillars and an expansive dining deck. On the inside the black and purple decor was replaced with knotty pine walls and enlarged historic photographs that tell the story of the lodge and park.

"It was very unfortunate that it burned down. When you go into national parks like at The Ahwahnee and Old Faithful you are in a 'lodge.' This one doesn't speak to it in the same way," said Jack Burns.

The historic Zion Lodge was lost, but the park's beauty is enhanced with noteworthy historic structures. In addition to the Deluxe Cabins, Underwood also designed the Women's Dormitory (1927); Zion Cafeteria/Inn (1934), now the Nature Center; the Men's Dormitory (1937); the Bake Shop (1931), later moved next to the Men's Dormitory and now used for storage; and a Mattress Shed, moved from Birch Creek next to the Men's Dormitory.

From 1926 through 1928, Underwood turned his attention to constructing utility buildings in the Birch Creek Area that included the Horse Barn, Machine Shop, and Auto/Bus Storage Sheds.

"There's such a direct link to the [original] lodge and Birch Creek buildings. They were built by the UP and designed by Underwood. What's neat was Underwood's approach to a utilitarian building and his choice of materials," explained Jack Burns of the simple frame structures.

Over the years, the various cabins were updated and modernized. During the 1970s and into the 1980s, many of these historic structures, including the Underwood-designed Deluxe Cabins and dormitories, were in jeopardy of being removed. In 1976 the swimming pool and Underwood's bathhouses were dismantled, and in 1984 the Standard Cabins were auctioned off and can be seen scattered around the state serving as summer cabins or storage sheds.

"The parks are great, but it's these buildings that show what man can do. I love these old buildings," said Carl Croft. "People too often forget about the buildings and the story never gets told."

In 1997 a historic structures report was filed and preservation plans outlined for the concessionaire, TWRS Recreational Services, and the National Park Service. Since then, the Deluxe, now called Western, Cabins have been restored in keeping with their historic ambiance. The acoustic paneled ceilings were removed, exposing the rafters and vaulted ceilings and giving the cabins their original dimensions. Pressed board paneling was also removed, the chair railings returned, and the walls repainted to the original ivory tone. The exteriors had remained very much as Underwood had designed them. "The theme of those buildings, what you see on the outside, needs to be carried through to the interior. I think overall it was successful," said Jack Burns of the project.

From April into October, visitors to Zion Canyon now see the park on foot or by shuttle bus. They have an opportunity to enjoy the canyon as early visitors once did. Around the lodge, they can loll on the lawn, walk along pathways between the historic cabins and buildings, play board games in the lobby, or sit on the lodge balcony.

"I can take the same old walks behind the lodge today," said Judi Rozelle as she recalled her childhood. "And I get that same old feeling."

NOTE

1. The Wylie Camp was located at the mouth of a small side canyon just south of where Zion Lodge stands today.

21 | The Zion Tunnel

From Slickrock to Switchback

DONALD T. GARATE

On July 4, 1930, Zion ceased to be a box canyon. Automobiles could now drive up a narrow series of switchbacks and through a mile-long tunnel blasted out of solid rock and access U.S. 89, connecting Zion to Bryce Canyon National Park to the north and the North Rim of the Grand Canyon to the south. Here, historian Donald Garate tells how the engineering marvel was constructed.

A MONUMENTAL TASK: WORK BEGINS

By the summer of 1927, building of the Zion–Mt. Carmel Highway was ready to begin. Area promoters, prominent politicians, and the United States Park Service under the capable direction of Stephen T. Mather had convinced a reluctant Congress that the project would work. Money was there, and the contract was let on September 8 of that year to Nevada Contracting Company of Fallon, Nevada.

The project was divided into four sections. Section #1 was the 3.6 miles of switchbacks between the Virgin River and the west entrance to the tunnel. Section #2 was the tunnel itself, and Section #3 was the stretch of road from the east tunnel entrance to the Park boundary. Section #4 was outside the Park and would largely be paid for by the State of Utah. The contract for that section of the road went to Raleigh-Lang Construction Company of Springville, Utah.

The first six men hired by Nevada Contracting Company started work on clearing the road right-of-way up Pine Creek Canyon on September 27, 1927. Under the leadership of the company's superintendent, Stanley Bray, the number of men would swell from six to over two hundred in the next couple of years. And, subcontractors and other companies working on the project would hire many more than that.

As men were brought onto the job, they were divided into two crews: one was a road crew building the switchbacks, and the other was a mining crew to build the tunnel. Locals were hired for most of the jobs with the exception of the crew bosses for the tunnel construction. These were a group of sixteen hard rock miners, brought onto the job from all over the United States and Canada, who oversaw the local men hired as tunnel workers and were under the direction of Tunnel Boss Richard N. Scott....

AN ENGINEERING MARVEL: DRIVING THE PILOT TUNNEL

It was decided that the most economical and quickest way to bore the tunnel would be to first drill a small shaft or pilot tunnel. When this was accomplished, another crew would follow and "ring drill" the pilot bore and blast it out to a full twenty-two feet wide and sixteen feet high. Since ventilation would be a problem in a tunnel slightly over a mile long, five windows, or galleries, were planned and the tunnel would be no more than forty feet inside the cliff face. Just before construction began, engineers decided to build a sixth gallery.

A "Pioneer Trail" was built along the face of the cliff to provide access to these galleries. Work on the tunnel began in early November at Galleries #1 and #6. When these galleries were into the mountain the desired depth, crews began drilling both directions from both galleries around the clock.

When the connection between Galleries #1 and #6 was made, work had already begun on Gallery #2. When the pilot bore was blasted out of the mountain at the west entrance, crews were drifting both directions from #2, and work had commenced at #3 where a 235-foot tramway had been built to carry materials and equipment from the Pioneer Trail to the cliff face.

When the Pioneer Trail reached the site of Gallery #4, it was found that the gallery would be two hundred feet above. So, rather than try to build scaffolding up the outside of the wall, a nearly vertical shaft, or stope, was drilled to the level of the tunnel floor, and the fourth gallery was blasted out from inside the mountain.

When the last connection was made between Galleries #3 and #4, the crews began drifting east from #4. When they reached the point for Gallery #5, they again blasted it out from the inside of the mountain at a point along Pine Creek where the canyon walls are about twenty feet apart, and yet, from the level of the tunnel it is several hundred feet to the canyon floor.

After completing the fifth gallery, the workers continued drifting east until the pilot bore broke out of the mountain on the side of a cliff above Pine Creek.

THE SWITCHBACKS

As work was progressing in the pilot shaft, crews were pushing the road up the steep side of the talus slope toward a point the engineers had marked for the tunnel's West Portal. Both the tunnel crew and the road crew hoped to be the first to arrive at the site. A spirit of competition intensified daily as each crew neared the ultimate destination. A rough preliminary road arrived at the site on February 9, 1928. Four days later the miners blasted out of the mountain at the same point.

The road crew's equipment consisted of one P&H 1¾-yard power shovel, two ¾-yard shovels, a fleet of several chain-driven "bulldog" Mack dump trucks, and lots of dynamite. As the road progressed up the mountain, each of the switchbacks was given a name: "Skinny Bend" describing the first; "Carl's Bend" for Carl Bergdahl, a job supervisor; "Sandwich Rock" for a huge boulder of like appearance; "Nevada Switchback" for the contractor; and "Spring Bend" for the spring from which water was piped to the Contractor's Camp.

Much difficulty was encountered at the Nevada Switchback. The mountainside kept sluffing away as the road progressed, leaving an unsightly scar. This particular point on the road was by far the worst, but the entire 3.6 miles was subject to rock slides. Retaining walls had to be built along much of the road to hold it on the side of the mountain.

It was a rock slide on the switchbacks that caused one of the two fatal casualties during the nearly three years the route was under construction. An enormous sandstone boulder pinned Mac McClain against the tracks of one of the power shovels. The other death occurred in the pilot tunnel

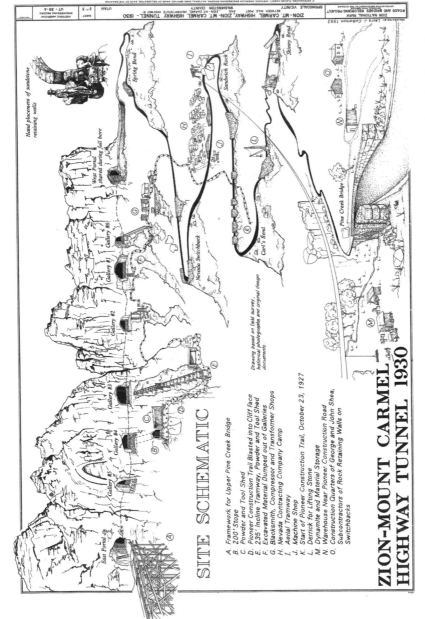

Schematic of Zion Mt. Carmel Tunnel. Created by Laura J. Culberson, Historic American Engineering Record. Courtesy of Library of Congress Prints and Photographs Division, Washington, DC.

on the night of July 1, 1928, when the connection was made between Galleries #3 and #4. Johnny Morrison, a crew boss and hard rock miner from Canada, lost his life from inhaling too much sand and dynamite fumes.

DRIVING THE FULL BORE

Five days after the pilot tunnel reached the west entrance on February 13, 1928, separate crews began "ring drilling" to expand the shaft to its full size. For this operation a drill was placed on a heavy iron spindle in the middle of the floor of the pilot shaft. One hole was drilled straight up into the ceiling. Then the drill was rotated and a series of holes was drilled from that point down to the floor on each side. When the seventeen holes constituting the "ring" were complete, the drill was moved down the tunnel three feet and another series of holes drilled. When twelve of these rings were complete, a blasting crew would load and touch them off, blasting out thirty-six feet of full bore tunnel.

The enormous rubble pile would then be cleared away. Unlike the pilot shaft in which the debris was hauled in mining cars and dumped out the galleries, the contractor's Mack trucks backed into the full bore shaft and hauled the blasted material down onto the switchbacks, dumping it wherever fill was needed. For loading the trucks inside the tunnel, the contractor brought an Erie Power Shovel onto the job. This compact piece of equipment operated on compressed air to cut down on the amount of exhaust fumes inside the shaft.

This was a mechanized operation that did not require the numbers of men that the pilot tunneling did. Work progressed rapidly, and although the ring drillers had started three months later than the pilot crew, they would only be one month behind them when they blasted out of the mountain on the east side.

Dynamite blasts could be heard daily coming from the switchbacks. The noise of explosions was also heard in succession at each of the galleries as blasting occurred inside the tunnel. This, coupled with the echoes made by each detonation, kept Pine Creek Canyon in constant reverberation.

COMPLETION OF A MONUMENTAL TASK

On Sunday, September 16, 1928, the pilot crew holed through at the east entrance. It had taken 313 days to get to that point. At that time the ring drillers were already east of the fifth gallery, and the Erie Air Shovel was working right at the gallery itself. The ring drilling was completed to the entrance on October 19. The following day at 6:00 p.m. the little air shovel completed cleaning the shaft. It had taken eleven months and twelve days to blast the tunnel through the mountain. Now the only thing left to do was blast the uneven places, or "shoot the tights," as the miners said.

As soon as a temporary bridge was built across Pine Creek at the east entrance, power shovels and dump trucks were moved out through the tunnel. Work was begun building the road toward the Park's east boundary to meet the Raleigh-Lang Company whose workers were nearing the boundary from the west. Much blasting had to be done to make cuts in the slickrock country on the east. A short road tunnel and four water tunnels to carry water under the road were built. Many rock culverts and retaining walls also had to be created.

The Reynolds-Ely Construction Company of Springville contracted to build the bridges on the route and Ora Bundy Construction of Ogden did all the curbs, paving, and other finish work.

By the end of 1929 the road was nearly completed. In fact, a car could be driven over the entire route, but it was not yet open to the public. That would not come until the formal dedication on July 4, 1930. Even then, the finishing touches on the Pine Creek Bridge were not completed. The contractor's foreman had made the bridge such a work of art that he missed the completion deadline by six days. The last rock work was finished on July 10, 1930.

22 | Polemic

Industrial Tourism and the National Parks

EDWARD ABBEY

Edward Abbey wrote extensively of the issues facing the American West and its natural wonders, and he has become an icon for civil disobedience in the service of the natural world. In this excerpt from the 1968 classic Desert Solitaire, *Abbey, writing as a seasonal park ranger in the then-remote Arches National Monument, argues for the exclusion of the automobile from Zion and the other national parks.*

I was sitting out back on my 33,000-acre terrace, shoeless and shirtless, scratching my toes in the sand and sipping on a tall iced drink, watching the flow of evening over the desert. Prime time: the sun very low in the west, the birds coming back to life, the shadows rolling for miles over rock and sand to the very base of the brilliant mountains. I had a small fire going near the table—not for heat or light but for the fragrance of the juniper and the ritual appeal of the clear flames. For symbolic reasons. For ceremony. When I heard a faint sound over my shoulder I looked and saw a file of deer watching from fifty yards away, three does and a velvet-horned buck, all dark against the sundown sky. They began to move. I whistled and they stopped again, staring at me. "Come on over," I said, "have a drink." They declined, moving off with casual, unhurried grace, quiet as phantoms, and disappeared beyond the rise. Smiling, thoroughly at peace, I turned back to my drink, the little fire, the subtle transformations of the immense landscape before me. On the program: rise of the full moon.

It was then I heard the discordant note, the snarling whine of a jeep in low range and four-wheel-drive, coming from an unexpected direction, from the vicinity of the old foot and horse trail that leads from Balanced Rock down toward Courthouse Wash and on to park headquarters near Moab. The jeep came in sight from beyond some bluffs, turned onto the dirt road, and came up the hill toward the entrance station. Now operating a motor vehicle of any kind on the trails of a national park is strictly forbidden, a nasty bureaucratic regulation which I heartily support. My bosom swelled with the righteous indignation of a cop: by God, I thought, I'm going to write these sons of bitches a ticket. I put down the drink and strode to the housetrailer to get my badge.

Long before I could find the shirt with the badge on it, however, or the ticket book, or my shoes or my park ranger hat, the jeep turned in at my driveway and came right up to the door of the trailer. It was a gray jeep with a U.S. Government decal on the side—Bureau of Public Roads—and covered with dust. Two empty water bags flapped at the bumper. Inside were three sunburned men in twill britches and engineering boots, and a pile of equipment: transit case, tripod, survey rod, bundles of wooden stakes. (*Oh no!*) The men got out, dripping with dust, and the driver grinned at me, pointing to his parched open mouth and making horrible gasping noises deep in his throat.

"Okay," I said, "come on in."

It was even hotter inside the trailer than outside but I opened the refrigerator and left it open and took out a pitcher filled with ice cubes and water. As they passed the pitcher back and forth I got the full and terrible story, confirming the worst of my fears. They were a survey crew, laying out a new road into the Arches.

And when would the road be built? Nobody knew for sure; perhaps in a couple of years, depending on when the Park Service would be able to get the money. The new road—to be paved, of course—would cost somewhere between half a million and one million dollars, depending on the bids, or more than fifty thousand dollars per linear mile. At least enough to pay the

salaries of ten park rangers for ten years. Too much money, I suggested—
they'll never go for it back in Washington.

The three men thought that was pretty funny. Don't worry, they said,
this road will be built. I'm worried, I said. Look, the party chief explained,
you *need* this road. He was a pleasant-mannered, soft-spoken civil engineer
with an unquestioning dedication to his work. A very dangerous man. Who
needs it? I said; we get very few tourists in this park. That's why you need
it, the engineer explained patiently; look, he said, when this road is built
you'll get ten, twenty, thirty times as many tourists in here as you get now.
His men nodded in solemn agreement, and he stared at me intently, waiting to see what possible answer I could have to that.

"Have some more water," I said. I had an answer all right but I was sav-
ing it for later. I knew that I was dealing with a madman.

As I type these words, several years after the little episode of the gray jeep
and the thirsty engineers, all that was foretold has come to pass. Arches
National Monument has been developed. The Master Plan has been ful-
filled. Where once a few adventurous people came on weekends to camp
for a night or two and enjoy a taste of the primitive and remote, you will
now find serpentine streams of baroque automobiles pouring in and out,
all through the spring and summer, in numbers that would have seemed
fantastic when I worked there: from 3,000 to 30,000 to 300,000 per year,
the "visitation," as they call it, mounts ever upward. The little campgrounds
where I used to putter around reading three-day-old newspapers full of
lies and watermelon seeds have now been consolidated into one master
campground that looks, during the busy season, like a suburban village:
elaborate housetrailers of quilted aluminum crowd upon gigantic camper-
trucks of Fiberglas and molded plastic; through their windows you will see
the blue glow of television and hear the studio laughter of Los Angeles;
knobby-kneed oldsters in plaid Bermudas buzz up and down the quaintly
curving asphalt road on motorbikes; quarrels break out between campsite
neighbors while others gather around their burning charcoal briquettes
(ground campfires no longer permitted—not enough wood) to compare
electric toothbrushes. The Comfort Stations are there, too, all lit up with

electricity, fully equipped inside, though the generator breaks down now and then and the lights go out, or the sewage backs up in the plumbing system (drain fields were laid out in sand over a solid bed of sandstone), and the water supply sometimes fails, since the 3,000-foot well can only produce about 5 gpm—not always enough to meet the demand. Down at the beginning of the new road, at park headquarters, is the new entrance station and visitor center, where admission fees are collected and where the rangers are going quietly nuts answering the same three basic questions five hundred times a day: (1) Where's the john? (2) How long's it take to see this place? (3) Where's the Coke machine?

Progress has come at last to the Arches, after a million years of neglect. Industrial Tourism has arrived.

What happened to Arches Natural Money-mint is, of course, an old story in the Park Service. All the famous national parks have the same problems on a far grander scale, as everyone knows, and many other problems as yet unknown to a little subordinate unit of the system in a backward part of southeastern Utah. And the same kind of development that has so transformed Arches is under way, planned or completed in many more national parks and national monuments. I will mention only a few examples with which I am personally familiar:

The newly established Canyonlands National Park. Most of the major points of interest in this park are presently accessible, over passable dirt roads, by car—Grandview Point, Upheaval Dome, part of the White Rim, Cave Spring, Squaw Spring campground, and Elephant Hill. The more difficult places, such as Angel Arch or Druid Arch, can be reached by jeep, on horseback, or in a one- or two-day hike. Nevertheless the Park Service had drawn up the usual Master Plan calling for modern paved highways to most of the places named and some not named.

Grand Canyon National Park. Most of the south rim of this park is now closely followed by a conventional high-speed highway and interrupted at numerous places by large asphalt parking lots. It is no longer easy, on the South Rim, to get away from the roar of motor traffic, except by descending into the canyon.

Navajo National Monument. A small, fragile, hidden place containing two of the most beautiful cliff dwellings in the Southwest—Keet Seel and

Betatakin. This park will be difficult to protect under heavy visitation, and for years it was understood that it would be preserved in a primitive way so as to screen out those tourists unwilling to drive their cars over some twenty miles of dirt road. No longer so: the road has been paved, the campground enlarged and "modernized," and the old magic destroyed.

Natural Bridges National Monument. Another small gem in the park system, a group of three adjacent natural bridges tucked away in the canyon country of southern Utah. Formerly you could drive your car (over dirt roads, of course) to within sight of and easy walking distance—a hundred yards?—of the most spectacular of the three bridges. From there it was only a few hours walking time to the other two. All three could easily be seen in a single day. But this was not good enough for the developers. They have now constructed a paved road into the heart of the area, *between* the two biggest bridges.

Zion National Park. The northwestern part of this park, known as the Kolob area, has until recently been saved as almost virgin wilderness. But a broad highway, with banked curves, deep cuts, and heavy fills, that will invade this splendid region, is already under construction.

Capitol Reef National Monument. Grand and colorful scenery in a rugged land—south-central Utah. The most beautiful portion of the park was the canyon of the Fremont River, a great place for hiking, camping, exploring. And what did the authorities do? They built a state highway through it.

Lee's Ferry. Until a few years ago a simple, quiet, primitive place on the shores of the Colorado, Lee's Ferry has now fallen under the protection of the Park Service. And who can protect it against the Park Service? Powerlines now bisect the scene; a 100-foot pink water tower looms against the red cliffs; tract-style houses are built to house the "protectors"; natural campsites along the river are closed off while all campers are now herded into an artificial steel-and-asphalt "campground" in the hottest, windiest spot in the area; historic buildings are razed by bulldozers to save the expense of maintaining them while at the same time hundreds of thousands of dollars are spent on an unneeded paved entrance road. And the administrators complain of *vandalism*.

I could easily cite ten more examples of unnecessary or destructive development for every one I've named so far. What has happened in these particular areas, which I chance to know a little and love too much, has happened, is happening, or will soon happen to the majority of our national parks and national forests, despite the illusory protection of the Wilderness Preservation Act, unless a great many citizens rear up on their hind legs and make vigorous political gestures demanding implementation of the Act.

There may be some among the readers of this book, like the earnest engineer, who believe without question that any and all forms of construction and development are intrinsic goods, in the national parks as well as anywhere else, who virtually identify quantity with quality and therefore assume that the greater the quantity of traffic, the higher the value received. There are some who frankly and boldly advocate the eradication of the last remnants of wilderness and the complete subjugation of nature to the requirements of—not man—but industry. This is a courageous view, admirable in its simplicity and power, and with the weight of all modern history behind it. It is also quite insane. I cannot attempt to deal with it here.

There will be other readers, I hope, who share my basic assumption that wilderness is a necessary part of civilization and that it is the primary responsibility of the national park system to preserve *intact and undiminished* what little still remains.

Most readers, while generally sympathetic to this latter point of view, will feel, as do the administrators of the National Park Service, that although wilderness is a fine thing, certain compromises and adjustments are necessary in order to meet the ever-expanding demand for outdoor recreation. It is precisely this question which I would like to examine now.

The Park Service, established by Congress in 1916, was directed not only to administer the parks but also to "provide for the enjoyment of same in such manner and by such means as will leave them unimpaired for the enjoyment of future generations." This appropriately ambiguous language, employed long before the onslaught of the automobile, has been understood in various and often opposing ways ever since. The Park Service, like any other big organization, includes factions and factions. The Developers, the dominant faction, place their emphasis on the words *"provide for the enjoyment."* The Preservers, a minority but also strong, emphasize the words *"leave them unimpaired."* It is apparent, then, that we cannot decide the question of development versus preservation by a simple referral to holy writ or an attempt to guess the intention of the founding fathers; we must make up our own minds and decide for ourselves what the national parks should be and what purpose they should serve.

The first issue that appears when we get into this matter, the most important issue and perhaps the only issue, is the one called *accessibility*. The Developers insist that the parks must be made fully accessible not only to people but also to their machines, that is, to automobiles, motorboats, etc. The Preservers argue, in principle at least, that wilderness and motors are incompatible and that the former can best be experienced, understood, and enjoyed when the machines are left behind where they belong—on the superhighways and in the parking lots, on the reservoirs and in the marinas.

What does accessibility mean? Is there any spot on earth that men have not proved accessible by the simplest means—feet and legs and heart? Even Mt. McKinley, even Everest, have been surmounted by men on foot. (Some of them, incidentally, rank amateurs, to the horror and indignation of the professional mountaineers.) The interior of the Grand Canyon, a fiercely hot and hostile abyss, is visited each summer by thousands and thousands of tourists of the most banal and unadventurous type, many of them on foot—self-propelled, so to speak—and the others on the backs of mules. Thousands climb each summer to the summit of Mt. Whitney, highest point in the forty-eight United States, while multitudes of others wander on foot or on horseback through the ranges of the Sierras, the Rockies, the Big Smokies, the Cascades, and the mountains of New England. Still more hundreds and thousands float or paddle each year down the currents of the Salmon, the Snake, the Allagash, the Yampa, the Green, the Rio Grande, the Ozark, the St. Croix, and those portions of the Colorado which have not yet been destroyed by the dam builders. And most significant, these hordes of nonmotorized tourists, hungry for a taste of the difficult, the original, the real, do not consist solely of people young and athletic but also of old folks, fat folks, pale-faced office clerks who don't know a rucksack from a haversack, and even children. The one thing they all have in common is the refusal to live always like sardines in a can—they are determined to get outside of their motorcars for at least a few weeks each year.

This being the case, why is the Park Service generally so anxious to accommodate that other crowd, the indolent millions born on wheels and suckled on gasoline, who expect and demand paved highways to lead them in comfort, ease, and safety into every nook and corner of the national parks? For the answer to that we must consider the character of what I call Industrial Tourism and the quality of the mechanized tourists—the Wheelchair Explorers—who are at once the consumers, the raw material, and the victims of Industrial Tourism.

Industrial Tourism is a big business. It means money. It includes the motel and restaurant owners, the gasoline retailers, the oil corporations, the road-building contractors, the heavy equipment manufacturers, the state and federal engineering agencies, and the sovereign, all-powerful automotive industry. These various interests are well organized, command more wealth than most modern nations, and are represented in Congress with a strength far greater than is justified in any constitutional or democratic sense. (Modern politics is expensive—power follows money.) Through Congress the tourism industry can bring enormous pressure to bear upon such a slender reed in the executive branch as the poor old Park Service, a pressure which is also exerted on every other possible level—local, state, regional—and through advertising and the well-established habits of a wasteful nation.

When a new national park, national monument, national seashore, or whatever it may be called is set up, the various forces of Industrial Tourism, on all levels, immediately expect action—meaning specifically a road-building program. Where trails or primitive dirt roads already exist, the Industry expects—it hardly needs to ask—that these be developed into modern paved highways. On the local level, for example, the first thing that the superintendent of a new park can anticipate being asked, when he attends his first meeting of the area's Chamber of Commerce, is not "Will roads be built?" but rather "When does construction begin?" and "Why the delay?"

(The Natural Money-Mint. With supersensitive antennae these operatives from the C. of C. look into red canyons and see only green, stand among flowers snorting out the smell of money, and hear, while thunderstorms rumble over mountains, the fall of a dollar bill on motel carpeting.)

Accustomed to this sort of relentless pressure since its founding, it is little wonder that the Park Service, through a process of natural selection, has tended to evolve a type of administration which, far from resisting such pressure, has usually been more than willing to accommodate it, even to encourage it. Not from any peculiar moral weakness but simply because such well-adapted administrators are themselves believers in a policy of economic development. "Resource management" is the current term. Old foot trails may be neglected, back-country ranger stations left unmanned, and interpretive and protective services inadequately staffed, but the administrators know from long experience that millions for asphalt can always be found; Congress is always willing to appropriate money for more and bigger paved roads, anywhere—particularly if they form loops. Loop drives are extremely popular with the petroleum industry—they bring the motorist right back to the same gas station from which he started.

Great though it is, however, the power of the tourist business would not in itself be sufficient to shape Park Service policy. To all accusations of excessive development the administrators can reply, as they will if pressed hard enough, that they are giving the public what it wants, that their primary duty is to serve the public not preserve the wilds. "Parks are for people" is the public-relations slogan, which decoded means that the parks are for people-in-automobiles. Behind the slogan is the assumption that the majority of Americans, exactly like the managers of the tourist industry, expect and demand to see their national parks from the comfort, security, and convenience of their automobiles.

Is this assumption correct? Perhaps. Does that justify the continued and increasing erosion of the parks? It does not. Which brings me to the final aspect of the problem of Industrial Tourism: the Industrial Tourists themselves.

They work hard, these people. They roll up incredible mileages on their odometers, rack up state after state in two-week transcontinental motor marathons, knock off one national park after another, take millions of square yards of photographs, and endure patiently the most prolonged discomforts: the tedious traffic jams, the awful food of park cafeterias and roadside eateries, the nocturnal search for a place to sleep or camp, the dreary routine of One-Stop Service, the endless lines of creeping traffic, the smell of exhaust fumes, the ever-proliferating Rules & Regulations, the fees and the bills and the service charges, the boiling radiator and the flat tire and the vapor lock, the surly retorts of room clerks and traffic cops, the incessant jostling of the anxious crowds, the irritation and restlessness of their children, the worry of their wives, and the long drive home at night in a stream of racing cars against the lights of another stream racing in the opposite direction, passing now and then the obscure tangle, the shattered glass, the patrolman's lurid blinker light, of one more wreck.

Hard work. And risky. Too much for some, who have given up the struggle on the highways in exchange for an entirely different kind of vacation—out in the open, on their own feet, following the quiet trail through forest and mountains, bedding down at evening under the stars, when and where they feel like it, at a time when the Industrial Tourists are still hunting for a place to park their automobiles.

Industrial Tourism is a threat to the national parks. But the chief victims of the system are the motorized tourists. They are being robbed and robbing themselves. So long as they are unwilling to crawl out of their cars they will not discover the treasures of the national parks and will never escape the stress and turmoil of those urban-suburban complexes which they had hoped, presumably, to leave behind for a while.

How to pry the tourists out of their automobiles, out of their back-breaking upholstered mechanized wheelchairs and onto their feet, onto the strange warmth and solidity of Mother Earth again? This is the problem which the Park Service should confront directly, not evasively, and which it cannot resolve by simply submitting and conforming to the automobile habit. The automobile, which began as a transportation convenience, has become a bloody tyrant (50,000 lives a year), and it is the responsibility of the Park Service, as well as that of everyone else concerned with preserving both wilderness and civilization, to begin a campaign of resistance. The automotive combine has almost succeeded in strangling our cities; we need not let it also destroy our national parks.

It will be objected that a constantly increasing population makes resistance and conservation a hopeless battle. This is true. Unless a way is found to stabilize the nation's population, the parks cannot be saved. Or anything else worth a damn. Wilderness preservation, like a hundred other good causes, will be forgotten under the overwhelming pressure of a struggle for mere survival and sanity in a completely urbanized, completely industrialized, ever more crowded environment. For my own part I would rather take my chances in a thermonuclear war than live in such a world.

Assuming, however, that population growth will be halted at a tolerable level before catastrophe does it for us, it remains permissible to talk about such things as the national parks. Having indulged myself in a number of harsh judgments upon the Park Service, the tourist industry, and the motoring public, I now feel entitled to make some constructive, practical, sensible proposals for the salvation of both parks and people.

(1) No more cars in national parks. Let the people walk. Or ride horses, bicycles, mules, wild pigs—anything—but keep the automobiles and the motorcycles and all their motorized relatives out. We have agreed not to drive our automobiles into cathedrals, concert halls, art museums, legislative assemblies, private bedrooms, and the other sanctums of our culture; we should treat our national parks with the same deference, for they, too, are holy places. An increasingly pagan and hedonistic people (thank God!), we are learning finally that the forests and mountains and desert canyons are holier than our churches. Therefore let us behave accordingly.

Consider a concrete example and what could be done with it: Yosemite Valley in Yosemite National Park. At present a dusty milling confusion of motor vehicles and ponderous camping machinery, it could be returned to relative beauty and order by the simple expedient of requiring all visitors, at the park entrance, to lock up their automobiles and continue their tour on the seats of good workable bicycles supplied free of charge by the United States Government.

Let our people travel light and free on their bicycles—nothing on the back but a shirt, nothing tied to the bike but a slicker, in case of rain. Their bedrolls, their backpacks, their tents, their food and cooking kits will be trucked in for them, free of charge, to the campground of their choice in the Valley, by the Park Service. (Why not? The roads will still be there.) Once in the Valley they will find the concessioners waiting, ready to supply whatever needs might have been overlooked, or to furnish rooms and meals for those who don't want to camp out.

The same thing could be done at Grand Canyon or at Yellowstone or at any of our other shrines to the out-of-doors. There is no compelling reason, for example, why tourists need to drive their automobiles to the very brink of the Grand Canyon's south rim. They could *walk* that last mile. Better yet, the Park Service should build an enormous parking lot about ten miles south of Grand Canyon Village and another east of Desert View. At those points, as at Yosemite, our people could emerge from their steaming shells of steel and glass and climb upon horses or bicycles for the final leg of the journey. On the rim, as at present, the hotels and restaurants will remain to serve the physical needs of the park visitors. Trips along the rim would also be made on foot, on horseback, or—utilizing the paved road which already exists—on bicycles. For those willing to go all the way from one parking lot to the other, a distance of some sixty or seventy miles, we might provide bus service back to their cars, a service which would at the same time effect a convenient exchange of bicycles and/or horses between the two terminals.

What about children? What about the aged and infirm? Frankly, we need waste little sympathy on these two pressure groups. Children too small to ride bicycles and too heavy to be borne on their parents' backs need only wait a few years—if they are not run over by automobiles they will grow into a lifetime of joyous adventure, if we save the parks and *leave them unimpaired for the enjoyment of future generations*. The aged merit even less sympathy: after all they had the opportunity to see the country when it was still relatively unspoiled. However, we'll stretch a point for those too old or too sickly to mount a bicycle and let them ride the shuttle buses.

I can foresee complaints. The motorized tourists, reluctant to give up the old ways, will complain that they can't see enough without their automobiles to bear them swiftly (traffic permitting) through the parks. But this is nonsense. A man on foot, on horseback, or on a bicycle will see more, feel more, enjoy more in one mile than the motorized tourists can in a hundred miles. Better to idle through one park in two weeks than try to race through a dozen in the same amount of time. Those who are familiar with both modes of travel know from experience that this is true; the rest have only to make the experiment to discover the same truth for themselves.

They will complain of physical hardship, these sons of the pioneers. Not for long; once they rediscover the pleasures of actually operating their own limbs and senses in a varied, spontaneous, voluntary style, they will complain instead of crawling back into a car; they may even object to returning to desk and office and that dry-wall box on Mossy Brook Circle. The fires of revolt may be kindled—which means hope for us all.

(2) No more new roads in national parks. After banning private automobiles the second step should be easy. Where paved roads are already in existence they will be reserved for the bicycles and essential in-park services, such as shuttle buses, the trucking of camping gear and concessioners' supplies. Where dirt roads already exist they too will be reserved for nonmotorized traffic. Plans for new roads can be discarded and in their place a program of trail-building begun, badly needed in some of the parks and in many of the national monuments. In mountainous areas it may be desirable to build emergency shelters along the trails and bike roads; in desert regions a water supply might have to be provided at certain points— wells drilled and handpumps installed if feasible.

Once people are liberated from the confines of automobiles there will be a greatly increased interest in hiking, exploring, and back-country pack-trips. Fortunately the parks, by the mere elimination of motor traffic, will come to seem far bigger than they are now—there will be more room for more persons, an astonishing expansion of space. This follows from the interesting fact that a motorized vehicle, when not at rest, requires a volume of space far out of proportion to its size. To illustrate: imagine a lake approximately ten miles long and on the average one mile wide. A single motorboat could easily circumnavigate the lake in an hour; ten motorboats would begin to crowd it; twenty or thirty, all in operation, would dominate the lake to the exclusion of any other form of activity; and fifty would create the hazards, confusion, and turmoil that make pleasure impossible. Suppose we banned motorboats and allowed only canoes and rowboats; we would see at once that the lake seemed ten or perhaps a hundred times bigger. The same thing holds true, to an even greater degree, for the automobile. Distance and space are functions of speed and time. Without expending a single dollar from the United States Treasury we could, if we wanted to, multiply the area of our national parks tenfold or a hundredfold—simply by banning the private automobile. The next generation, all 250 million of them, would be grateful to us.

(3) Put the park rangers to work. Lazy scheming loafers, they've wasted

too many years selling tickets at toll booths and sitting behind desks filling out charts and tables in the vain effort to appease the mania for statistics which torments the Washington office. Put them to work. They're supposed to be rangers—make the bums range; kick them out of those overheated air-conditioned offices, yank them out of those overstuffed patrol cars, and drive them out on the trails where they should be, leading the dudes over hill and dale, safely into and back out of the wilderness. It won't hurt them to work off a little office fat; it'll do them good, help take their minds off each other's wives, and give them a chance to get out of reach of the boss—a blessing for all concerned.

They will be needed on the trail. Once we outlaw the motors and stop the road-building and force the multitudes back on their feet, the people will need leaders. A venturesome minority will always be eager to set off on their own, and no obstacles should be placed in their path; let them take risks, for Godsake, let them get lost, sunburnt, stranded, drowned, eaten by bears, buried alive under avalanches—that is the right and privilege of any free American. But the rest, the majority, most of them new to the out-of-doors, will need and welcome assistance, instruction, and guidance. Many will not know how to saddle a horse, read a topographical map, follow a trail over slickrock, memorize landmarks, build a fire in rain, treat snake-bite, rappel down a cliff, glissade down a glacier, read a compass, find water under sand, load a burro, splint a broken bone, bury a body, patch a rubber boat, portage a waterfall, survive a blizzard, avoid lightning, cook a porcupine, comfort a girl during a thunderstorm, predict the weather, dodge falling rock, climb out of a box canyon, or pour piss out of a boot. Park rangers know these things, or should know them, or used to know them and can relearn; they will be needed. In addition to this sort of practical guide service the ranger will also be a bit of a naturalist, able to edify the party in his charge with the natural and human history of the area, in detail and in broad outline.

Critics of my program will argue that it is too late for such a radical reformation of a people's approach to the out-of-doors, that the pattern is too deeply set, and that the majority of Americans would not be willing to emerge from the familiar luxury of their automobiles, even briefly, to try the little-known and problematic advantages of the bicycle, the saddle horse, and the footpath. This might be so; but how can we be sure unless we dare the experiment? I, for one, suspect that millions of our citizens, especially the young, are yearning for adventure, difficulty, challenge—they will respond with enthusiasm. What we must do, prodding the Park Service into the forefront of the demonstration, is provide these young people with the opportunity, the assistance, and the necessary encouragement.

How could this most easily be done? By following the steps I have proposed, plus reducing the expenses of wilderness recreation to the minimal level. Guide service by rangers should, of course, be free to the public. Money saved by *not* constructing more paved highways into the parks should be sufficient to finance the cost of bicycles and horses for the entire park system. Elimination of automobile traffic would allow the Park Service to save more millions now spent on road maintenance, police work, and paper work. Whatever the cost, however financed, the benefits for park visitors in health and happiness—virtues unknown to the statisticians—would be immeasurable.

Excluding the automobile from the heart of the great cities has been seriously advocated by thoughtful observers of our urban problems. It seems to me an equally proper solution to the problems besetting our national parks. Of course it would be a serious blow to Industrial Tourism and would be bitterly resisted by those who profit from that industry. Exclusion of automobiles would also require a revolution in the thinking of Park Service officialdom and in the assumptions of most American tourists. But such a revolution, like it or not, is precisely what is needed. The only foreseeable alternative, given the current trend of things, is the gradual destruction of our national park system.

Let us therefore steal a slogan from the Development Fever Faction in the Park Service. The parks, they say, are for people. Very well. At the main entrance to each national park and national monument we shall erect a billboard one hundred feet high, two hundred feet wide, gorgeously filigreed in brilliant neon and outlined with blinker lights, exploding stars, flashing prayer wheels, and great Byzantine phallic symbols that gush like geysers every thirty seconds. (You could set your watch by them). Behind the fireworks will loom the figure of Smokey the Bear, taller than a pine tree, with eyes in his head that swivel back and forth, watching YOU, and ears that actually twitch. Push a button and Smokey will recite, for the benefit of children and government officials who might otherwise have trouble with some of the big words, in a voice ursine, loud and clear, the message spelled out on the face of the billboard. To wit:

> Howdy folks. Welcome. This is your national park, established for the pleasure of you and all people everywhere. Park your car, jeep, truck, tank, motorbike, motorboat, jetboat, airboat, submarine, airplane, jetplane, helicopter, hovercraft, winged motorcycle, snowmobile, rocketship, or any other conceivable type of motorized vehicle in the world's biggest parkinglot behind the comfort station immediately to your rear. Get out of your motorized vehicle, get on your horse, mule, bicycle or feet, and come on in. Enjoy yourselves. This here park is for *people*.

23 | Zion Park, Town Clash over Development

MAURA DOLAN

An enormous movie theater opened in 1994 in Springdale, just outside Zion's main entrance. In this article for the Los Angeles Times, *published as plans went forward on construction, reporter Maura Dolan explores the tensions between accessibility and authenticity, conservation and economic growth.*

Springdale Mayor Robert Ralston maneuvered his Ford LTD through the winding back roads of this labyrinth of sculpted, multicolored canyons and smugly shook his finger at a cluster of modest, boxy-looking houses for park employees.

"Did the park ask the town if they could build that?" demanded the 69-year-old mayor, peering out from beneath his royal-blue baseball cap at one of the prefabricated park dwellings. "They didn't ask the town nothing. But they try and tell us what we can do."

Ralston bitterly blames Zion National Park officials for stirring up a national dispute over a piece of private property that borders the park's gates in tiny Springdale. Developers want to build a four-story, big-screen theater on the site—located across a river from the park's largest campground—to feature a film about Zion.

If the theater is built, tourists could experience Zion's soaring sandstone walls in air-conditioned comfort—without entering the park. "Vacations for Couch Potatoes" was how an article in a grocery store tabloid described the project.

To Ralston and other town leaders, the theater represents badly needed tax revenue for Springdale. To members of Congress, a national environmental group, and actor-activist Robert Redford, the development project threatens to desecrate a national treasure.

But the feud here is over more than just the theater. It is a tug of war over the future of Springdale and other small "gateway" towns under pressure to cash in on soaring park visitation with increased commercial development.

"As visitation to parks continues to increase, we are seeing more and more commercial ventures to make a buck off the parks," said Terri Martin, regional director of the Washington-based National Parks and Conservation Assn., a park watchdog group.

"These small rural towns are easy victims for big, million-dollar investors who often threaten to pack up their bags and go home if they don't get exactly what they want."

Northern California–based World Odyssey Inc. came to Springdale four years ago to look for a theater site. Kieth Merrill, an Oscar-winning filmmaker and a principal in the firm, had helped develop big-screen films for theaters outside the Grand Canyon, at Niagara Falls, and at the Alamo.

He and his partners hoped that Zion would be the next of many more national parks to have one of these huge theaters. The developers already had an eye on West Yellowstone and had considered Yosemite as a possible location, rejecting it for the foreseeable future because of logistic problems.

The concept behind the theaters, according to World Odyssey Vice President Tim Kelly, is to provide visitors with an "extension of the (park) experience." The 55-foot-high by 70-foot-wide screens "make you feel you are more than there."

"There are certain areas of the park that are difficult to reach unless you are very athletic, and we're going to bring them into the film," said Kelly, vice president for development.

But the multimillion-dollar theater complex, as first envisioned by Odyssey, ran into immediate trouble. In addition to a 350-seat theater, the developer wanted to build a lodge with at least 120 rooms, substantially larger than any motel in town. The National Park Service said it was not opposed to such a project in Springdale; it just did not want it located next door.

Zion officials complained that the development would increase congestion at the park's entrance, where long lines of cars back up for miles in the summer. A proposal to build the complex in a style that was supposed to resemble the surrounding canyons, complete with crags and curves, also triggered considerable dismay.

"It was different…abrasive," said Larry Wiese, assistant Zion superintendent. "It looked very false."

When Mark Austin, 39, who heads a local anti-development group, saw the plans, he "could not help thinking of Disneyland."

The developers also wanted to remove a hill from the site. Steve Heaton, who owns the land and is a partner in the development, still cannot understand why there was so much fuss over the idea of leveling the sage-and-juniper-dotted hill.

"To me, it looks like a dumb hill," said the jean-clad Utah businessman, a green cap shading his face from the bright morning sun. "I think it's completely out of place."

The developers made repeated concessions.

The building style that offended the Park Service and local activists was abandoned, and World Odyssey agreed to adopt the architectural motif of the National Park Service. The theater would be built with rock and dark wood. The proposed lodge would have 80 rooms, not 120, and the theater would be nestled into the base of the hill to mask its height.

But as word of the plans filtered out, thousands of letters from Zion lovers poured into the two-room Springdale town hall, the park's headquarters, and World Odyssey.

Nineteen members of the House Interior and Insular Affairs Committee wrote to Odyssey and complained that the development would "intrude on the majestic scenery of one of our nation's most treasured national parks."

Redford sent a note to Odyssey's Merrill. "The light and noise generated by such a development is not conducive to such a serene location," the actor wrote.

The pressure on Springdale to decide its future was intense. A community of 300, the 1-mile-wide by 5-mile-long town has been at a crossroads over development ever since Zion's popularity began to rise a decade ago.

Dubbed "Yosemite in Technicolor" by its admirers, the park attracted 2.34 million visitors this year and is expected to lure more than 3 million a year during the next decade.

Even with the soaring park crowds, Springdale has retained its sleepy feeling. There are few sidewalks or paved roads. Only the small motels and gift shops advertising Indian goods betray its new status as a tourist destination. At night, the neon signs along the main street glow.

But if the theater is approved at the park's entrance, it will "send a message to future developers that large-scale development is welcome in Springdale," complained Louise Excell, 44, a former member of the town's planning and zoning commission and a native of the town.

Fighting Excell over the theater are the mayor, town officials, and development advocates. They want to develop more attractions for tourists and thus build a tax base that would pay for sidewalks and paved roads.

"A man has a right to do what he wants with his property" is their refrain, and it echoes powerfully through these canyons.

Town meetings are strained by the divisions over development. Shouting matches are prone to break out over zoning decisions, and a sheriff's deputy has been installed to keep peace at Town Council sessions.

Excell accuses the mayor of trying to punish her for opposing development by challenging the liquor license for her parents' motel and restaurant.

Ralston does not deny that he challenged the license but insists he has "no vendetta against anyone." He complains that his critics reported him to authorities for digging behind his hillside trailer house on land that is endangered desert tortoise habitat.

On greeting a visitor for the first time, the white-haired mayor inquired: "Did you hear about me being in trouble with the town and the tortoise?"

Some Odyssey representatives, frustrated by all the fuss, have threatened to abandon the theater project in Springdale if approval does not come soon. They blame environmentalists for stirring up all the trouble.

"Somebody has chosen this site, this project, to make a stand," complains World Odyssey's Kelly. "Why? I don't know. Ask that environmental group."

The answer, according to the National Parks and Conservation Assn., may be found by looking at other gateway communities.

The approach to Tennessee's Great Smoky Mountains National Park is a gaudy, neon-lit 15-mile commercial strip that includes a recreational theme park. Outside Rocky Mountain National Park is a huge water slide.

At West Yellowstone, a developer has proposed creating a grizzly bear theme park, complete with live bear exhibits, the big-screen theater, and a luxury hotel.

"The American public is becoming increasingly turned off by gateway communities that have allowed development that either intrudes on park scenery or is simply tacky or over commercialized," said the park association's Martin.

So far, nobody has managed to stop the theater project here. Town officials say they expect to grant the developer a conditional-use permit within the next few weeks for a 12,000-square-foot theater and adjoining 12,000-square-foot retail complex.

Odyssey officials in turn have dropped their request for the lodge, at least for now. They have promised the Park Service to scour the town for an alternative site, even if they get the permit to develop by the park's entrance.

The Park Service seems mollified by the developer's pledges. "World Odyssey has been very upfront, and when they tell me they are going to continue to look for alternative sites, I have no reason not to believe them," said Wiese.

But Heaton, one of the development partners, said recently that there was "zero chance" the company would choose another site. The Park Service, said town activist Excell, overestimates its influence.

If the developers persist in trying to build by the park, Congress probably will introduce legislation to buy the site, according to a staff member of the House Interior Committee.

Ralston is ready to wage battle with these "outsiders" from Congress.

"We just got through war in the Middle East and what was the reason for it?" he asked. "Outsiders. Outsiders jumped into Kuwait. And that's what we're looking at here. Outsiders telling the people of Springdale what to do."

Part 5

Senses of Place

Angels Landing. Photograph by J. K. Hillers, 1873. Hillers was part of the Powell Survey. Courtesy of U.S. Geological Survey Photographic Library, Denver, Colorado.

24 | The Land That God Forgot

JUANITA BROOKS

An important historian of the American West in the twentieth century, Juanita Brooks here writes of the natural wonders that have lured tourists to her southern Utah home. Included in this 1958 article are colorful descriptions of the scenic drives and breathtaking trails to be found in Zion.

The desert of the southwest knows no artificial boundaries. Sliced through by the Colorado River and its tributaries, it sprawls and stretches to pale miniature mountains against distant horizons. Except for one brief period in the spring it is dun-colored, but given rain in January and February it bursts into life almost as if by magic. Suddenly every scraggy bush is standing in a bunch of grass which thins as it fans out into the open, but which in wet seasons becomes an almost solid carpet. The first blossoms are the delicate annuals—bluebells, buttercups, sugar flowers, and sego lilies. Then come the red cups of the slippery elm, the purple spikes of the sage, the pink sand-verbenas, and the flame-tipped Indian paintbrush. The vivid cacti and the tall stems of the yucca, heavy with waxen bells, appear last, like royalty making a dramatic entrance after all the common folk have assembled. It is as if Mother Nature would compensate for the brief blooming by giving it extra color and perfume.

But such loveliness cannot last. By June the grass is burned to a crisp, the little annual flowers are only blown bits of refuse, the dry yucca pods rattle upon their long dead stalks. Each plant which survives the summer heat has made its own adaptation—the leaves of the creosote covered with gum, the yucca spines and cactus thorns all encased in heavy cellophane.

Before cars and good roads erased the distance, men learned to make their trips through the desert between September and May while the weather was moderate. Even then they must linger at the creeks and springs, follow the river beds as far as possible, and make long forced drives across country to water. If they *must* travel during the summer months, they adopted the habits of the desert animals, moving in the late afternoon through the night and taking shelter during the day in the shade of cliffs or sand caves or, if they were fortunate, under trees beside a stream.

The terrain is still a monotony to be endured, an area where the traveler may ride a whole day without seeing a living thing—bird, beast, or reptile. Such is the nature of the desert. One who would know its secrets must take time to live intimately upon the ground, must listen and watch through many nights to become aware of even a small part of the activity of this strange land....

St. George today is a tourist center where modern motels and restaurants daily furnish accommodations for more than a thousand people, most of them en route to the National Parks. It is interesting to note that the very liabilities of the early settlers are the greatest assets of their descendants. This multi-colored land, with its barren, fantastically eroded hills, which then seemed such a curse, is now a blessing. Its very wildness, its untamed grandeur, provides "gold in them thar hills" of a kind that only increases with the intangibles which each visitor carries away.

From St. George through the village of Washington, also settled as a part of the cotton industry, you pass on through Hurricane Valley with its luscious fruits and berries and its ditch hanging high along the hillside, up and up a winding road to the top of the plateau. Stop here and look back at the scene behind you, just in case you don't come back this way.

Directly below you Hurricane covers the valley, a patch-work quilt in neat squares. To your right clumps of green mark the location of ranches or settlements, and beyond stretches the wasteland cut through by ridges and punctuated with upthrust masses of violent red rock standing on end.

To the left rolling hills stretch out, one blanketed with some fifty acres of bright cerise sand, rippling and as clear of vegetation as beach sand, a miniature Sahara. Away and beyond this tucked-in corner stretches the desert.

Pioneer travelers, measuring these distances in terms of days and nights on the road, of hours plodding across a sandy stretch or up a grade to a summit, called the whole area "the land which God forgot." This view to them was not something to admire but the place where they must live; these colors spoke to them more of sterility than beauty.

You now stand almost midway between the two lanes of traffic through Utah—U.S. 91,[1] which you left some twenty miles back, and U.S. 89, which lies ahead. For nearly three hundred miles they run parallel, much of the way only forty miles apart, and joining them in a sort of magic circle are the scenic wonders of Zion, Bryce, and Cedar Breaks, all within a circumference of 150 miles. Today instead of being the land that God forgot, it is the land that man remembers and tells his friends about, reinforcing his telling with pictures of unbelievable quality. It is a land to return to again and again, for no one can ever wholly see it, so responsive and sensitive is it to the hours and the seasons.

Back on your way again, you ride across a level plateau, the skyline ahead a teasing lure to hurry you on. Close against your left is another flat elevation, the top held together with a tight band of hard rock from which the layers of softer earth burst away in flounces and billows and folds, horizontally striped, like permanent models for the abundant skirts of the Navajo maidens. On top of one elevation you may catch a glimpse of buildings and mechanisms connected with the government experiment known as "Project Smart." Here Dummy Sam is repeatedly being catapulted from a cockpit at a speed greater than that of sound—thrown through the air over the edge of the cliff to test the various effects on a jet pilot similarly ejected. No, visitors are not admitted except by special permission and when accompanied by authorized attendants.[2]

Rockville and Springdale are little one-street rows of houses crowded between the Virgin River and the hills. Now for the first time you are close to the stream. Innocent looking, isn't it? Hardly large enough to be called a river, it ripples along, shallow and cheerful. You could take off your shoes and stockings and wade it almost anywhere without wetting your knees.

Yet it was this same stream in flood that washed out the early village at Pocketville—houses, barns, and all—and then swung back in demoniac glee to scoop out the land upon which Duncan was going to establish another settlement. It has been said that the stream daily carries out of the canyon 180 carloads of ground rock.

After you reach the ranger station at Zion, make haste slowly. Pull up at the first viewpoint, stop, and get out for a general over-all impression of the place—the Three Patriarchs on the one side and the Watchman on the other guarding the entrance. Past this point the Indians would venture during the day, but would not let the evening catch them there. There is something so overwhelming about the place as the canyon narrows that they shrank away in awe, afraid of too close association with the spirits that whispered among the rocks.

Drive to the Temple of Sinawava, the end of the road for cars, and then get out and take time to enjoy this indescribable place. The general feeling is of mass—sheer cliffs that stretch up and up. How high? Why try to conceive the number of feet of several Empire State Buildings placed one on top of the other? The impression is of mass and height overwhelming, red walls in variegated shades, sheer, hard as honed steel. There is vegetation, of course, but so little that it is dwarfed and lost on the blank upper reaches. Close on the trails, aspens take the edge off the magnitude of what towers above and beyond the stretch of the imagination.

Follow to the trail's end at the edge of the Narrows, where the stream rushes out as from a huge pipe in an opening, only twenty feet wide in some places, between the two thousand feet of sheer ledge, clean-cut and polished. It is said by those who have followed through this canyon, entering from above and coming down with the streams during low-water time, that the defile is so narrow and the slit of blue sky so far above that the stars can be seen in midday. Here you may see the work of the stream more clearly, as it has cut its channel at the rate of an inch or two a year, and continues still to grind down the stone.

Linger in the Park as long as you can; your time will be well spent. Go on the guided tours and listen to the stories of those who have background to help you see what you look at. Or, with one of the "self-guided tour" booklets to direct you, explore for yourself.

You might try to hike up Angel's Landing, for it is not too strenuous, leading as it does by winding trails up the back to bring you suddenly to the top and the edge of the cliff. Now you can get a better view of the still higher walls that surround you, and, even at this elevation, things take on a different aspect as you sense the distance both up and down.

Do not attempt to climb Lady Mountain on the west rim unless you are in condition, but if you are, tackle it with the assurance that the effort will be richly rewarded. There are no words coined to describe the magnificence of the view from here, the expanse of unexplored land that opens to the west, numberless peaks whose tops are on a level with the high plateau, divided by a labyrinth of abysmal chasms. Beyond them the view stretches out as though to the end of the earth. Is it thirteen mountain ranges that you can count? Some say more, some less, depending on the strength of their eyes and imaginations. But it is an unforgettable experience.

Perhaps you do not care to hike at all. It is almost as well, for you can sit quietly in the shade of one canyon wall and look at the other; you can close your eyes and feel the spirit of this place. Stop where you can contemplate the Great White Throne, the unconquered peak scaled by only one human being—a seasoned mountain climber proud of his achievements in the Alps. He would win added fame by being the first to reach the top of this monolith! For one night his signal fire glowed on top of the crest, and that was all. Searching parties were sent out; airplanes flew over. It was futile, for the man had disappeared completely, and the mountain stood in silent disdain of their puny efforts.[3]

If you are fortunate enough to witness the moon rise over the canyons, you will understand better why people can believe in elves and fairies, and why the Indians might shun the eerie shapes that the moonlight conjures up. Or you might happen to be there for one of the brief summer showers when each cliff has its own waterfall, a misty, varicolored veil. But at any hour of any ordinary day Zion Canyon will provide pictures for your memory album.

Leave the canyon by way of the Zion–Mount Carmel tunnel, one of the engineering feats of the world. You snake your way up the mountain side and enter the darkness. But stop at the windows to look back at the canyons and cliffs and to get perspective. It is almost like a summary at the end of an interesting chapter, tying the individual points together and showing them in relation to each other.

The scenery beyond Zion to the east is varied and interesting—the checkerboard mountain with its bare slope neatly marked into squares, the wooded hills, the open valleys, and the patches of cleared land. At Mount Carmel Junction the road joins U.S. 89....

Back at Cedar City on U.S. 91 you fall again into the stream of life, but the memory of these natural beauties will be as a fresh breeze across your face, the whole experience something in the nature of a baptism. Surely this is not the land which God forgot, but the one He has preserved inviolate to minister to the troubled heart of man.

NOTES

1. The approximate route of present-day Interstate 15.
2. The U.S. Air Force operated the Supersonic Military Air Research Track on Hurricane Mesa from 1954 to 1961. Its purpose was to test ejection systems for jet fighters and bombers. Thomas G. Alexander and Rick J. Fish, "The Defense Industry of Utah," *Utah History Encyclopedia*, ed. Allan Kent Powell (Salt Lake City: University of Utah Press, 1994), 131.
3. The story of William H. Evans's attempt in 1927 to scale the Great White Throne and his subsequent rescue are recounted in chapter 16.

25 | Rough Hike through the Wrong Canyon

EDWIN O. REED

In this magazine article, Edwin Reed describes how a wrong turn and a flash flood turned what was to have been a moderate family hike down the Zion Narrows into a fight for survival in Orderville Canyon.

At Zion National Park the muddy, rushing Virgin River emerges from between sheer, steep canyon walls into the relative quietness of Zion Canyon. In places this river flows through a canyon over one thousand feet deep, eight feet wide at the bottom, and only slightly wider at the top. Each year a few adventuresome souls make the eleven-mile hike from the North Fork of the Virgin River through the "Narrows" into Zion Canyon. These people can testify to the beauties and the dangers of such a hike. It is necessary to wade the muddy, swift-flowing river most of the way, and in case of a heavy storm the water level can rise several feet within minutes.

In July, 1963, I wrote to the National Park Service at Zion inquiring about a hike through the Narrows with my family. A few days later the answer came:

You and your family should experience no difficulties on your planned Narrows hike provided the weather co-operates. Special equipment is not necessary.

We arrived at Zion National Park on Saturday afternoon, August 17, eager and ready for the hike. There were four hikers: Jimmy—age nine, Karin—age eleven, Margo—age twelve, and Daddy—pushing forty. My wife Alice and six-year-old Kristeen would stay behind.

Margo and I went to the Park Headquarters to get a hiking permit. Assistant Chief Ranger Lukens warned us that it was not the best time of the year to make such a trip, and asked us to postpone the trip if the weather looked threatening the following day.

The sky was cloudless the next morning and the air was clear, crisp, and still. Hurriedly, we ate breakfast.

The National Park Service information sheet gave directions for the twenty-five mile drive to the North Fork. Just a short distance past the eastern boundary of the Park we turned down a gravel road, which gradually deteriorates into a twisting, climbing, narrow dirt road. Finally Alice announced that we had driven twenty-five miles. A half mile farther on was a canyon but the ranch which the information sheet listed was not there. We drove another three miles. The road only became more treacherous. We studied the information sheet for more clues. It seemed that the canyon three miles back should have been our starting point and the ranch must be downstream from there.

After backtracking, we made our way down a wash to the canyon floor. As we reached the bottom, Alice drove away, but not before telling us that she had put a rope in my pack which we might find a need for.

Soon the canyon walls disappeared and we found ourselves in a long, narrow valley. A few minutes later we encountered a small group of cattle and a jeep road.

Now we were all convinced that this was the ranch and our trip should proceed from this point. But at the end of the canyon was a waterfall with a 150-foot drop. Fortunately, Margo remembered a cattle trail about a hundred yards back. Sure enough, the cattle trail headed downward to the left of the waterfall and dead-ended just ten feet above the river bed. We eased ourselves into the river.

Ahead we could see the canyon walls climbing higher and higher above the river as the water gushed its way downstream. In some places we had to walk in the rushing creek which was over Jimmy's hips. There *was* a narrow bank on one side or the other in most places but it was muddy, wet, and slippery from previous high water.

A half mile ahead was the first of several narrows. Several times I tried to touch both canyon walls at the same time upon the kids' request. Each time the canyon was a foot or two wider than my outstretched arms.

Karin strode ahead to learn of the wonders of this fantastic canyon. Then she stopped us with an excited whisper: "That's a canyon wren you hear whistling ahead." We were skeptical, but around the next bend there were, indeed, a pair of canyon wrens flying down the chasm ahead.

By now the sun was almost overhead, revealing the fantastic colors of the rocky walls which enclosed us. Jimmy and Karin soon discovered that the same colors were duplicated in the small rocks lying on the river bank, and proceeded to stuff their pockets to capacity. When they ran out of pockets they then begged me to carry the overflow.

At 1:00 when we sat down to eat lunch, everyone was happy and exhilarated. We guessed we were over halfway to the north entrance of Zion, where Alice and Kristeen would meet us. Through the canyon opening a thousand feet overhead we could see a thin sliver of beautiful, blue sky and one thin, white cloud.

Our serene mood came to an abrupt end after lunch when we found our way was completely blocked by a twenty-foot waterfall. The canyon walls soared straight up for a thousand feet on each side of the cascade. I was perplexed—no one had mentioned this obstacle. Then I remembered Alice's parting gift. Carefully I tied the rope around Margo's chest and lowered her slowly to the base of the falls. Jimmy and Karin followed in the same method. Next I tied the rope around a huge boulder and rappelled down the face of the rock. It was my first attempt at this mountain climbing technique, and I was thankful it went so well. Lastly, I used Margo's Scout knife and stood on tiptoe to salvage fifteen feet of the rope.

This challenge whetted Margo's interest and she wanted to take the lead. The next quarter mile was easy. Suddenly Karin screamed in terror and came running back. I scrambled to the top of a huge boulder to see what had happened. Margo had jumped from the boulder into a pool of quicksand! Already she was hip deep as she struggled toward firm ground just a few feet away. Quickly Margo sprawled forward on all fours and I shouted encouragement as she crawled to safety. She staggered to her feet, a muddy mess from head to toe. With a determined smile, she pointed out where the rest of us could jump safely onto solid sand.

Farther on we came to another hurdle—a twelve-foot waterfall this time. We would have to jump right through the center of the waterfall into a swirling pool below. A test pole showed that the water was over our heads and it might be as much as a sixty-foot swim through turbulent water.

This called for a family conference. The vote was three to one to proceed—with Karin our lone dissenter. I jumped in and swam wildly for shallow water. Next I found a long slender log. I waded back into the pool up to my shoulders and pushed the log ahead of me toward the falls. I asked Karin to jump into the water and swim to the pole. Bravely, she dived headfirst and came up spouting muddy water. She made the fifteen-foot swim to the pole and I reeled her to safety. Jimmy and Margo followed in the same manner.

Soon Jimmy noticed that the narrow strip of sky overhead was turning a grayish-black. Quickly we hurried downstream. I kept a close watch on the water level but it didn't rise. At each break in the canyon wall I looked to see how high we could climb in case of flood waters. Within thirty minutes thunder began to roll ominously and lightning flashed overhead.

The thundering skies permitted no time for a family consultation. There was a break in the canyon wall ahead and we made a quick climb to safety. We stopped a full sixty feet above the river, where Margo straddled a small tree while the rest of us wrapped ourselves in toboggan-like fashion behind her. With our remaining piece of rope, I secured the four of us to the tree.

For twenty minutes we waited while the thunder and lightning increased. Suddenly the skies opened up and the storm released a tremendous downpour of rain. It was 4:15 P.M.

Hail pelted us and rain drenched us thoroughly. Suddenly tremendous waterfalls began gushing over the cliffs on the opposite canyon wall. Margo and I gazed in wonder at the spectacle, but Jimmy and Karin were too depressed to care.

The flooding rains continued unrelentingly for forty-five minutes; gradually the downpour began to moderate. Within an hour and a half the storm was over. When the rain stopped the waterfalls disappeared. We waited another hour till the river was down to within a foot of its former level and some blue sky showed overhead.

Carefully we worked ourselves down to the river bed again. In the next hour we swam through two swift-moving pools, scrambled over rocks, waded several rapids, and climbed down one waterfall. But our frantic flight was hopeless: it was getting dark.

We climb[ed] the rocks to a small, level spot fifty feet above the river, then lifted out rocks to form a foxhole so no one could fall. Karin began to cry. I explained to the youngsters that we were *not* in serious trouble (though my fingers were crossed). One thing we had to do was huddle together for warmth—and keep our spirits up.

Quietly, we took stock of our situation. There was no dry wood, no matches, and no food. During our wild swims I had lost a contact lens and my watch. Jimmy and Karin had a few caustic comments about anyone who would allow three children and their father to make such a rugged hike, but Margo pointed out that the park ranger had neither encouraged nor discouraged us. "We have only ourselves to blame," she concluded.

Karin complained of the cold so I huddled around her. Margo and Jimmy sat together in Spartan silence. I tried to keep track of the time by watching a star move across the sky. It was a slow, cold, and tedious pastime.

There was a lot of time for thinking. It was fairly obvious that we were in the wrong canyon, but just where were we? This miserable canyon *might* merge with the Virgin River. Tomorrow we would have to continue hiking downstream—unless the obstacles became worse.

By midnight we four were wrapped around each other for warmth. This worked reasonably well and the youngsters fell into fitful naps. Another two hours and my hips began to get sore from lying against the rocks. Regularly, I would have to arouse everyone so we could shift to a new position and relieve the soreness.

The hour before dawn was the worst. All of us were too cold to sleep. Someone would start shivering violently and, contagiously, we would all shiver.

Dawn breaks slowly in a deep canyon. After thirty minutes of increasing light, we ventured back to the river bed. Our first hurdle was a fifty-foot swim. Twice I started to jump but didn't. Then I thought of the three brave ones behind me. I jumped in and swam for the shallowness of the rapids. Again I found a long log so that each youngster had a ten-foot swim and a forty-foot ride while hanging to the log. Ahead, the way looked easier.

A half mile ahead, just around a bend in the canyon, our river merged with a slightly larger river. Was it the Virgin? Karin gave a weak cry of joy.

The river was a little swifter and deeper now, but there weren't any more waterfalls. Jimmy had some trouble swinging his sixty-six pounds against the swift rapids, so I held his hand as we crossed and recrossed the river several times. Our excitement mounted—were we getting close?

Around the next bend there was a sign stating that five people had been killed there during a flash flood in September, 1961! Slowly, the enormity of our accomplishment penetrated our minds. We had mastered the hazards of a flash flood, a frigid night among the rocks, and an unknown canyon! We looked at each other—a cold, pathetic, and hungry foursome, but we were happy inside.

Later, after being reunited with my wife and Kristeen, I visited with Chief Ranger Armstrong. Our unknown canyon was Orderville Canyon, a canyon reserved for good swimmers with mountain climbing equipment. No one had tackled the canyon in three years. The Park Service felt sure that three children could not master the hazards of Orderville Canyon and only our timely arrival prevented a search party from entering the canyon at the starting point of our hike.

Will the Reeds ever hike down the narrows of the muddy Virgin? Perhaps, but never during the thunderstorm season and never again will we tackle Orderville Canyon.[1]

NOTE

1. Forty-eight years later, Reed's daughter Karin Leperi wrote a follow-up article recalling the flash flood and a return trip she made to Zion. Karin Leperi, "Return to Zion Canyon," *Country Extra*, September 2011, 52–54, http://www.adventuremedianews.com/clients/123122/images/CedCityReturntoZion.pdf.

26 | Canyons, Colours, and Birds

An Interview with Olivier Messiaen

HARRIET WATTS

Olivier Messiaen secured his position as one of the twentieth century's most important composers when he wrote Quartet for the End of Time *as a French prisoner of war in World War II. Three decades later, after he was commissioned to write an orchestral work in celebration of the bicentennial of the United States, he found his muse in the canyons of southern Utah. As he explains here, the piece he wrote—*From the Canyon to the Stars—*incorporates the colors and bird songs he found in Zion and its neighboring canyons.*

H.W. [Harriet Watts]: What made you choose southern Utah as the source of inspiration for your last symphony?

O.M. [Olivier Messiaen]: [...] It was a commission for a work in honour of the United States. I thought it over a long time, I looked at my geography books, at all the books I have at home, over 7,000, and into a special series of books I own, *Les Marveilles du Monde*. This series has everything, the Sphinx of Egypt, extraordinary things, and I said to myself, the grandest and the most beautiful marvels of the world must be the canyons of Utah. So, I'll have to get to Utah. At that time I was in the process of recording in Washington [DC] with Mr. Dorati my work *La Transfiguration*, and I called up my impresario, Mr. Breslin, and I said to him, "I want to go to Bryce

Canyon." "What's that?" he exclaimed, and I explained, "Bryce Canyon is the most beautiful thing in the United States." "Oh?" "So," I said, "You'll have to find a way for me to get there." He was horrified: "But it's so far away." I said "Well, it's either that or the Islands of Hawaii." "Oh, no, that's even further," he said. So, the matter was settled, we were to go to Bryce Canyon....

I knew that Bryce Canyon was beautiful, because I had read all about it, I looked at pictures of it, but it was even more beautiful than in the photographs. It's quite amazing; first, it's so big, immense, it's a landscape of nothing but cliffs and boulders in fantastic shapes. There are castles, towers, dungeons, there are turrets, bridges, towers, windows, and then, even more beautiful, there are the colours. Everything is red, all sorts of reds: red-violet, a red-orange, rose, dark red carmine, scarlet red, all possible varieties of red, an extraordinary beauty. I observed all of this very carefully, I wrote it all down, notation after notation....

Colours are very important to me because I have a gift—it's not my fault, it's just how I am—whenever I hear music, or even if I read music, I see colours. They correspond to the sounds, rapid colours which turn, mix, combine, and move with the sounds. Like the sounds they are high, low, quick, long, strong, weak, etc. The colours do just what the sounds do. They are always changing, but they are marvelous and they reproduce themselves each time one repeats the same sound complex. It's a theory that's a bit complicated, but I'll explain how it works. Take a note, any note, and there is a corresponding colour. If you change the note, even by a semitone, it's no longer the same colour. With the twelve semitones the colour never remains the same. But once you reach the octave, you have the original colour again. It recommences with the high octaves and with the low octaves. In the higher octaves, it becomes progressively more diluted with white, and in the lower octaves, it is mixed with black so that it's darker....

So, if you have a note a fifth above a yellow note, you'll see a violet; if you have a fifth at blue, you'll see an orange. I've often carried out these experiments with my students at the conservatory; they all thought I was crazy, but that's of no importance. I do it anyway, because I'm convinced of the results.

Bryce Canyon was of special interest to me. That's because it had all those wonderful colours, and I wanted to put them into music. So, the piece I composed about Bryce Canyon is red and orange, the colour of the cliffs. I proceeded on through the canyons. Next I was at Cedar Breaks. The name is very difficult to translate into French. Cedar is the word for "cedres," but there aren't any cedars there. Breaks, well, that's like a "trou," a hole, I don't know how one should say that in French, perhaps "l'abime des cedres" (the abyss of cedars). Anyway, it's a very impressive spot, an immense amphitheatre with an enormous slash in the earth, very, very, deep, it is frightening, and the feeling I had there was religious. I composed a piece entitled, "Cedar Breaks is the Gift of Fear." Fear in a religious sense, not the sort of fear one has of the police, but a fear which is a reverence before something sacred. One senses a divine presence, something which is sacred, one is subjugated to this feeling, the gift of fear. I felt that Cedar Breaks gave one that sense of fear.

After Cedar Breaks, I continued on to Zion Park. The cliffs there are also very beautiful, but less red, less fantastic. The atmosphere is more somber, serene, more sacred, even more celestial. I believe that it is indeed celestial, because the Mormons, who discovered this place, called it Zion Park. Zion in the Bible is the synonym of Jerusalem, not of the earthly Jerusalem, but of the celestial city itself, thus, the gift of heaven. So, I did like the Mormons and composed a piece which is called "Zion Park and the Celestial City." My work concluded with paradise, the piece composed for Zion Park.

At Zion, it was still springtime, the season of love and song for the birds. In Zion there were the most beautiful birds of all. First, and perhaps most important, there was the cassis [Cassin's] finch with a lovely, lovely voice, flute-like with a charming timbre, a marvelous virtuoso. The bird itself is red. Then there was the grey vireo which is very imperative, it's the drill-master of birds (co mo! co mo!) and then a wonderful singer, the western meadowlark. It has a yellow breast with a black hood. Its song is incredible, very limpid, with many harmonics. Each note carries five or six harmonics; it's one of the greatest songbirds of the United States. There were numerous specimens of all three types, the cassis finch, the grey vireo, the western meadowlark in Zion Park. After seeing and taking notes on all this, I composed my work on the canyons. I'd seen the canyons from two different perspectives. I'd seen them from on high, with the vertigo of the abyss, that's important, one sees vast black holes against the red of the cliffs. Afterwards my wife and I went down the trails, very carefully, never leaving the paths and we made our way to the depths, all the way to the bottom. From the depths of the abyss, we could see the path circling very high above us, and that is what inspired the title of my work, *From the Canyons to the Stars*, one progresses from the deepest bowels of the earth and ascends towards the stars.

From the titles of all the pieces in the composition, you'll see that they're suggestive of Utah. The first piece is called "The Desert," a place where one is all alone, and after that, the second movement is called "The Orioles," which refers to the orioles of the United States. The next piece is "That which is Written in the Stars." Written in the stars are those terrible words, Mene Tekel Upharsin which mean weigh, count, divide.[1] The stars are weighed, counted, and divided. Afterwards there is a solo bird piece called "White-Browed Robin." Then there is the piece to "Cedar Breaks and the Gift of Fear," or the reverence for the sacred. Next there is a piece for solo horn which is called "Interstellar Appeal," one calls for help in the midst of the stars, to the void between the stars, and then there is "Bryce Canyon and the Red-Orange Cliffs," that's the principal piece, the chant of victory, and then there is another piece to the stars called "The Resurrected." It is situated beyond death and is for those who have been resurrected. It is the song of the star Aldebaran. It is not the resurrected who sing, but the stars themselves, because it seems that stars do sing. One can record vibrations from stars, each star has its own vibration and produces a note....

Afterwards, there is an extensive piano solo which is called "The Polyglot Mockingbird," that famous mockingbird which one finds all over the United States, even at Washington, DC, and especially throughout California. I've heard it in Pasadena, in Santa Barbara, in San Francisco, all over California. Then there is a piece to a bird called "The Wood Thrush." After that, in remembrance of my phone call to my impresario and his exclamation "Bryce Canyon, it's so far away" and my reply, "if it's not Bryce Canyon, it will be the islands of Hawaii," recalling that reference to Hawaii, I've included a piece on the birds of Hawaii. It is called "Omao, Leiothrix, Elepaio, Shamn [Shama]." These are all birds that one finds in Hawaii. And the four names together constitute a verse line, an Alexandrine,[2] "Omao, Leiothrix, Elepaio, Shama." Then finally one ends in paradise, like the Mormons who believed that they had discovered the celestial Jerusalem at Zion Park. The last piece is called "Zion Park and the Celestial City."...

H.W.: One last question for you, Monsieur Messiaen. How do you feel about having your own mountain now in Utah, Mount Messiaen?[3]

O.M.: Ah, it's just incredible and very touching. When I told my impresario about it, he was amazed. When I told my publisher M. Leduc in Paris about it, he was astounded, too. He couldn't imagine that there would be a mountain anywhere with my name; at first he laughed, but then he almost cried. And we plan to go back there soon. It's a great excuse to see Utah again, and, in any case, it seems to me that I now have the obligation to present myself before those three cliffs. They're there waiting for me.

NOTES

1. This refers to the mysterious writing on the wall that Daniel interpreted concerning King Belshazzar, in the fifth chapter of Daniel in the Old Testament.
2. That is, a poetic line of twelve syllables.
3. On August 5, 1978, the state of Utah renamed a rock formation near Parowan, Utah, "Mount Messiaen" in honor of the composer.

27 | The Spirit of Kinesava

LYMAN HAFEN

Lyman Hafen is executive director of the Zion Natural History Association. He is also a remarkable chronicler of southern Utah, and very few know Zion Canyon as intimately as he does. In this essay, Hafen describes a mystical encounter on a blistering summer day atop Angels Landing.

I do not recommend a climb to the top of Angels Landing at midday in July. Unless, of course, you feel compelled to it, as I did some years ago. The result could be heatstroke, dehydration, or one of many forms of disorientation resulting from an overdose of the sun. Even if you dress lightly, wear a hat, cover yourself with sun-screen, and carry plenty of water, the canyon is likely to play tricks on you. Or it could be the spirit of Kinesava.

At noonday I set out. There was no one else on the trail. The sun, a searing globe of fire, hovered directly above, leaving only a compressed shadow at my feet. I had a bottle of water hooked to my belt and a stash of beef jerky in my pocket. Within minutes I understood why no one else was on the trail. This would go down as one of the hottest days on record in Zion. Anyone in his right mind would have tarried beneath the cottonwoods along the river, soaking his toes in the cool rushing water and waiting out the sun until evening. But I did not on that day fall into the aforementioned category.

It wasn't bad at first. I shuffled along at a limber clip, intent on reaching the top for what reason heaven only knew. Then the paved trail slowly transformed from moderate to steep. My legs grew heavy. Sweat saturated my hat band and streamed down my face. I could feel the heat radiating out of the rocks. The sun hit me at 110 degrees Fahrenheit, but the oven effect of the rocks took it to broiling range.

Before long my vision began to blur and my mind started to swirl. As I pushed upward, a long, strange word worked its way into my thoughts. Mukuntuweap. I had heard the word before, had seen it in books, and knew that it was the Indian name for this canyon. The word had come back to me now and it rolled over and over, beating a rhythm through my body. *Moo-koon-too-weep.*

"The Indians call the canyon through which the river runs, Mu-koon-tu-weap, or Straight Canyon," John Wesley Powell wrote. I knew that some of the early white settlers thought the word meant "the place of the gods," or simply "God's land." Tuweap, I knew, means ground, earth, or place. And I knew there were several other theories, including the possibility that the canyon was named for a chief among the Parrusits named Mukun.

I kept climbing toward the sun with the word Mukuntuweap slogging through my head like a loose cottonwood log on the river. I should have stopped and drunk some water, should have at least lingered a moment in one of those shady corners where the air swirls a few degrees cooler and a hint of green clings to the moist sandstone. But I kept going. Kept climbing. Couldn't stop. Not now.

Not until I heard the whistle did I stop. It was a shrill, piercing whistle that sounded once, then was gone. I turned and looked behind me. Had it come from below or above? I looked up the canyon wall, up through the shimmering waves of Navajo Sandstone. Nothing. Then I looked down. Down through the hot wavering air to the canyon bottom. Nothing. I took off my hat and wiped my wrist across my brow.

By the time I reached the long series of switchbacks called Walter's Wiggles my spirit and body had begun to disassociate. My body slowed with each step, but my spirit pushed on. My spirit pulled and tugged at my mortal frame, threatening to leave it on its own if flesh and bone could not keep pace. Midway up the Wiggles I heard a loud cry. It was a yell, one strong syllable of a holler that carried across the canyon and echoed back at me. I stopped again. Frozen this time. There was no one below me. No one above me. No one anywhere I could see who might have made the sound.

I turned in a circle and struggled to determine which way was up. Lifting my chin to the next ridge I caught sight of a human form. It scurried along the rim just long enough for me to see it, then disappeared into shadow. I was shaking now. I had to sit down. I fell forward onto the closest flat rock, broke the fall with my outstretched arms, and rolled over onto my back beneath the pounding sun.

It's hard to say how long I lay there. When I finally arose I set out with fresh strength and renewed courage and bounded effortlessly up to the summit. Ascending the narrow spine, up the last stretch to the platform of Angels Landing, I disregarded the chains and pipe railings that I had always carefully clung to before. The canyon floor was one step away, a thousand feet straight down. Yet I felt no need to anchor myself. It was as if my feet were not touching the ground anyway. I had never felt quite this buoyant, quite this full of joy, quite this close to heaven.

Then, at the top, at the far edge of the landing where you can reach out with your eyes and gather in more of God's creation than at any other spot on earth, I saw the man.

He was perched on the ledge, squatting on his haunches. His weathered skin, dark and deep red, looked as old as the rock of the far canyon wall. He wore only a short sash of rabbit skin around his waist. His hair, long and thick and coarse like a horse's mane, flashed hot black in the sun. And his face, his squinted, windblown face, looked straight at me—black flint eyes shimmering with understanding and with an implicit kindness that set me immediately at ease.

I didn't move for a long time. Finally a gentle breeze whiffed across the landing and I half expected it to carry this vision away. But the man still sat there on his haunches and peered at me with those glimmering black eyes and a hint of a smile on his face.

"Who *are* you?" I finally asked.

He shifted slightly on his bare, leathery feet and lifted his arm toward me. Crooked fingers dangled from his outstretched hand. He seemed to want me to come closer.

I took a few steps forward. "Are you the one who whistled?" I said.

He smiled.

"Are you the one who yelled?"

He smiled again.

"That was you on the ledge above me, wasn't it?"

The old Indian began to chuckle. It was a laugh unlike anything I'd ever heard. High pitched, almost like crying.

"Kinesava," he finally said. His voice passed gently into my ears, as if from an ancient cavern where sound is made of smooth beautiful rocks tumbling softly against one another.

"You are Kinesava?" I said.

"No," the man said. "You have been deceived by Kinesava. He is the one of changeable moods. He will yell at you or whistle, or make a strange noise. But he will remain invisible. He might reveal himself in the form of a man in the distance somewhere, then he will disappear when you approach him. Sometimes he builds fires in places where no man can climb. He pushes the rocks that fall down, and sometimes he frightens the deer when you hunt. On such days it is better to go home."

"If you're not Kinesava, then who are you?" I asked.

"It makes no never mind," he said. And then he went on. "In a friendly mood Kinesava will help you. He will soothe the deer so they are not frightened and lure them to where they are easily found. Then you must show your appreciation and leave meat for Kinesava. When you come back, the meat will be gone and Kinesava will not play pranks on you for a time."

What could I say? I stood there and nodded my head.

"Or it could have been Wainopits," the old man went on. "He is always at cross purposes and causes no end of trouble. He hides in the shadows. He is intent upon evil. It is Wainopits who will visit your camp and bring sickness to it. He will cause all sorts of dire calamities. Wherever he is present, it is best to run away."

"Why are you telling me this?" I asked.

The old Indian finally stood up from his haunches and took a step toward me. He was short and stooped but his eyes never lost contact with mine. "In the shadows of Mukuntuweap anything might happen," he said. "The ancient ones lived here. But my people, the Parrusits, seldom came into this canyon. When we came, it was only by day. Kinesava is a good spirit, but he will play tricks on you. Wainopits will not rest until he undoes you. Be careful when you enter Mukuntuweap. Do not do foolish things. Kinesava has little patience. Wainopits has none at all."

"Won't you tell me who you are?" I asked.

"I am the last Parrusit," the old man finally admitted. He stretched his stick-like arm and pointed with crumpled fingers across the canyon. "We lived along this river, *Pa'rus*, for many generations. Once we were a thousand in number. We hunted deer and rabbits and ate the berries and the plants the land afforded. When white men came we started to disappear. More white men came and more of the Parrusits disappeared. We have been gone for many years now. They say the last Parrusit died in 1945. But they do not know of me. They do not know that one last Parrusit still roams this country with a warning for those who will listen."

"Tell me more," I said.

The old Indian did not hesitate. "Once the earth was smooth and plain. But one day Shinob told Kusav to place his quiver at a short distance from where they stood that it might be a mark for him to shoot. Then Shinob sent an arrow from his bow. The arrow struck the quiver, but glanced and plowed its way about the face of the earth in every direction. The arrow dug deep gorges and canyons, making valleys, plowing up mountains, hills, and rocks. In this way the river courses were made and the hills and mountains were made and the big broken rocks were scattered about the country."

The old Parrusit lay his feeble hand upon my shoulder and continued his story. "Before this time all people had lived in one community. They were all brothers and sisters. But when the canyons and the mountains were made the people scattered, for there was now a great diversity of country and each people found their own place. When the people had separated they ceased to speak their ancient language. Each one adopted a new language which has been handed down. They also lost their wisdom because of their disagreements. These changes were a great wonder among the people. Each saw the changes of the others, but did not see the transformation in themselves. Each supposed that he spoke the original language and that the rest had lost it. This is how the quarrels and the separation began."

The old man let go of my shoulder and squatted down again. I sat on a rock near him. There was a long silence. He seemed to be finished. I did not like the silence so I asked him something. I asked him what Mukuntu-weap means.

"Mukuntuweap is this place," he said, extending his arm and drawing it around in a half circle.

"What does it mean in my language?" I asked.

He answered the question with another question. "For you, what is this place?" he asked.

"It is among the most glorious places on earth for me," I said. "It is a place apart, a place I can come to and feel closer to heaven."

The old man reached over and touched my chest. I felt his fingers pushing at my heart. "You are right," the old man said. "That is Mukuntuweap."

My eyes opened to nothing but white light. An explosion of sun filled the entire sky. The fingers still tapped on my chest. They were the feet of a crow dancing upon my prostrate body. As I lifted my chin the crow spread his wings in my face and fluttered off into the canyon. I sat up on the rock and brushed myself off. It was several minutes before I could stand with any semblance of balance. When I finally got my bearings I drew a long drink of water from my bottle, then reached into my pocket and pulled out a strip of jerky. I set the meat upon the rock and started down Walter's Wiggles toward the river and the shade of the cottonwoods.

28 | Kolob Backcountry

Paradise Found

Paul W. Rea

Kolob Terrace is a popular lookout point for people traveling on Interstate 15 south of Cedar City, but few venture beyond the parking lot. In this excerpt from Canyon Interludes, *naturalist writer Paul Rea describes encounters with wildlife and a mammoth arch while backpacking in a lesser-known corner of Zion National Park.*

Among the spectacles of the Colorado Plateau, few surpass the high plateaus of southern Utah and northern Arizona. Here in addition to the usual beauties offered by the red-rock country, one finds a crowning glory: large trees. The luxuriant foliage that drapes the rocks here at Kolob Terrace rivals that of Zion Canyon, itself a plant lover's nirvana. Like Mayan pyramids overgrown with greenery, the burnt-orange sandstone bluffs round into the domes so characteristic of Zion. In most of the park, cliff tops appear blond where water has dissolved much of the lime and iron that cement the quartz crystals, but here the Navajo sandstone bluffs retain more of their red pigments. Our route toward Kolob Arch skirts this balcony of red and green. From all we've heard, this should be one of the great hikes in the Southwest.

Major geologic factors explain these spectacular walls and domes. In essence, winds piled up vast dunes that were flooded, covered, lifted up, and eroded down to become the Colorado Plateau. When the sands accumulated, this area lay even with present-day Central America. Since that time, tectonic plate movement caused the continent to drift two thousand miles northward. Despite its origin in the Age of Dinosaurs, the Navajo sandstone contains few fossils because few plants and animals lived in the hot desert sands.

The "Great Sand Pile" reached its highest point here in southwest Utah, and the resulting Navajo sandstone stands fully two thousand feet thick in Zion Canyon. But upheavals that began about thirteen million years ago lifted this rock several thousand feet higher yet in the Kolob section. The upthrust of this colossal block exposed it to the elements that carve the domes, towers, slots, and ruddy walls along this trail.

We're skirting the Hurricane Fault, the west-facing escarpment that runs for almost three hundred miles from the Wasatch Mountains to Grand Canyon. Viewed from the air, this long cliff marks the west side of the Grand Staircase. Perched behind these sandstone bluffs, the swaled, corrugated Kolob Terrace represents a middle step on the stairs. Above this shelf, the Gray Cliffs of Cedar Canyon and Pink Cliffs of Bryce Canyon reach the top landings. Downstairs from Kolob Terrace lie the White Cliffs of Zion, the Vermilion Cliffs of Kanab, the Belted Cliffs of Colorado City, and finally the Kaibab Limestone bluffs of the Grand Canyon. As it scales the six thousand feet from the Colorado River to Bryce Canyon, the Grand Staircase reveals nearly two billion years of the earth's history.

Runoff from Kolob Terrace not only carves the canyons we'll explore but nourishes a unique blend of plants from the Rocky Mountains, the Great Basin, the Sierra Nevadas, and the Arizona desert. Considering the fact that much of the park is bare rock, this variety is amazing. Zion is a place of specialized adaptations to micro niches; standard zones often don't apply because micro climates vary widely in a short space. A cactus may thrive on a sunny ledge a few feet from the lush hanging gardens of ferns and monkey flowers, the special habitat required by the Zion snail, a species found nowhere else.

We parked at Lee's Pass, named for John D. Lee, a complex and controversial figure who secretly used this route on his way to Hop Valley and beyond. Since the Mormon church commissioned him to explore it, Lee knew southwest Utah as well as any white man. His well-known troubles began in 1857 when Paiute Indians harassed over a hundred non-Mormon emigrants camped at Mountain Meadows, thirty miles west of here. When the immigrant party circled its wagons and repulsed the Paiutes, inflicting casualties, Mormon leaders became fearful. Would the attack activate the U.S. Army, which was already poised to invade Utah? Would the Indians turn on the Mormon settlers?

Following instructions, Lee and others first offered to help the emigrants, then led them into a trap: the Mountain Meadows Massacre. The Mormons fell on the men as the Indians attacked the women and children. Weeks later wolves still chewed on the bodies. The distinguished Western writer Wallace Stegner rightly described the tragedy as an outburst of "hatred and misunderstanding that had been building for a long time."[1]

Excommunicated and forced into exile, Lee often took remote routes such as the trail we're hiking. After he'd sequestered himself for years at Lee's Ferry on the Colorado River, he was eventually tried and brought before a firing squad. To his dying breath Lee contended that Brigham Young "sacrificed me through his lust for power." Though Lee, a multiple murderer, never denied his involvement in the massacre, he also bore the guilt of a tribe that had disowned its shadow.

A thousand feet above us, the last of the rounded Five Fingers marks the western reach of the red rock plateau. Like most drainages that incise Kolob Terrace along cracks in the rock, those between the fingers run east and west. The trail continues south, first along cottonwood-lined Timber Creek, then heads through pinyon and juniper country.

Butterflies probe the brilliant orange blossoms clustered on a handsome bush, its dark-green leaves set against a background of gray sage and red rock. Anchored to deep, drought-resistant tubers, butterfly weed (or orange milkweed) blooms in warm colors that make it attractive for landscaping. These butterflies face a risk, however, for pollination in the milkweed family can prove fatal. Rather than floating freely for grain-by-grain transfer, this pollen sticks together in a waxlike mass. With great strength relative to their weight, visiting insects must free the waxy platelets of pollen or become trapped in the flower. When things work well, their pollen-laden feet inadvertently grasp the protruding pistil of the flower. Mass fertilization ensues.

With its diversified flora offering nectar throughout warmer months, Zion attracts several varieties of butterflies. Buckeyes, small but strikingly colored butterflies with blue eyespots, often dash after others of their kind and then ascend in a whirlwind. California sisters resemble white-striped admirals except for the pumpkin-orange dots that glow like tail lights. Azures, painted ladies, tiger swallowtails, and common sulphurs (whose color probably suggested the term "butter fly") all add to the already diverse palette.

As La Verkin Creek enters from the east, we look around the historic *Corrales*, where for decades ranchers paused with their herds. Feet and hooves have compacted the soil, leading the Zion Natural History Association to advise against camping on such trampled areas. From here the trail heads into the complex of verdant buff-and-salmon canyons that we'll explore.

Like a painted bird on a Christmas tree, a western tanager swoops from a treetop, flashing its red head, yellow-orange body, and black tail. Tanagers are birds of the tropics, reaching their zenith on the lower slopes of the Andes where several species may feed from the same tree at the same time. In the summer males flaunt their colors for breeding, but in the fall, for protection during migration, they molt into the dull greenish-yellow of their mates. With their bursts of flamboyance, tanagers bring the tropics to temperate North America. Bird lovers now recognize the crucial importance of preserving winter habitat for "our" summer songbirds.

Skies darken as clouds engulf Timber Top Mountain. When the trail climbs into conifers, drops begin to tingle my scalp. While we munch carrots under a spreading ponderosa, the drizzle wanes into mist. A cloud burns off as Gregory Peak, named for pioneer geologist Herbert E. Gregory, blazes in the late-afternoon light.

Campsites nestle in shady groves. No sooner do we put down our burdens than a rock squirrel tears into my pack. We yell, make coarse gestures, and even charge the marauder, but it doesn't scurry far. To prevent further problems, Barbara guards the packs while I drift down to the stream. Its banks lined with bright green horsetails, it rushes brick red after the rain. A Say's phoebe, gray with a sharp beak, shoots out to snap a mosquito. On the banks grow plants commonly found in the East, such as Solomon's seal and black raspberries. Just downstream a buck kinks his neck to scratch his steaming back with the tip of his antler.

This area is well known for wildlife. When trapper-traders William Wolfkill and George C. Yount traipsed through southwest Utah in the winter of 1831–32, Yount marveled at what they saw in the Virgin River valley: "The elk, deer, and antelope, driven from the mountains by the snow and piercing cold, were basking, with their frolicsome fawns, unaware and unintimidated by the sight of man. They would flock around like domestic sheep or goats, and would almost feed from the hand."[2]

Where there was plentiful prey, there were also predators. Unfortunately, however, hunters, trappers, and ranchers had exterminated the Mexican gray wolves well before establishment of the park. Mountain lions, on the other hand, proved more difficult to kill. Their preference for fresh meat made them difficult to poison, and they hid on ledges where they could evade a pack of howling hounds. Much as a house cat can reach a counter, cougars can spring up cliffs several times their height.

These magnificent cats now prowl Kolob Terrace, but, because their territories are so large, they often stray from the park. When cougars prey on livestock and a rancher reports the loss, the Utah Division of Wildlife traps the cougar for release in areas needing predators. But other ranchers prefer to "bag their lion" like a Teddy Roosevelt—or find it profitable to guide outstate trophy hunters whose challenge amounts to hitting a large target crouched in a small tree. Cougars are defiantly wild, and there are people who need to destroy any creature that defies human domination. Perhaps Captain Ahab, who hated the whale he couldn't kill, didn't go down with the *Pequod*.

Mountain lions have also faced accusations of killing off the bighorn sheep here in Zion. Actually, though, there were additional causes. When the deer population expanded, bighorns were less able to compete, so their numbers dwindled. In addition, reintroduced bighorns have multiplied slowly in Zion because of diseases contracted from domestic sheep. Small parks such as Zion and Bryce Canyon present special challenges. Both have lost about a third of their original species, and the reintroduction of mobile species such as wolves alarms the locals. It's extremely difficult to restore full diversity in a complex ecosystem that's been evolving for thousands of years.

In the morning we face the rock squirrels again, so we stuff our food into a sack and suspend it from the end of a bough. But the sack's weight bows it down and squirrels jump *that* high to reach bird feeders. I know—I've been outsmarted by them before. Finally we select a stronger branch, clean any crumbs from around our site, and set off to play.

Our first stop is Kolob Arch, at 310 feet possibly the largest in the world. Despite its size, the arch itself is not overwhelming because it sits so high up the cliff. Unlike many arches on the Colorado Plateau, Kolob is not essentially the work of percolating water. Instead, it is a free-standing arch, one formed through exfoliation. Where the weight of the rock creates bulges along stress planes, cracking and peeling loosen surface slabs that slough off during freezes. As time goes on, expansion and contraction accelerate this process. Much like Great Arch near the Zion Tunnel, Kolob has exfoliated itself deeply into the cliff, finally causing its ceiling to fall in. Because Kolob is open at the top, it does not protect the cliff beneath it from eroding still more rapidly than before.

Few hikers continue past Kolob Arch. Although the lovely trail to the Arch is graced with pink phlox, scarlet penstemons, lavender shooting stars, and other wildflowers, it scarcely hints at the marvels just beyond. We follow the stream that has, for only a few million years, abraded this soft sandstone like a continuously grinding belt sander. Yesterday's shower speeded up the belt and added new abrasives.

For another mile past the arch, these exquisite narrows remain pristine, free from bootprints. Far above, cross-bedded planes sweep through long arcs on the canyon walls. Fresh fractures appear clean and buff against the older, darker surfaces. Seeps spot these cliffs to reveal where moisture percolates through the porous sandstone, making them resemble the Redwall limestone bluffs in the Grand Canyon. However, these sheer walls rise over a thousand feet in two stages, separated by a distinct seep line where water reaches a harder layer which it follows until it oozes out. Strong enough to support itself on a cliff face but soft enough for streams to chisel, Navajo sandstone forms absolutely magnificent cliffs.

Well up the sheer face, a narrow shelf supports a band of trees. Tall conifers too high up for even a tree hugger to identify look like props in a museum showcase. The upper wall frames lovely water streaks, long stripes that accentuate the curvature. This second face, too, is crowned with twisted trees standing defiantly against a blue slice of sky.

These glorious walls glow like a pumpkin in the midmorning sunlight.

In such narrow canyons the reflected overtones can render the colors richer. Flavored by this tangerine light, mist drifts from beneath an overhang where lacy maidenhair ferns decorate the walls. Like Weeping Rock in Zion Canyon, this shallow cave drips tears that wobble in the air like soap bubbles.

The air seems slightly tinted by iron, full of grains from the sandstone cliffs. This is broad daylight turned palpable, not photons simply striking and bouncing off a surface, not rock merely absorbing some wavelengths of light to impart color, but sublime luminescence imbued with the spirit of matter. This beauty animates me, dissolving any feelings of estrangement into the sandstoned air. I react to illusory appearances, momentarily disregarding the hard-rock realities that lie beneath the gorgeous surfaces.

Far overhead, their wings backlit by the sun, hundreds of swallows twitter and cavort. Cliff swallows winter in Paraguay and Brazil, flying thousands of miles each way and nesting in huge colonies. These colonies serve as communication centers where unsuccessful hunters watch successful ones feeding their nestlings, then follow them to the best places to grab bugs. However, parasitism also characterizes swallow colonies. Laying eggs in neighboring nests is common, even rampant. Nor is this the result of confusion among similar nests, for some females wait until the owner is distracted, then pop out an egg in as little as fifteen seconds. Exuberant fliers that they are, swallows understandably prefer soaring to brooding eggs.

In the creek a slate-gray water ouzel, or dipper, bobs on rocks to remind me of how I first beheld ouzels under a bridge in Yosemite. In his *The Mountains of California*, John Muir sang paeans to his favorite bird:

> He is a singularly joyous and lovable little fellow, about the size of a robin, clad in a plain waterproof suit of bluish gray....In both winter and summer he sings, sweetly, cheerily, independent alike of sunshine and of love, requiring no other inspiration than the stream on which he dwells.

Water ouzels dive into pools where they hunt insect larvae. And they aren't fooled by caddis fly grubs that cover themselves with sticks and stones, either.

Where huge slabs of sandstone clog the slot, we pull ourselves up and over, each time marking the best route to climb back down. After running nearly straight, apparently along a north/south joint, this slot opens into a spectacular amphitheater. Black-and-white streaks decorate an enormous stone knob. Tufts of grass and moss—plus a limber pine seedling, its boughs like bottle brushes—all cling to the peeling rock.

How appropriate that, as far as we can tell, this magical alcove doesn't have a name. Sequestered behind those slab barriers, this is a magical place that few people see. Perhaps it's better off unnamed, for blank places on the map are less likely to risk the overuse experienced by some of Zion's backcountry, such as The Subway.

On the way back I freeze. Just a yard ahead, its head buried under loose rock, lies a colorful serpent. Its strikingly colored body, larger than my thumb, looks almost enameled. Barbara cautions me to stand back, which I do, though I'd prefer to see as much as possible. Yes, I definitely do have a way of letting beauty blind me to danger. Then I recall that "Red and yellow, kill a fellow. Red and black, venom lack." Rings encircle the body, but the red ones do not meet the yellow. Red rings are bordered on either side by black. This is a harmless Arizona mountain kingsnake, a constrictor of lizards and other snakes. I linger for a closer look.

My skin feels sticky as I recline on a flagstone, legs in a pool, snacking on limp carrots and stale peanuts. Mmmm, good. Gauzy-winged damselflies dance with Tinkerbell wings in the dappled light. Their bowed bodies glowing a phosphorescent blue, they often perch near sunny spots so that small flying insects wandering into the sunshine are easier to see. Several damselflies light softly on stream grasses beside my canteen. After a mating display of arched abdomens, a male fastens his tail behind a female's head. Later she will curl her abdomen around to meet his, suggesting a most holistic union of mind and body.

A small black water snake two feet long wriggles into the pool. Head held high, it glides up and rests on a rock ledge. It remains calm, perhaps more so than we do, ignoring both us and the damselflies. It then swims downstream, much at home in the gentle current.

Buzz. Leaf litter flies as two antagonists fight to the death. A yellow jacket is assaulting a large digger bee, its wings a blur in the dust. Gradually the yellow jacket pins the bee, going at it with chewing mouth and stinging tail. While its jaws bite the bee's head off, its stinger repeatedly stabs the bee's abdomen. The decapitated bee's wings buzz intermittently. What's the conflict here? This yellow jacket may want the bee's burrow, since both nest in the soil. It's more likely, though, that this yellow jacket is a sterile female worker seeking protein to feed larvae. After an episode like this, it's difficult to understand why most bees live alone. There's greater safety in numbers, but bees that live in hives must pay a price for their greater security.

As I stare at this savage scene, I'm both shocked and fascinated. When nature seems as beautiful or as suited to human needs as it does right now, I forget that it can also be so "red in tooth and claw."

Back at camp we're in for another shock; the rodents have struck again—and I've been outsmarted once more. Familiar debris litters the ground near our stuff sack. The varmints have chewed through the cord to drop our sack of food. Though it's humbling to be outwitted by rock squirrels, the loss is more serious. Without our dried dinners, peanuts, granola, and dried apples, we're short on food. Barbara wants to hike out; I argue that the little beasties didn't take our coffee, oranges, peanuts, or brandy. We should be able to get by on these and then hike out early. When I promise her a rib eye at Milt's Stage Stop near Cedar City, she agrees to stay.

After the cleanup we set out for Hop Valley. A half mile down La Verkin Creek we come to a fork. Ringed by golden columbine, a sizable spring gushes from the hillside. The streamside trail follows La Verkin and Willis creeks past more springs into slot canyons, some of them classic narrows. Surrounded by Wilderness Study Areas, this is one of the wildest areas of the park, one where large pines and firs, rushing waters, waterfalls, pools for bathing, and solitude are the rule.

The Hop Valley trail is also spectacular. From the creek the trail climbs into a thick grove of maples and box elders. Domes and towering cliffs rise in nearly all directions. The cross-bedding characteristic of wind-deposited sandstones often guides erosional forces, determining by their tilt whether the rock will become a dome or a cliff. Where the Navajo sandstone is exposed on these great rock faces, the curvatures of ancient dunes define the sweeping contours. The sandstone domes of Zion present the crests of petrified dunes, frozen in time. Except for Gregory Butte, which balds at 7,700 feet, these rounded cliffs are trimmed with green.

Hop Valley first presents wide, rolling terrain covered by scrub oaks and ponderosas, then it changes to broad meadows with blue lupines, or bluebonnets. Since lupines are poisonous to cattle, their numbers have probably increased as decades of grazing have reduced more palatable plants. Other changes have resulted from protracted grazing. Sage, pinyon, and juniper often invade lands denuded of their natural grasses. Farther on, where slump-and-slide dams once backed up the stream to create a lake, the valley widens. Its floor resembles a golf course, complete with sand traps and fairways. An eagle sails into the valley, stirring the ravens.

Most of this long valley is an inholding owned by Bud Lee, a descendent of John D. For years Bud has run cattle in these verdant meadows from May through October, but the cattle also stray into the park, where they do damage. Private inholdings disrupt national parks when their owners insist on uses that conflict with park values. Why, one wonders, can the government condemn private land for highways, railroads, power lines, and pipelines but not for unified national parks? Here in Utah, at least, one answer is that the Park Service has felt intense hostility from locals, especially ranchers, and has tried to appease them.

On the final trail back, other campers tell tales of woe. They thought they'd be clever and hide food in their tent, but they too were outsmarted. Squirrels chewed into their tent, found their food and fought over it, smearing blood and excrement. Normally rock squirrels eat acorns plus the seeds of currant, cactus, and yucca, all of them plentiful in this area. Did these rodents become dependent on human handouts? Or did they overpopulate, leading them to become excessively aggressive? When animals lose their fear of humans, could they turn their residual anger on us? Naturalists often remark that in areas frequented by humans the wildlife comes forward, whereas in truly wild areas it runs the other way. These squirrels parallel the fearless deer that one finds around many campgrounds. Contrary to "the Bambi syndrome," such seemingly tame, cute animals are not as benign as their liquid eyes might suggest. On more than one occasion they've chewed off my bootlaces or carried off my hat, both of which cause problems when you're camped in the backcountry.

The other campers decide to hike out, but I forget to make an offer for what remains of their food. Damn! To ignore the hunger pangs, I imagine spending time to select just the right twigs for a small, low-impact fire and whittling as I toss shavings on the fire. But no, this is a national park where no backcountry fires are allowed. Besides, freed from cooking we have more time to observe everything. If full vitality involves being totally present, nature delivers like little else.

But writing offers full involvement too—should I watch the woodpeckers or scribble in my journal? New England poet and essayist Donald Hall mused on contentment and "absorbedness":

> The hour of bliss is the lost hour....I lose the hour—inhabiting contentment—in my lucky double absorption with work and with land. At the desk, writing and trying to write, I do not even know that I will die. The whole of me enters the hand that holds the pen that digs at word-weeds, trying to set the garden straight.[3]

For total absorbedness one watches, writes, reads, gardens, converses, makes love, or whatever.

Toward dusk, as clouds move in, we exchange massages to feel less like we've been sent to our rooms without supper. Rain infuses the woods with an immense throb of energy, pitter-pattering the tent with insistent rhythms. We snuggle into our bags, drifting slowly toward sleep, relaxed but excited. I sense along with Thomas Merton that rain "reminds me again and again that the whole world runs by rhythms I have not yet learned to recognize."[4]

Once the last drips from the oak have ceased, droplets of light ooze through the nylon from a sky of pearls. Outside, the Summer Triangle is swimming beside the ghostly, gauzy Milky Way. As the skies clear fully, I hear the stars hum and listen to the music of the spheres.

Living in a city, where light pollution limits our view of the cosmos, I'd forgotten the splendor of the night sky. Here, thankfully, we're a hundred and fifty miles from the gaudy glare of Las Vegas. Air pollution also clouds our capacity for wonder, our ability to commune with a universe that is so much more than "virtual" dots on a screen. Today most people settle for a surrogate sky in a planetarium where viewers gasp in astonishment as the dull city heavens burst into their former brilliance. Under an empty sky or one filled only with blinking lights from airplanes, our engagement with the stars that so fascinated our ancestors lapses into disconnection with realms beyond our own.

I awaken to thunks on our tent. These are just too regular, so I suspect that a squirrel is dropping pine cones. Perhaps I've got rodents on my mind. We slug down coffee and tear into the one last orange, thinking we'll need a double caffeine and fructose buzz to cover the seven miles. With no delay for washing dishes, we're off by eight. Over a thousand feet above us Gregory Butte gleams in the early light, tiger-striped by last night's rain. An evening primrose, a common night bloomer, looks shriveled after its night of glory.

Raindrops bead the knee-high golden buckwheat beside the trail. This is the local version of the wild buckwheat appearing as sulphur flowers and umbrella plants in the Rockies. Throughout the West, wherever differences in moisture, salinity, soil type, exposure, and animal foraging occur, different species of buckwheat adapt to specific eco-niches. Perhaps the most dramatic adaptation to aridity is *Eriogonum inflatum*, the bottle plant that stores water in its bloated stems.

Beside the buckwheat, sphinx moths mate in the moist shade. Their colors are muted but bold, their forewings dark brown with a beige band, their hind wings mostly pink. Named for their large caterpillars that rear up like a sphinx, these remarkable insects are sometimes called "hawk-moths" because of their swooping flight or, more appropriately, "hummingbird moths" because of their hovering movements and rapid wingbeats. Unlike most moths, their antennae aren't feathery to locate food in the dark. Instead, their eyes are highly developed to spot bright-colored flowers during the day.

Sphinx moths lack hearing organs, possibly because they wouldn't be able to hear above their whir in flight. Stout-bodied and strong-winged, these insects buzz from flower to flower, often at dusk. As they hang above a flower, their pink color visible through the blur of their wings, they grasp the petal with two legs while their long proboscis uncoils to penetrate the flower as if in a passionate embrace. To fuel their high-energy metabolism, they require nectar with a lot of sugar. Burning all this fuel makes it necessary for them to release heat, which they do by perspiring from their wings and by circulating extra air through their respiratory system. Who could dismiss these marvels as mere bugs?

The sphinx moths don't amuse Barbara, though: "You're an interesting guy to hike with, Paul, but not on an empty stomach." Like a horse galloping for the barn, she heads for her oats, non-stop. Pulling on blinders, I force myself to bypass the kingbird on the branch, the butterflies on the pleurisy-root bush, and the baby grouse, almost invisible among the rice grass and sage. A curious coyote probably gives us more time than we give it. Barbara remarks that she'd complain about her sore feet if they didn't keep her mind off her belly. Hunger hits me too. I feel weak, and not just from the heat. After groaning up the last grade, we heave our packs somewhere near our van.

While I drive, she scavenges like a rodent for crackers, bits, pieces, crumbs. At Milt's Stage Stop we wolf down rib-eye steaks like ravenous carnivores. But my conscience nags. How can we object to overgrazing and then eat beef? Sure, we human critters are omnivores so it's natural for us to eat meat. Everything considered, though, I vow to consume even less red meat. Starting tomorrow. Over coffee, we rave about these glorious higher canyons of Zion. Their altitude and moisture keep them cooler, and the extra water supports more varied and prolific flora and fauna than in lower desert areas. When the Mormon pioneers named this Kolob area after the star nearest Heaven, they weren't far wrong. This might make a good place to live. . . .

Three years later we moved to Cedar City, only eighteen minutes away.

NOTES

1. Wallace Stegner, *Mormon Country* (Lincoln: University of Nebraska Press, 1981), 86.
2. Quoted in Herbert E. Gregory, *Geology and Geography of the Zion Park Region, Utah and Arizona* (Washington, DC: Government Printing Office, 1950), 17.
3. Donald Hall, "The One Hour," *Habitat: Journal of the Maine Audubon Society* 9, no. 6 (December 1992), 18.
4. Thomas Merton, *Raids on the Unspeakable* (New York: New Directions, 1966), 9.

29 | Zion Pioneers and Spirituality in the Land of Zion

EILEEN M. SMITH-CAVROS

Land use is a source of persistent controversy in the American West, and the theology and practices of Latter-day Saint immigrants to the Great Basin have always played a central role in the debates. For the Mormon settlers of the area in and around what is now Zion National Park, this was not principally a scenic wonderland but a wilderness to be tamed (or at least in which to eke out an existence). The following excerpt from Pioneer Voices of Zion Canyon *includes oral histories with the children and grandchildren of the original settlers of the upper Virgin River valley. Here the Zion Canyon natives attempt to reconcile tensions between religious devotion, economic realities, and an environmental ethic.*

Most of the residents of Zion Canyon during the Pioneer Voices era were members of the Church of Jesus Christ of Latter-day Saints. Much of their daily lives revolved around their spiritual beliefs, sense of family, and community connections. Philip Hepworth, born in 1916 in Zion Canyon, commented about how he felt they were perceived as Mormon settlers in relation to land and the park:

About the religion connection…we went to church and practically everybody in Springdale belonged to the Mormon Church, they were LDS and it influenced their lives…We were like a happy family…we were taught to work and be honest and thrifty and all of the virtuous things of life. We were taught that as we grew up…There was an erroneous rumor that went around for years. You used to hear that "the natives, they don't appreciate that park, we've got to get in there and preserve it so they don't destroy it. They want places to farm, they don't want a park to look at." But that was a mistaken idea. All the people I know…they loved that park. They loved those mountains…I've always, all my life I've continued to love nature and the outdoors because I grew up in it.

[Victor] Hall affirms, "It is a generally accepted notion that the early Mormon settlers were blind to the beauties of Zion Canyon, their energies being directed to the task of extracting a livelihood from a hostile environment. Such was not the case."[1]

A *Pioneer Voices* interviewee described the interaction between her ancestry and land ethic:

I'm proud of my pioneer heritage. These are the people who came and settled this part of the country. And they're strong people and I'm proud of that. I'm proud to be a part of that, those people. And they're what built this area up. And so I take pride in the fact that those were my ancestors, those were my people [who did] that. And when things don't look right or things get messed around I take it personally. You know…it means a lot to me, this area…I try to take care of my piece of the earth here. I try to remember my ancestors. I think that's one reason that I am so interested in genealogy and doing these histories…is because I admire those people so much.

Another pioneer interviewee noted the stereotype that he felt was incorrect of Mormon settlers as oblivious to the natural world around them.

The Mormons didn't attribute any spiritual…that is, "life"…to the mountains, like maybe the Native Americans do. You see they think everything has a spirit. I don't think we looked at the mountains [like that]. Though we admired them and were happy to live among…the mountains…A lot of people had the idea that the Mormons, the early settlers, didn't appreciate the beauty of the area. And of course I think the reason is that they didn't have a lot to say about it and they didn't write about it very much. Because they were busy twenty-four hours a day making a living. And didn't have much time to lay around…however, I'm sure they did have an appreciation. A lot of people noticed well. Joseph Black who was one of the first settlers in there. He was a young man and he is evidently reputed to be the first one to hike on up the canyon beyond Springdale and come back raving about the beauty to the extent that people got to calling it "Joe's Glory." So somebody noticed the beauty.

Della Higley reaffirmed the pioneer link to the land. "I feel that the pioneers were in love with the canyon…I don't know—what you would call it. But they appreciated the land and they appreciated the beauty that was here."

Many of them did notice the beauty of the canyon in spite of their challenging lives in Zion. Alma Cox, born in 1919, commented:

I've always…thought about the beauties of nature and God's creations and…[it] always amazes me what the Lord has done when He's created this earth for us. And the park also. I remember when I was postmaster why, I was postmaster for a long, long time [in Rockville] and the tourists would come down…after they'd been up in the park and they'd have a bunch of cards that they had bought and they wanted 'em cancelled out so they could go to their homes and some of the people they come and [said], "Just a big pile of rocks," and others would [say], "Oh, it was magnificent! Magnificent, those sheer ledges going up there." And you couldn't imagine…the difference in people! Ha. I guess it all depends on the eyes of the beholder I suppose…but most of 'em, most of 'em really enjoyed…one lady says, "This is just like being in the Celestial Kingdom." Well, she was talking about Rockville. She was talking about Rockville. "This is just like being in the Celestial Kingdom."

In addition, the lives of the Mormon settlers and the park intersected when it came to livelihood as well as philosophy. Betsy Alford, born in 1938 in Springdale, and her sister Janis Kali, born 1936, were interviewed for the Pioneer Voices Project and are both current Zion National Park employees. Descendants of a Mormon pioneer family, First Acting Zion Superintendent Walter Ruesch was their maternal grandfather, their paternal grandfather was District Supervisor of the Civilian Conservation Corps (CCC), and their father was Zion CCC foreman. They provided insight on how their heritage and spirituality were interconnected with a land ethic. Alford noted, "I think there's something spiritual myself that talks to you here [in Zion]. I've always felt it. I could be gone a day, I could be gone weeks, I could be gone years…but I keep coming back to the land, coming back to this area…it gathers you in and says 'okay, you're home and you're safe.' And I think part of that was because of grandpa [Walter Ruesch]…a very rough-spoken man and every other word was a swear word."

Her sister Janis Kali continued, "I also remember [Grandpa's] great love for this park. He was a woodcarver and I remember he carved a sign…He nailed it up to one of the trees in the [Zion] campground and it said 'This is God's country. Don't make it look like Hell.' I think it was a mistake to take that down because it was a part of this history and it was a part of the way we felt about our connection to the land."

The daughter of chief ranger Donal Jolley, also of Mormon pioneer heritage, remembered how her father felt about protecting and preserving the park. When asked if they ever ate sego lilies, as many settlers had, Lorna [Jolley] Kesterson replied:

> No. My dad was pretty strict about what we were doing. I'll tell you this one story about my dad. They were making a movie up in Zion with Tom Mix and they had their cameras set up and there was one branch of a tree that was right in the way, so they kept after Dad to cut that down so they wouldn't have to move their camera. But he wouldn't do it. So Tom Mix offered him a cowboy hat if he'd cut that branch off but Dad wouldn't cut it and didn't get the cowboy hat either. That's the way he was: very strict, strict with regulations.

An ethic of stewardship toward the natural world was a part of the Zion pioneer experience, even though this was often at odds with the fervent struggle to survive and persevere in what to the settlers surely seemed an unforgiving land. The pioneers derived lasting joy from the land and found an anchoring sense of place in its midst. If this historically based sense of place and stewardship towards nature is acknowledged as integral to the Zion pioneer experience, it follows that responsibility to the natural world must also have an integral role in the heritage of Zion pioneers: for past, present, and future. This acknowledgement can be beneficial both to the land of Zion and to its human inhabitants....

Another pioneer mused on the transition from tradition to modernity in Zion Canyon:

> They were very quiet years. But I know that, the people were very, very concerned with each other and for their animals. And we were very concerned about the wild animals because they would get the farm animals if they could...And...it was hard living here...But the people loved the land they loved the reason they were here. They took good care of everything that they had and not a thing was wasted. I think people lived closer to the land in those days...I won't say they worshipped the land—they respected the land. And they knew that it was the way they would make a living. And nowadays that isn't the way they make their living, and so they don't have the same relationship that they used to have.

That relationship was embodied for many of the pioneers by their sense of independence tempered with safety as children in Zion of yesterday:

> We were so isolated, I guess, we didn't get out and learn the ways of the world. 'Cause we were very isolated here, maybe become too self-oriented. I don't know. But I think it did make a difference. 'Cause we were different from people who lived out in these bigger places. We just lived out in the sticks! We was hillbillies! [But] I'm glad I grew up here...I think it was good for us in a way. We had to make our own way. We learned to work hard and appreciate each other and we just

learned to love this canyon. And so maybe that does have an effect on our whole lives, I don't know. I think it probably did. But we made our own entertainment, we made our own food, everything had to be pretty much what we could do ourselves for a long, long time.

All interviewees, like Barbara (Terry) Bell, born in Rockville in 1918, seemed to share in common a belief that their childhood in Zion was a cherished time:

Well, I'm sure that…having been raised in a small town, I think it's to my advantage as far as that goes. I can't see my dad doing anything else than what he did for a living [running the Rockville mercantile]. And while we weren't rich, we always had enough to eat and clothes to wear. So I don't ever regret not…having gone, you know, farther afield.

Another explained how the past tied into the present. "I've always felt that the people in this area have very strong spirits. Otherwise they wouldn't have been chosen to come down here in this desolate desert country. And they stuck it out here and raised their families and I've always been very, very proud of my pioneer heritage. When I think of what they went through so that I could have the life I've got now."

The power of heritage and place continued to tug at many long after their childhood was over and the journey to adulthood was underway. One explained, "Well, it was great for me [living in Zion]. I always enjoyed it. When we left for employment purposes, like when I went to California, I was there a couple of years, I couldn't wait to get back to Zion. Same way when I was in the service for a year and eight months. Come back to Zion."

And "come back to Zion" many did. Sometimes, bringing their children and grandchildren with them to share the joy.

One interviewee explained it thusly:

I've always enjoyed the out-of-doors. I've always enjoyed plants and flowers and…especially birds [and] animals. I don't do any hiking anymore; I don't have the ability to. But I think being acquainted with Zion and Cedar Mountain is what shaped me into what I am. And I have a granddaughter who I taught into the out-of-doors who wouldn't otherwise. You know, city girl, never get away from town...I used to take her with me up there [to Zion National Park]. That was many years later, of course. But it was because of how I had grown up. And the out-of-doors was always part of our life. And Zion was one of those important points in that.

Dan Crawford was born in 1914 in a cabin on Oak Creek. That cabin is gone and only traces remain of the irrigation ditches that once surrounded it. Children who once played there in the shadow of Steamboat Mountain are 90 years old now. Even the name of the mountain has changed. Today's visitors know it as the West Temple. Crawford summed up that moment in the history of Zion that was for him the world of childhood. "I thought that every place in the world had mountains around, and I thought they all had a river running past. I grew up and enjoyed the land...Best place in the world, I guess...I assumed I'd always live there." Interviewee Philip Hepworth echoed this sentiment when he explained of his Zion Canyon childhood, "It was just a wonderful life...I'd kinda like to go back and live it over."

The name of the canyon, "Zion" means "sanctuary." It has served as such for animals, plants, and humans for centuries. The pioneers of Zion used natural resources to survive, and like all of us do every day, they left an imprint on the land. But the land left an imprint on them, as well. In a sense, we are all their descendants. We have inherited their history; their heritage is our lesson. Although families struggled with the land of Zion and its elements, they loved that land, and many of them never left it. Others who left it, have returned to it. All of them preserve it, at least in their memories. These Zion pioneers have more in common with those who came before and with we who came after, than they have differences. The land is a part of us and it always has been. And we still depend on it in many and complex ways, from its resources to its respite. Like the pioneers in their time of transition, those who care about Zion Canyon today strive to adjust to more visitors, more imprints on the land, and more challenges to natural resources from inside and outside the park boundaries than we have ever known before. The "pioneers" of today may be measured in how they respond to these challenges and the ensuing choices. Perhaps our best guide may be the voices of the pioneers that echo in Zion Canyon and remind us of what we have.

NOTE

1. Victor Hall, "A History of Rockville," 44. Manuscript. Val A. Browning Library Special Collections, Dixie State College of Utah.

Further Reading

GEOLOGY AND ENVIRONMENTAL HISTORY

Crampton, C. Gregory. *Standing Up Country: The Canyon Lands of Utah and Arizona.* Tucson, AZ: Rio Nuevo, 2000.

Fillmore, Robert. *The Geology of the Parks, Monuments, and Wildlands of Southern Utah.* Salt Lake City: University of Utah Press, 2000.

Gregory, Herbert E. *A Geologic and Geographic Sketch of Zion National Park.* Washington, DC: Government Printing Office, 1950.

Hamilton, Wayne L. *The Sculpturing of Zion: Guide to the Geology of Zion National Park.* Springdale, UT: Zion Natural History Association, 1984.

NATIVE PEOPLES

Euler, Robert C. *The Paiute People.* Phoenix, AZ: Indian Tribal Series, 1972.

Hebner, William Logan, and Michael L. Plyler. *Southern Paiute: A Portrait.* Logan: Utah State University Press, 2010.

Plog, Stephen. *Ancient Peoples of the American Southwest.* 2nd ed. London: Thames and Hudson, 2008.

Reeve, W. Paul. *Making Space on the Western Frontier: Mormons, Miners, and Southern Paiutes.* Champaign: University of Illinois Press, 2006.

Trimble, Stephen. *The People: Indians of the American Southwest.* Santa Fe, NM: School of American Research Press, 1993.

EXPLORATIONS AND SETTLEMENT

Crawford, J. L. *Zion Album: A Nostalgic History of Zion Canyon.* Springdale, UT: Zion Natural History Association, 1986.

Smart, William B., and Donna T. Smart, eds. *Over the Rim: The Parley P. Pratt Exploring Expedition to Southern Utah, 1849–50.* Logan: Utah State University Press, 1999.

Swanson, Frederick H. *Dave Rust: A Life in the Canyons.* Salt Lake City: University of Utah Press, 2008.

Woodbury, Angus M. *A History of Southern Utah and Its National Parks.* 2nd ed. Springdale, UT: Zion National History Association, 1997.

Worster, Donald. *A River Running West: The Life of John Wesley Powell.* New York: Oxford University Press, 2001.

DEVELOPMENT AND PRESERVATION

Clark, John, and Melissa Clark. *Opening Zion: A Scrapbook of the National Park's First Official Tourists*. Salt Lake City: Bonneville Books, 2010.

Farmer, Jared. *Glen Canyon Dammed: Inventing Lake Powell and the Canyon Country*. Tucson: University of Arizona Press, 2004.

Hinton, Wayne K., and Elizabeth A. Green. *With Picks, Shovels, and Hope: The CCC and Its Legacy on the Colorado Plateau*. Missoula, MT: Mountain Press, 2008.

Markoff, Dena S., et al. *The Outstanding Wonder: Zion Canyon's Cable Mountain Draw Works*. Springdale, UT: Zion Natural History Association, 1978.

Nash, Roderick Frazier. *Wilderness and the American Mind*. 4th ed. New Haven, CT: Yale University Press, 2001.

Reisner, Marc. *Cadillac Desert: The American West and Its Disappearing Water*. Rev. ed. New York: Penguin, 1993.

Rothman, Hal K. *Devil's Bargains: Tourism in the Twentieth-Century American West*. Lawrence: University Press of Kansas, 1998.

Sellars, Richard West. *Preserving Nature in the National Parks: A History*. New Haven, CT: Yale University Press, 1997.

Worster, Donald. *Rivers of Empire: Water, Aridity, and the Growth of the American West*. New York: Oxford University Press, 1992.

VOICES OF CANYON COUNTRY

A Century of Sanctuary: The Art of Zion National Park. Springdale, UT: Zion Natural History Association, 2008.

Geary, Edward A. *The Proper Edge of the Sky: High Plateau Country of Utah*. Salt Lake City: University of Utah Press, 2002.

Handley, George B. *Home Waters: A Year of Recompenses on the Provo River*. Salt Lake City: University of Utah Press, 2010.

Williams, Terry Tempest. *Refuge: An Unnatural History of Family and Place*. 2nd ed. New York: Vintage, 1992.

Williams, Terry Tempest, William B. Smart, and Gibbs M. Smith, eds. *New Genesis: A Mormon Reader on Land and Community*. Salt Lake City: Gibbs Smith, 1998.

Sources and Permissions

Abbey, Edward, "Polemic: Industrial Tourism and the National Parks," from *Desert Solitaire: A Season in the Wilderness* (New York: Simon and Schuster, 1968), 44–57. Reprinted by permission of Don Congdon Associates.

Barnes, Christine, "Zion Park Lodge," from *Great Lodges of the National Parks* (Bend, OR: W. W. West, 2002), 115–21. Reprinted by permission of the author.

Brooks, Juanita, "The Land That God Forgot," *Utah Historical Quarterly* 26, no. 3 (July 1958): 207–19. Reprinted by permission of The Utah State Historical Society.

Chesher, Greer K., "Zion's Story," from *Zion Canyon: A Storied Land* (Tucson: University of Arizona Press, 2007), 54–64. Reprinted by permission of the author.

Clark, Lewis F., "Amid the Mighty Walls of Zion," *National Geographic Magazine* 105, no. 1 (January 1954): 37–70. Reprinted by permission of Christopher Clark.

Crawford, J. L., "Flora and Fauna," from *Zion National Park: Towers of Stone*, 2nd ed. (Springdale, UT: Zion Natural History Association, 1991), 23–25, 29–33. Reprinted by permission of the Zion Natural History Association.

Dellenbaugh, Frederick S., "A New Valley of Wonders," *Scribner's Magazine* 35, no. 1 (January 1904): 1–18.

Dodge, Henry Irving, "All Aboard for Zion." Omaha: Union Pacific Railroad/Acorn Press, 1926. Reprinted by permission of the Union Pacific History Museum.

Dolan, Maura, "Zion Park, Town Clash over Development." *Los Angeles Times*, May 13, 1991. Reprinted by permission of the *Los Angeles Times*.

Dutton, Clarence E., "The Vermilion Cliffs, and Valley of the Virgen," from *Tertiary History of the Grand Cañon District* (Washington, DC: Government Printing Office, 1882), 54–60.

Eves, Robert L., "Water and the Geology of Zion National Park," from *Water, Rock, and Time: The Geologic Story of Zion National Park* (Springdale, UT: Zion Natural History Association, 2005), 53–63. Reprinted by permission of the Zion Natural History Association.

Fisher, Frederick Vining, "'The Canyon Sublime'; Mukuntuweap So Named," *Washington County News* (St. George, UT), October 12, 1916, 1.

Flanigan, David A., "Story of Zion Cable," *Washington County News* (St. George, UT), June 28, 1923, 4.

Fraser, George C., Journal, July 5–8 and 11, 1914, from *Journeys in the Canyon Lands of Utah and Arizona, 1914–1916*, edited by Frederick H. Swanson (Tucson: University of Arizona Press, 2005), 6–17.

Garate, Donald T., *The Zion Tunnel: From Slickrock to Switchback* (Springdale, UT: Zion Natural History Association, 1991). Reprinted by permission of the Zion Natural History Association.

Hafen, Lyman, "The Spirit of Kinesava," from *Mukuntuweap: Landscape and Story in Zion Canyon* (St. George, UT: Tonaquint Press, 1996), 27–41. Reprinted by permission of the author.

Jeffers, LeRoy, "Zion Canyon and the Colob Plateau," *Scientific American* 120, no. 7 (February 15, 1919): 144–45.

Knack, Martha C., *Boundaries Between: The Southern Paiutes, 1775–1995* (Lincoln: University of Nebraska Press, 2001), 10–13, 14, 15–16, 20, 28–29. Reprinted by permission of the University of Nebraska Press.

Larson, A. Karl, "Zion National Park with Some Reminiscences Fifty Years Later," *Utah Historical Quarterly* 37, no. 4 (Fall 1969): 408–25. Reprinted by permission of the Utah State Historical Society.

Messiaen, Olivier, and Harriet Watts, "Canyons, Colours, and Birds: An Interview with Oliv[i]er Messiaen," *Tempo* 33, no. 128 (March 1979): 2–8. Reprinted by permission of Cambridge University Press.

Nichols, Howard S., *Zion Canyon: Utah's New Wonderland via Salt Lake City and "Wylie Way"* (Los Angeles: Salt Lake Route, 1917).

Powell, John Wesley, "Origin of the Pai-Utes," from *Anthropology of the Numa: John Wesley Powell's Manuscripts on the Numic Peoples of Western North America, 1868–1880*, edited by Don D. and Catherine S. Fowler (Washington, DC: Smithsonian Institution Press, 1971), 78.

———, "An Overland Trip to the Grand Cañon," *Scribner's Monthly* 10, no. 6 (October 1875): 661–63.

Rea, Paul W., "Kolob Backcountry: Paradise Found," from *Canyon Interludes: Between White Water and Red Rock* (Salt Lake City: Signature Books, 1996), 169–86. Reprinted by permission of the author.

Reed, Edwin O., "Rough Hike through the Wrong Canyon," *Westways* 58, no. 7 (July 1966): 4–6. Reprinted by permission of Karin Leperi.

Ruess, Everett, Letters, August 1931, from *Everett Ruess: A Vagabond for Beauty*, edited by W. L. Rusho (Salt Lake City: Peregrine Smith Books, 1983), 54–59, 180–81. Reprinted by permission of the Waldo Ruess estate.

Smith-Cavros, Eileen M., "Zion Pioneers and Spirituality in the Land of Zion," from *Pioneer Voices of Zion Canyon* (Springdale, UT: Zion Natural History Association, 2006), 82–93. Reprinted by permission of the Zion Natural History Association.

Stegner, Wallace, "The Land Nobody Wanted …," from *Mormon Country* (Lincoln: University of Nebraska Press, 1981), 34–36, 45–51. Copyright © 1942 by Wallace Stegner; Copyright renewed © 1970 by Wallace Stegner. Used by permission of Brandt & Hochman Literary Agents, Inc. All rights reserved.

Woodbury, Angus M. "The Great White Throne—Has It Ever Been Climbed?" *The Westerner*, July 1930, 22–23, 54–55. Reprinted by permission of J. Walter Woodbury.